Python Essentials 1

by
The OpenEDG Python Institute

Open Education and Development Group
1013 Centre Road, Suite 403-A
Wilmington, DE
19805, United States

Second edition published in the USA in 2024 by the Open Education and Development Group

Copyright © 2023 Open Education and Development Group

ISBN: 979-8-9877622-4-0

All rights reserved. This book may not be copied or reproduced, in whole or in part, without the express written permission of the Open Education and Development Group. While the authors and publisher have taken every precaution in the preparation of this book, they assume no responsibility for any errors or omissions. Furthermore, authors and publisher assume no liability for any damages that result from the use of the information contained within this book.

Image credits

Portrait of Guido Van Rossum at the Dropbox headquarters in 2014
CC BY-SA 4.0, Photograph by Daniel Stroud.

Cover Design

Konrad Papka

Trademarks & Disclaimer

Every effort has been made by the publisher to provide information that is accurate. Any terms in this book that are known trademarks have been capitalized. The Open Education and Development Group makes no claims to the accuracy of such trademarks.

The Open Education and Development Group and its subsidiaries, including the OpenEDG Python Institute, is an independent organization with no affiliated links to any other organization, including the Python Software Foundation.

No warranty of fitness is implied as to the accuracy of the information contained within this book, although every effort has been made to ensure it is as accurate as possible. Neither the authors nor publisher assume liability for or responsibility to any person or entity that suffers loss or damage as result of the use of the information contained herein.

All the code examples in the book have been tested on Python 3.4, 3.6, 3.7, 3.8, and 3.9, and should work with any subsequent versions of Python 3.x.

Bulk purchase and custom book design

This book may be purchased in bulk in either ePUB or PDF format. Additionally, it may be possible to customize the layout of the book to suit your needs. To discuss these options, email services@openedg.org.

TABLE OF CONTENTS

Welcome to Python Essentials 1
    Learn Python – the language of today and tomorrow   xiv
    Introduction   xiv
    About the course   xiv
    Syllabus   xv
    Prepare for the PCEP-30-0x exam   xvi

Introduction to Python and Computer Programming

Chapter 1: Introduction to Programming   3
    Natural languages vs. programming languages   4
    What makes a language?   4
    Machine language vs. high-level language   4
    Compilation vs. Interpretation   5
    What does the interpreter do?   6
    Compilation vs. Interpretation – Advantages and Disadvantages   7

Chapter 2: Introduction to Python   9
    Who created Python?   10
    A hobby programming project   10
    What makes Python so special?   11
    Python rivals   11
    Where can we see Python in action?   11
    Why not Python?   12
    There is more than one Python   12
    Python implementations   13

Chapter 3: Downloading and Installing Python   17
    How to download, install, and configure Python   17
    Starting your work with Python   19
    Your very first program before your first program   19
    How to spoil and fix your code   22

Python Data Types, Variables, Operators, and Basic I/O Operations

Chapter 4: The "Hello, World!" Program   27
    The print() function   27
    Function arguments   28
    Function invocation   29
    LAB: Working with the print() function   30
    The print() function and its effect, arguments, and values returned   30
    Instructions   31
    Python escape and newline characters   32
    Using multiple arguments   33
    Positional arguments   33
    Keyword arguments   34

  LAB: The print() function and its arguments   35
  LAB: Formatting the output   36
  Summary   36
  Quiz   37

Chapter 5: Python literals   39
  Integers   40
  Floats   41
  Strings   43
  Boolean values   44
  LAB: Python literals — strings   45
  Summary   45
  Quiz   46

Chapter 6: Operators: data manipulation tools   47
  Basic operators   47
  Operators and their priorities   51
  Summary   53
  Quiz   54

Chapter 7: Variables   55
  Variable names   56
  How to create a variable   57
  How to use a variable   58
  How to assign a new value to an already existing variable   59
  Solving simple mathematical problems   60
  LAB: Variables   60
  Shortcut operators   61
  LAB: Variables — a simple converter   62
  LAB: Operators and expressions   63
  Summary   63
  Quiz   64

Chapter 8: Comments   67
  Marking fragments of code   68
  LAB: Comments   68
  Summary   69
  Quiz   70

Chapter 9: Interaction with the User   71
  The input() function with an argument   72
  The result of the input() function   72
  The input() function – prohibited operations   72
  Type casting, or type conversion   73
  More about input() and type casting   73
  String operators   74
  Type conversion once again   75
  LAB: Simple input and output   76
  LAB: Operators and expressions   76
  LAB: Operators and expressions 2   77
  Summary   78
  Quiz   79

Boolean Values, Conditional Execution, Loops, Lists and List Processing, Logical and Bitwise Operations

Chapter 10: Making decisions in Python — 83
- Comparison: equality operator — 83
- Exercises — 83
- Operators — 84
- Making use of the answers — 85
- LAB: Variables — Questions and answers — 86
- Conditions and conditional execution — 87
- Analyzing code samples — 91
- Pseudocode and introduction to loops — 93
- LAB: Comparison operators and conditional execution — 94
- LAB: Essentials of the if-else statement — 95
- LAB: Essentials of the if-elif-else statement — 96
- Summary — 98
- Quiz — 101

Chapter 11: Loops in Python — 103
- An infinite loop — 104
- The while loop: more examples — 105
- LAB: Guess the secret number — 106
- Looping your code with for — 107
- More about the for loop and the range() function with three arguments — 109
- LAB: Essentials of the for loop – counting mississippily — 110
- The break and continue statements — 111
- LAB: The break statement — Stuck in a loop — 113
- LAB: The continue statement — the Ugly Vowel Eater — 113
- LAB: The continue statement — the Pretty Vowel Eater — 114
- The while loop and the else branch — 115
- The for loop and the else branch — 116
- LAB: Essentials of the while loop — 116
- LAB: Collatz's hypothesis — 117
- Summary — 120
- Quiz — 122

Chapter 12: Logic and bit operations in Python — 125
- Logical expressions — 127
- Logical values vs. single bits — 127
- Bitwise operators — 127
- How do we deal with single bits? — 130
- Binary left shift and binary right shift — 132
- Summary — 134
- Quiz — 135

Chapter 13: Lists — 137
- Indexing lists — 138
- Accessing list content — 139
- Removing elements from a list — 140
- Negative indices are legal — 141
- LAB: The basics of lists — 142
- Functions vs. methods — 142

ix

Adding elements to a list: append() and insert()	143
Making use of lists	145
Lists in action	146
LAB: The basics of lists — the Beatles	147
Summary	148
Quiz	150

Chapter 14: Sorting simple lists: the bubble sort algorithm — 151

Sorting a list	153
The bubble sort — interactive version	154
Summary	155
Quiz	155

Chapter 15: Operations on lists — 157

Powerful slices	158
Slices — negative indices	159
The in and not in operators	161
Lists — some simple programs	161
LAB: Operating with lists — basics	163
Summary	164
Quiz	165

Chapter 16: Lists in advanced applications — 167

Two-dimensional arrays	168
Multidimensional nature of lists: advanced applications	170
Summary	172

Functions, Tuples, Dictionaries, Exceptions, and Data Processing

Chapter 17: Functions — 177

Decomposition	178
Where do functions come from?	179
Your first function	179
4.1.5 How functions work	181
Summary	183
Quiz	184

Chapter 18: How functions communicate with their environment — 185

Positional parameter passing	187
Keyword argument passing	188
Mixing positional and keyword arguments	189
Parametrized functions – more details	190
Summary	191
Quiz	193

Chapter 19: Returning a result from a function — 195

The return instruction	195
A few words about None	197
Effects and results: lists and functions	198
LAB: A leap year — writing your own functions	200
LAB: How many days: writing and using your own functions	200
LAB: Day of the year — writing and using your own functions	201

x

LAB: Prime numbers — how to find them	201
LAB: Converting fuel consumption	202
Summary	203
Quiz	205

Chapter 20: Scopes in Python — 207

Functions and scopes: the global keyword	209
How the function interacts with its arguments	209
Summary	211
Quiz	213

Chapter 21: Creating multi-parameter functions — 215

Sample functions: Triangles	218
Sample functions: Factorials	221
Fibonacci numbers	222
Recursion	223
Summary	224
Quiz	225

Chapter 22: Tuples and dictionaries — 227

Tuples	228
Dictionaries	230
Dictionary methods and functions	234
Tuples and dictionaries can work together	237
Summary	239
Quiz	245

Chapter 23: Exceptions — 247

When data is not what it should be	248
The try-except branch	249
The exception proves the rule	250
How to deal with more than one exception	250
The default exception and how to use it	251
Some useful exceptions	252
Why you can't avoid testing your code	253
When Python closes its eyes	254
Tests, testing, and testers	255
print debugging	256
Some useful tips	256
Unit testing – a higher level of coding	257
Summary	257
Quiz	260

Appendices

Appendix A: LAB Hints	263
Appendix B: LAB Sample Solutions	269
Appendix C: Answers	279
Appendix D: PCEP Exam Syllabus	286

WELCOME TO PYTHON ESSENTIALS 1

Learn Python – the language of today and tomorrow

This book is the first in a two-part Python Essentials series. It covers everything you need to know to start designing, writing, running, debugging, and improving Python programs at the foundational level. It also fully prepares you for the PCEP — Certified Entry-Level Python Programmer™ certification exam from the Python Institute.

Introduction

Python is one of the fastest growing programming languages in the world, and is used in almost every sector and industry, from gaming, to medicine, to nuclear physics. It is essential for any would-be programmer to have at least a foundational knowledge of Python. Luckily, Python is also one of the easiest programming languages to learn. With its focus on real-world words and syntax, a beginner learner of Python can start writing simple programs within minutes

Goals of this book

This book is designed to teach you the basics of Python programming, even if you have zero programming experience. Additionally, it prepares you to take the PCEP Python Certified Entry-Level Python Programmer™ exam, which can be taken through the OpenEDG testing platform TestNow™. At the end of this book, you will find the complete syllabus for the PCEP Python Certified Entry-Level Python Programmer™ exam

Learning Tools

EDUBE

The material found in this book may also be accessed online at www.edube.org. Here it is possible to take other courses such as JavaScript Essentials, or C/C++ Essentials, and progress to the intermediate and advances Python courses. Furthermore, through the Edube platform, you can purchase exam vouchers and schedule an exam.

SANDBOX

The Edube educational platform offers an interactive programming sandbox, where you can try out the code examples shown in this book. The Sandbox becomes available as soon as you create an account on Edube.

ANSWERS

Throughout this book you will find quizzes and exercises. You can find the answers, hints, and sample solutions and the back of the book in the Appendices.

About the course

Welcome to *Python Essentials 1*! This book has been designed and developed by the OpenEDG Python Institute and is based on the online course created in partnership with the Cisco Networking Academy. It has been created for anyone and everyone who wants to learn Python and modern programming techniques. It will particularly appeal to:

- aspiring programmers and learners interested in learning programming for fun and for job-related tasks;
- learners looking to gain fundamental skills and knowledge for an entry-level job role as a software developer, data analyst, or tester;
- industry professionals wishing to explore technologies that are connected with Python, or that utilize it as a foundation;
- team leaders, product managers, and project managers who want to understand the terminology and processes in the software development cycle to more effectively manage and communicate with production and development teams.

In this book you will be guided through hands-on practice materials, labs, quizzes, assessments, and tests to learn how to utilize the skills and knowledge gained from studying the resources and performing coding tasks, and interact with some real-life programming challenges and situations.

Syllabus

In this book you will learn:

- the universal concepts of computer programming;
- the syntax and semantics of the Python language;
- practical skills in resolving typical implementation challenges;
- how to use the most important elements of the Python Standard Library;
- how to install your runtime environment;
- how to design, develop, test, and debug simple Python programs.

The book is divided into four parts:

PART 1
Introduction to Python and computer programming

PART 2
Data types, variables, basic input-output operations, and basic operators

PART 3
Boolean values, conditional execution, loops, lists and list processing, logical and bitwise operations

PART 4
Functions, tuples, dictionaries, exceptions, and data processing

Prepare for the PCEP-30-0x exam

Dive into programming, learn Python from scratch, and prepare for the PCEP — Certified Entry-Level Python Programmer certification. *Python Essentials 1* is aligned with the *PCEP — Certified Entry-Level Python Programmer* certification, a professional credential that demonstrates the holder's understanding of the Python language syntax and semantics, as well as their proficiency in using the most essential elements of the language, tools, and resources to design, develop, and refactor simple Python programs. The certification holder knows the syntax of the Python language to a degree that allows them to work with variables, operators, control flow mechanisms, and functions, as well as understands the fundamentals of the Python data type system, exception handling, troubleshooting, debugging, and the runtime environment.

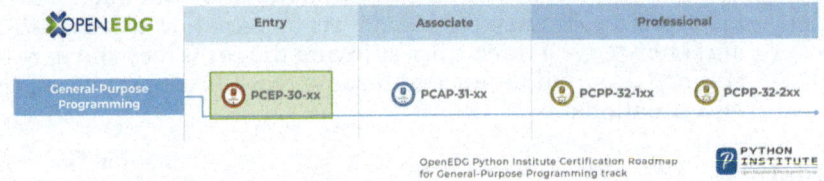

PCEP — Certified Entry-Level Python Programmer certification is an interim step to the *PCAP — Certified Associate in Python Programming* certification, and the starting point to launch a career in software development, Python programming, and related technologies. Becoming PCEP certified will help you stand out from other candidates and get your foot in the door. For more information about the *PCEP — Certified Entry-Level Python Programmer* certification, please visit www.PythonInstitute.org.

PART 1
INTRODUCTION TO PYTHON AND COMPUTER PROGRAMMING

ONE
INTRODUCTION TO PROGRAMMING

A program makes a computer usable. Without a program, a computer, even the most powerful one, is nothing more than an object. Similarly, without a player, a piano is nothing more than a wooden Computers are able to perform very complex tasks, but this ability is not innate. A computer's nature is quite different. It can execute only extremely simple operations. For example, a computer cannot understand the value of a complicated mathematical function by itself, although this isn't beyond the realms of possibility in the near future. Contemporary computers can only evaluate the results of very fundamental operations, like adding or dividing, but they can do it very fast, and can repeat these actions virtually any number of times.

Imagine that you want to know the average speed you've reached during a long journey. You know the distance, you know the time, you need the speed. Naturally, the computer will be able to compute this, but the computer is not aware of such things as distance, speed, or time. Therefore, it is necessary to instruct the computer to:

- accept a number representing the distance;
- accept a number representing the travel time;
- divide the former value by the latter and store the result in the memory;
- display the result (representing the average speed) in a readable format.

These four simple actions form a program. Of course, these examples are not formalized, and they are very far from what the computer can understand, but they are good enough to be translated into a language the computer can accept. Language is the keyword.

Natural languages vs. programming languages

A language is a means (and a tool) for expressing and recording thoughts. There are many languages all around us. Some of them require neither speaking nor writing, such as body language; it's possible to express your deepest feelings very precisely without saying a word. Another language you use each day is your mother tongue, which you use to manifest your will and to ponder reality.

Computers have their own language, too, called machine language, which is very rudimentary. A computer, even the most technically sophisticated, is devoid of even a trace of intelligence. You could say that it is like a well-trained dog — it responds only to a predetermined set of known commands. The commands it recognizes are very simple. We can imagine that the computer responds to orders like "take that number, divide by another and save the result". A complete set of known commands is called an instruction list, sometimes abbreviated to IL. Different types of computers may vary depending on the size of their ILs, and the instructions could be completely different in different models.

NOTE Machine languages are developed by humans.

No computer is currently capable of creating a new language. However, that may change soon. Just as people use a number of very different languages, machines have many different languages, too. The difference, though, is that human languages developed naturally. Moreover, they are still evolving, and new words are created every day as old words disappear. These languages are called natural languages.

What makes a language?

We can say that each language — machine or natural, it doesn't matter — consists of the following elements: an alphabet, which is a set of symbols used to build words of a certain language, such as the Latin alphabet for English, the Cyrillic alphabet for Russian, Kanji for Japanese, and so on; a lexis, aka a dictionary, a set of words the language offers its users — for example, the word "computer" comes from the English language dictionary, while "cmoptrue" doesn't, or the word "chat" is present both in English and French dictionaries, but their meanings are different; a syntax or a set of rules, either formal or informal, written or felt intuitively, used to determine if a certain string of words forms a valid sentence (e.g. "I am a python" is a syntactically correct phrase, while "I a python am" isn't); and finally semantics, a set of rules determining if a certain phrase makes sense. For example, "I ate a doughnut" makes sense, but "A doughnut ate me" doesn't.

Machine language vs. high-level language

The IL is, in fact, the alphabet of a machine language. This is the simplest and most primary set of symbols we can use to give commands to a computer. It's the computer's mother tongue. Unfortunately, this mother tongue is a far cry from a human mother tongue. We both (computers and humans) need something else, a common language for computers and humans, or a bridge between the two different worlds. We need a language in which humans can write their programs and a language that computers may use to execute the programs, one that is far more complex than machine language and yet far simpler than natural language.

Such languages are often called high-level programming languages. They are at least somewhat similar to natural ones in that they use symbols, words and conventions readable to humans. These languages enable humans to express commands to computers that are much more complex than those offered by ILs. A program written in a high-level programming language is called a source code (in contrast to the machine code executed by computers). Similarly, the file containing the source code is called the source file.

Compilation vs. Interpretation

Computer programming is the act of composing the selected programming language's elements in the order that will cause the desired effect. The effect could be different in every specific case — it's up to the programmer's imagination, knowledge and experience.

Of course, such a composition has to be correct in many senses. First, it must be alphabetically correct. A program needs to be written in a recognizable script, such as Roman, Cyrillic, etc. Next, it must be lexically correct. Each programming language has its dictionary and you need to master it; thankfully, it's much simpler and smaller than the dictionary of any natural language. It must also be syntactically correct. Each language has its rules and they must be obeyed. And finally, it needs to be semantically correct. In other words, the program has to make sense. Unfortunately, a programmer can also make mistakes with each of the above four senses. Each of them can cause the program to become completely useless.

Let's assume that you've successfully written a program. How do we persuade the computer to execute it? You have to render your program into machine language. Luckily, the translation can be done by a computer itself, making the whole process fast and efficient. There are two different ways of transforming a program from a high-level programming language into machine language.

The first is compilation — the source program is translated once by getting a file containing the machine code. For example, an *.exe* file if the code is intended to be run under MS Windows. Now you can distribute the file worldwide; the program that performs this translation is called a compiler or translator. However, this translating act must be repeated each time you modify the source code

Introduction To Programming

The second is interpretation — you, or any user of the code, can translate the source program each time it has to be run. The program performing this kind of transformation is called an interpreter, as it interprets the code every time it is intended to be executed. It also means that you cannot just distribute the source code as-is, because the end-user also needs the interpreter to execute it.

Due to some very fundamental reasons, a particular high-level programming language is designed to fall into one of these two categories. There are very few languages that can be both compiled and interpreted. Usually, a programming language is projected with this factor in its constructors' minds — will it be compiled or interpreted?

What does the interpreter do?

Let's assume once more that you have written a program. Now, it exists as a computer file: a computer program is actually a piece of text, so the source code is usually placed in text files.

NOTE It has to be pure text, without any decorations like different fonts, colors, embedded images or other media. Now you have to invoke the interpreter and let it read your source file.

The interpreter reads the source code in a way that is common in Western culture: from top to bottom and from left to right. There are some exceptions — they'll be covered later in the course. First of all, the interpreter checks if all subsequent lines are correct using the four aspects covered earlier.

If the compiler finds an error, it finishes its work immediately. The only result in this case is an error message. The interpreter will inform you where the error is located and what caused it. However, these messages may be misleading, as the interpreter isn't able to follow your exact intentions, and may detect errors at some distance from their real causes. For example, if you try to use an entity of an unknown name, it will cause an error, but the error will be discovered in the place where it tries to use the entity, not where the new entity's name was introduced. In other words, the actual reason is usually located a little earlier in the code, for example, in the place where you had to inform the interpreter that you were going to use the entity of the name.

If the line looks good, the interpreter tries to execute it (note: each line is usually executed separately, so the trio "read-check-execute" can be repeated many times — more times than the actual number of lines in the source file, as some parts of the code may be executed more than once). It is also possible that a significant part of the code may be executed successfully before the interpreter finds an error. This is normal behavior in this execution model.

You may ask now: which is better? The "compiling" model or the "interpreting" model? There is no obvious answer. If there had been, one of these models would have ceased to exist a long time ago. Both of them have their advantages and their disadvantages.

Compilation vs. Interpretation – Advantages and Disadvantages

COMPILATION

Advantages: The execution of the translated code is usually faster; only the user has to have the compiler — the end-user may use the code without it; the translated code is stored using machine language — as it is very hard to understand it, your own inventions and programming tricks are likely to remain your secret.

Disadvantages: the compilation itself may be a very time-consuming process — you may not be able to run your code immediately after making an amendment; you have to have as many compilers as hardware platforms you want your code to be run on.

INTERPRETATION

Advantages: you can run the code as soon as you complete it — there are no additional phases of translation; the code is stored using programming language, not machine language — this means that it can be run on computers using different machine languages; you don't compile your code separately for each different architecture.

Disadvantages: don't expect interpretation to ramp up your code to high speed — your code will share the computer's power with the interpreter, so it can't be really fast; both you and the end user have to have the interpreter to run your code.

What does this all mean for you?

Python is an interpreted language. This means that it inherits all the described advantages and disadvantages. Of course, it adds some of its unique features to both sets. If you want to program in Python, you'll need the Python interpreter. You won't be able to run your code without it. Fortunately, Python is free. This is one of its most important advantages. Due to historical reasons, languages designed to be utilized in the interpretation manner are often called scripting languages, while the source programs encoded using them are called scripts. Okay, let's meet Python.

TWO
INTRODUCTION TO PYTHON

Python is a widely-used, interpreted, object-oriented, and high-level programming language with dynamic semantics, used for general-purpose programming. And while you may know the python as a large snake, the name of the Python programming language comes from an old BBC television comedy sketch series called Monty Python's Flying Circus. At the height of its success, the Monty Python team were performing their sketches to live audiences across the world, including at the Hollywood Bowl. Since Monty Python is considered one of the two fundamental nutrients to a programmer (the other being pizza), Python's creator named the language in honor of the TV show.

Who created Python?

One of the amazing features of Python is the fact that it is actually one person's work. Usually, new programming languages are developed and published by large companies employing lots of professionals, and due to copyright rules, it is very hard to name any of the people involved in the project. Python is an exception. There are not many languages whose authors are known by name. Python was created by Guido van Rossum, born in 1956 in Haarlem, the Netherlands. Of course, Guido van Rossum did not develop and evolve all the Python components himself. The speed with  which Python has spread around the world is a result of the continuous work of thousands (very often anonymous) programmers, testers, users (many of them aren't IT specialists) and enthusiasts, but it must be said that the very first idea (the seed from which Python sprouted) came to one head — Guido's.

A hobby programming project

The circumstances in which Python was created are a bit puzzling. According to Guido van Rossum:

> In December 1989, I was looking for a "hobby" programming project that would keep me occupied during the week around Christmas. My office (...) would be closed, but I had a home computer, and not much else on my hands. I decided to write an interpreter for the new scripting language I had been thinking about lately: a descendant of ABC that would appeal to Unix/C hackers. I chose Python as a working title for the project, being in a slightly irreverent mood (and a big fan of Monty Python's Flying Circus).
>
> — Guido van Rossum

Python goals

In 1999, Guido van Rossum defined his goals for Python:

- an easy and intuitive language just as powerful as those of the major competitors;
- open source, so anyone can contribute to its development;
- code that is as understandable as plain English;
- suitable for everyday tasks, allowing for short development times.

About 20 years later, it is clear that all these intentions have been fulfilled. Some sources say that Python is the most popular programming language in the world, while others claim it's the second or the third. Either way, it still occupies a high rank in the top ten of the PYPL PopularitY of Programming Language and the TIOBE Programming Community Index. Python isn't a young language anymore. It is mature and trustworthy. It's not a one-hit wonder. It's a bright star in the programming firmament, and time spent learning Python is a very good investment.

What makes Python so special?

How does it happen that programmers, young and old, experienced and novice, want to use it? How did it happen that large companies adopted Python and implemented their flagship products using it? There are many reasons — we've listed some of them already, but let's go through them again in a little more detail.

Python is easy to learn — the time needed to learn Python is shorter than for many other languages; this means that it's possible to start the actual programming faster. It's easy to teach — the teaching workload is smaller than that needed by other languages; this means that the teacher can put more emphasis on general, language-independent, programming techniques, not wasting energy on exotic tricks, strange exceptions and incomprehensible rules. It's easy to use for writing new software — it's often possible to write code faster when using Python. It's easy to understand — it's also often easier to understand someone else's code faster if it is written in Python. And finally, it's easy to obtain, install and deploy — Python is free, open and multi-platform; not all languages can boast that.

Python rivals

Python has two direct competitors, with comparable properties and predispositions. These are Perl, a scripting language originally authored by Larry Wall, and Ruby, a scripting language originally authored by Yukihiro Matsumoto. The former is more traditional and more conservative than Python, and resembles some of the old languages derived from the classic C programming language. In contrast, the latter is more innovative and more full of fresh ideas than Python. Python itself lies somewhere between these two creations. The Internet is full of forums with infinite discussions on the superiority of one of these three over the others, should you wish to learn more about each of them.

Where can we see Python in action?

We see it every day and almost everywhere. It's used extensively to implement complex Internet services like search engines, cloud storage and tools, social media and so on. Whenever you use any of these services, you are actually very close to Python, although you wouldn't know it. Many developing tools are implemented in Python. More and more everyday-use applications are being written in Python.

Lots of scientists have abandoned expensive proprietary tools and switched to Python. Lots of IT project testers have started using Python to carry out repeatable test procedures. The list is long.

Why not Python?

Despite Python's growing popularity, there are still some niches where Python is absent, or is rarely seen. We don't often see Python in low-level programming, sometimes called "close to metal" programming. If you want to implement an extremely effective driver or graphical engine, you wouldn't use Python. We also haven't seen it used too much in applications for mobile devices, although this territory will most likely be conquered someday.

There is more than one Python

There are two main kinds of Python, called Python 2 and Python 3. Python 2 is an older version of the original Python. Its development has since been intentionally stalled, although that doesn't mean that there are no updates to it. On the contrary, the updates are issued on a regular basis, but they are not intended to modify the language in any significant way. They rather fix any freshly discovered bugs and security holes. Python 2's development path has reached a dead end already, but Python 2 itself is still very much alive. Python 3 is the newer, or to be more precise, the current, version of the language. It's going through its own evolutionary path, creating its own standards and habits.

These two versions of Python aren't compatible with each other. Python 2 scripts won't run in a Python 3 environment and vice versa, so if you want the old Python 2 code to be run by a Python 3 interpreter, the only possible solution is to rewrite it, not from scratch, of course, as large parts of the code may remain untouched, but you do have to revise all the code to find all possible incompatibilities. Unfortunately, this process cannot be fully automatized. It's too hard, too time-consuming, too expensive, and too risky to migrate an old Python 2 application to a new platform, and it's even possible that rewriting the code will introduce new bugs into it. It's easier, and more sensible, to leave these systems alone and to improve the existing interpreter, instead of trying to work inside the already functioning source code.

Python 3 isn't just a better version of Python 2 — it is a completely different language, although it's very similar to its predecessor. When you look at them from a distance, they appear to be the same, but when you look closely, though, you notice a lot of differences. If you're modifying an old existing Python solution, then it's highly likely that it was coded in Python 2. This is the reason why Python 2 is still in use. There are too many existing Python 2 applications to discard it altogether.

NOTE If you're going to start a new Python project, you should use Python 3, and this is the version of Python that will be used during this course.

It is important to remember that there may be smaller or bigger differences between subsequent Python 3 releases. For example, Python 3.6 introduced ordered dictionary keys by default under the CPython implementation. The good news, though, is that all the newer versions of Python 3 are backward compatible with the previous versions of Python 3. Whenever meaningful and important, we will always try to highlight those differences in the course. All the code samples you will find during the course have been tested against Python 3.4, Python 3.6, Python 3.7, Python 3.8, and Python 3.9.

Python implementations

In addition to Python 2 and Python 3, there is more than one version of each. According to the Python wiki page, an *implementation* of Python refers to "a program or environment, which provides support for the execution of programs written in the Python language, as represented by the CPython reference implementation." The *traditional* implementation of Python, called CPython, is Guido van Rossum's reference version of the Python computing language, and it's most often called just "Python". When you hear the name *CPython*, it's most probably used to distinguish it from other, non-traditional, alternative implementations.

But, first things first. There are the Pythons which are maintained by the people gathered around the PSF (Python Software Foundation), a community that aims to develop, improve, expand, and popularize Python and its environment. The PSF's president is Guido von Rossum himself, and for this reason, these Pythons are called canonical. They are also considered to be reference Pythons, as any other implementation of the language should follow all standards established by the PSF.

Guido van Rossum used the "C" programming language to implement the very first version of his language and this decision is still in force. All Pythons coming from the PSF are written in the "C" language. There are many reasons for this approach. One of them, probably the most important, is that thanks to it, Python may be easily ported and migrated to all platforms with the ability to compile and run "C" language programs — virtually all platforms have this feature — which opens up many expansion opportunities for Python. This is why the PSF implementation is often referred to as CPython. This is the most influential Python among all the Pythons in the world.

Cython is one of a possible number of solutions to the most painful of Python's traits — the lack of efficiency. Large and complex mathematical calculations may be easily coded in Python, much easier than in "C" or any other traditional language, but the resulting code execution may be extremely time-consuming.

How are these two contradictions reconciled? One solution is to write your mathematical ideas using Python, and when you're absolutely sure that your code is correct and produces valid results, you can translate it into "C". Certainly, "C" will run much faster than pure Python. This is what Cython is intended to do — to automatically translate the Python code, clean and clear, but not too swift, into "C" code, complicated and talkative, but agile.

Another version of Python is called Jython. "J" is for "Java". Imagine a Python written in Java instead of C. This is useful, for example, if you develop large and complex systems written entirely in Java and want to add some Python flexibility to them. The traditional CPython may be difficult to integrate into such an environment, as C and Java live in completely different worlds and don't share many common ideas. Jython can communicate with existing Java infrastructure more effectively. This is why some projects find it useful and necessary.

> **NOTE** The current Jython implementation follows Python 2 standards. There is no Jython conforming to Python 3, so far.

The PyPy logo is a rebus. Can you solve it? It means: a Python within a Python. In other words, it represents a Python environment written in Python-like language named RPython (Restricted Python). It is actually a subset of Python. The source code of PyPy is not run in the interpretation manner, but is instead translated into the C programming language and then executed separately. This is useful because if you want to test any new feature that may be (but doesn't have to be) introduced into mainstream Python implementation, it's easier to check it with PyPy than with CPython. This is why PyPy is rather a tool for people developing Python than for the rest of the users. This doesn't make PyPy any less important or less serious than CPython, of course. In addition, PyPy is compatible with the Python 3 language.

MicroPython is an efficient open source software implementation of Python 3 that is optimized to run on microcontrollers. It includes a small subset of the Python Standard Library, but it is largely packed with a large number of features such as interactive prompt or arbitrary precision integers, as well as modules that give the programmer access to low-level hardware. Originally created by Damien George, an

Australian programmer, who in the year 2013 ran a successful campaign on Kickstarter, and released the first MicroPython version with an STM32F4-  powered development board called pyboard. In 2017, MicroPython was used to create CircuitPython, another one open source programming language that runs on the microcontroller hardware, which is a derivative of the MicroPython language.

There are many more different Pythons in the world. You'll find them if you look, but this course will focus on CPython.

THREE
DOWNLOADING AND INSTALLING PYTHON

There are several ways to get your own copy of Python 3, depending on the operating system you use. Linux users most probably have Python already installed — this is the most likely scenario, as Python's infrastructure is intensively used by many Linux OS components. For example, some distributors may couple their specific tools together with the system and many of these tools, like package managers, are often written in Python. Some parts of graphical environments available in the Linux world may use Python, too.

If you're a Linux user, open the terminal/console, and type:

```
python3
```

At the shell prompt, press *Enter* and wait. If you see something like Figure 3.1. Then you don't have to do anything else. If Python 3 is absent, then refer to your Linux documentation in order to find out how to use your package manager to download and install a new package — the one you need is named python3 or its name begins with that.

All non-Linux users can download a copy at https://www.python.org/downloads/.

How to download, install, and configure Python

Because the browser tells the site you've entered the OS you use, the only step you have to take is to click the appropriate Python version you want. In this case, select Python 3. The site always offers you the latest version of it.

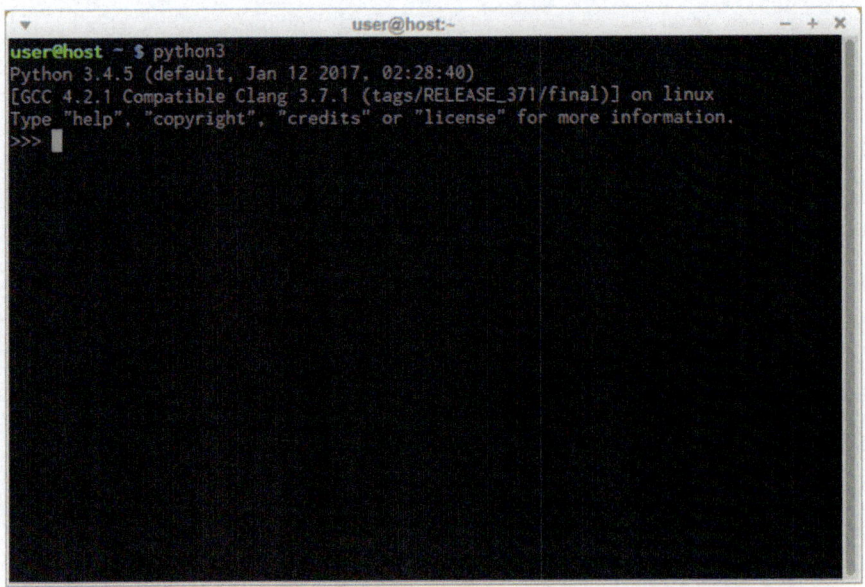

Figure 3.1

If you're a Windows user, start the downloaded *.exe* file and follow all the steps. Leave the default settings the installer suggests for now, with one exception — look at the checkbox named *Add Python 3.x to PATH* and check it. This will make things easier. If you're a macOS user, a version of Python 2 may already have been preinstalled on your computer, but since we will be working with Python 3, you will still need to download and install the relevant *.pkg* file from the Python site.

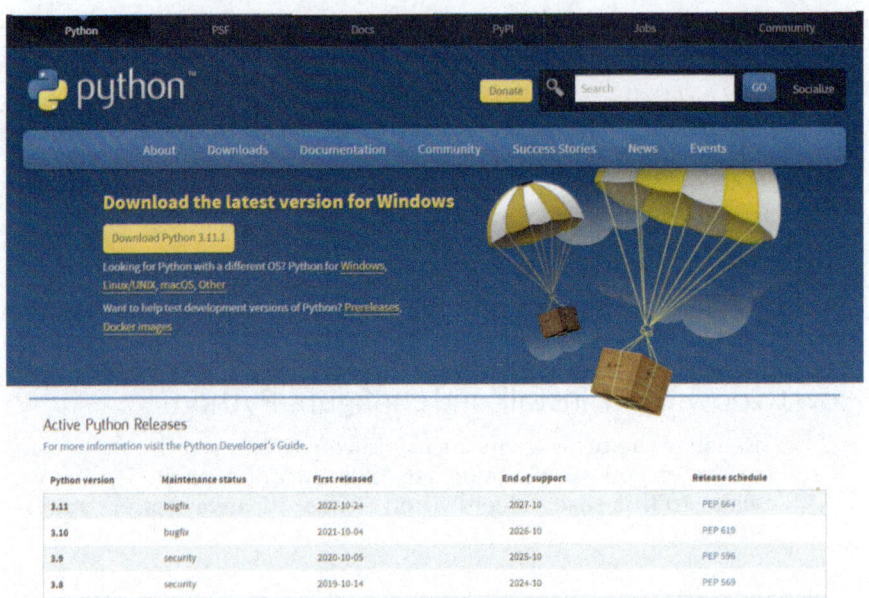

Figure 3.2

Starting your work with Python

Now that you have Python 3 installed, it's time to check if it works and make the very first use of it. This will be a very simple procedure, but it should be enough to convince you that the Python environment is complete and functional. There are many ways of utilizing Python, especially if you're going to be a Python developer. To start your work, you need the following tools:

- an editor which will support you in writing the code (it should have some special features, not available in simple tools); this dedicated editor will give you more than the standard OS equipment;
- a console in which you can launch your newly written code and stop it forcibly when it gets out of control;
- a tool named a debugger, able to launch your code step-by-step, which will allow you to inspect it at each moment of execution.

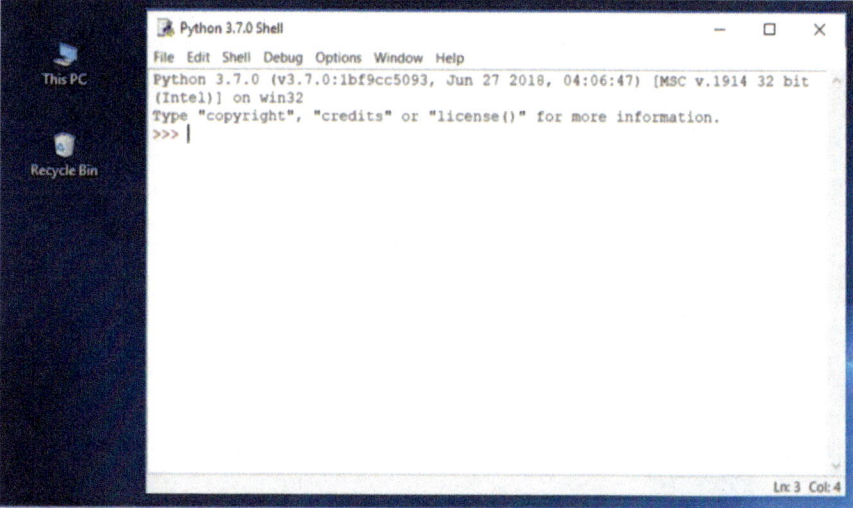

Figure 3.3

Besides its many useful components, the Python 3 standard installation contains a very simple but extremely useful application named IDLE. IDLE is an acronym: Integrated Development and Learning Environment. Navigate through your OS menus, find IDLE somewhere under Python 3.x and launch it. This is what you should see:

Your very first program before your first program

It is now time to write and run your first Python 3 program. It will be very simple, for now. The first step is to create a new source file and fill it with code. Click *File* in the IDLE menu and choose *New file*. As you can see in Figure 3.4, IDLE opens a new window for you. You can use it to write and amend your code.

Downloading And Installing Python   19

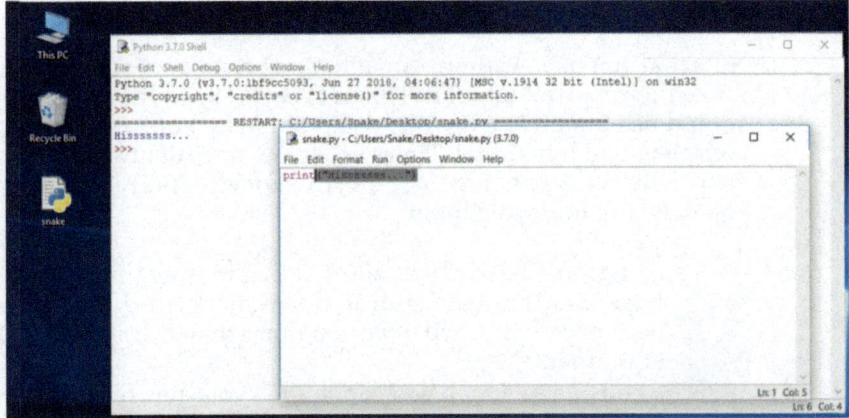

Figure 3.4

This is the editor window. Its only purpose is to be a workplace in which your source code is treated. Do not confuse the editor window with the shell window. They perform different functions. The editor window is currently untitled, but it's good practice to start work by naming the source file.

Click *File* in the new window, then click *Save as...*, select a folder for the new file — the desktop is a good place for your first programming attempts — and chose a name for the new file (Figure 3.5).

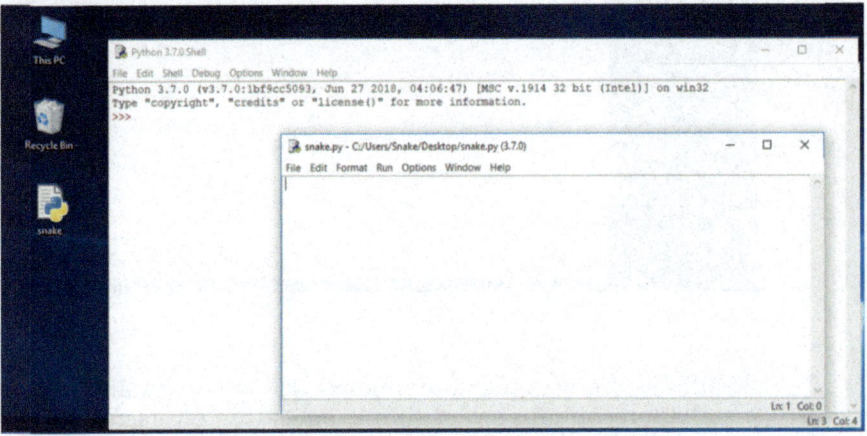

Figure 3.5

NOTE Don't set any extension for the file name you are going to use. Python needs its files to have the *.py* extension, so you should rely on the dialog window's defaults. Using the standard *.py* extension enables the OS to properly open these files.

Now put just one line into your newly opened and named editor window (Figure 3.6). The line looks like this:

```
print("Hisssssss...")
```

Chapter 3

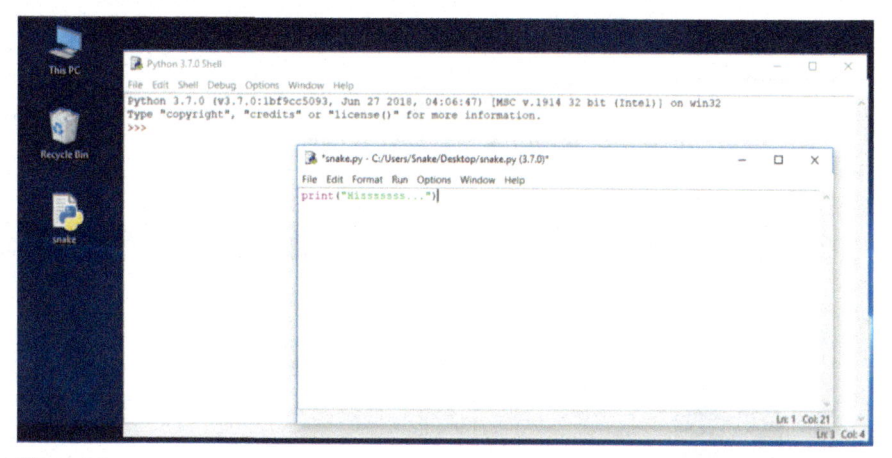

Figure 3.6

We're not going to explain the meaning of the program right now. You'll find a detailed discussion in the next chapter. Take a closer look at the quotation marks. These are the simplest form of quotation marks, called neutral, straight, dumb, etc. and are commonly used in source files. Do not try to use typographic quotes (curved, curly, smart, etc.), used by advanced text processors, as Python doesn't accept them.

Save the file (*File -> Save*) and run the program (*Run -> Run Module*). If everything goes okay and there are no mistakes in the code, the console window will show you the effects caused by running the program (Figure 3.7). In this case, the program hisses. Try to run it once again. And once more. Now close both windows now and return to the desktop.

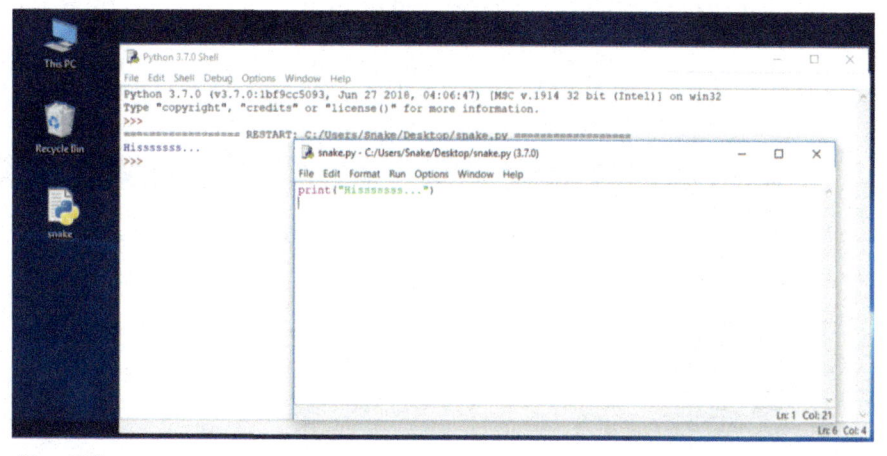

Figure 3.7

Downloading And Installing Python   21

How to spoil and fix your code

Now start IDLE again. Click *File, Open*, point to the file you saved previously and let IDLE read it in. Try to run it again by pressing *F5* when the editor window is active. As you can see, IDLE is able to save your code and retrieve it when you need it again.

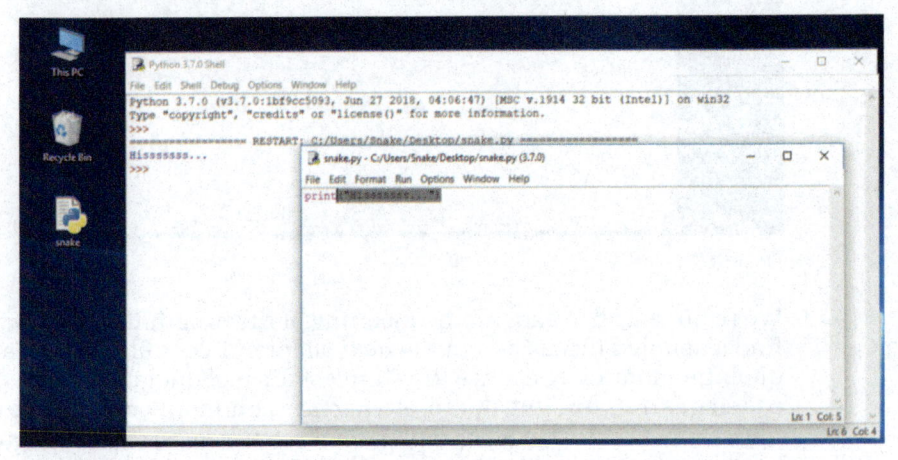

Figure 3.8

IDLE contains one additional and helpful feature. First, remove the closing parenthesis. Then enter the parenthesis again. Your code should look like this:

```
Hisssssss...
```

Every time you put the closing parenthesis in your program, IDLE will show the part of the text limited with a pair of corresponding parentheses (Figure 3.8). This helps you to remember to place them in pairs. Remove the closing parenthesis again. The code becomes erroneous. It contains a syntax error now (Figure 3.9). IDLE should not

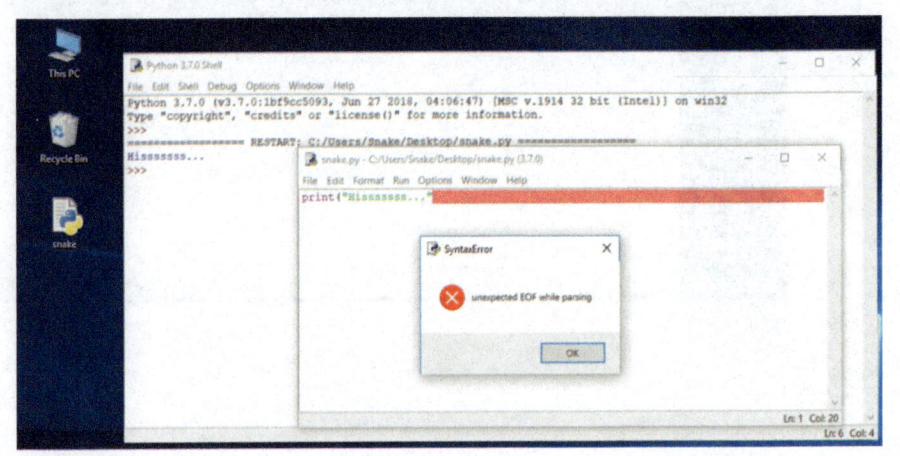

Figure 3.9

let you run it. Try to run the program again. IDLE will remind you to save the modified file. Follow the instructions. Watch all the windows carefully. A new window appears — it says that the interpreter has encountered an EOF (*end-of-file*) although, in its opinion, the code should contain some more text. The editor window shows clearly where it happened.

Fix the code now. It should look like this:

```
print("Hisssssss...")
```

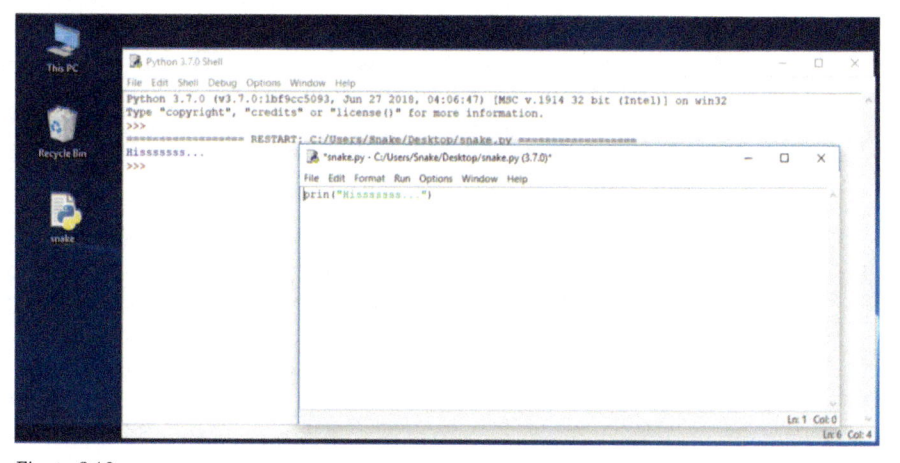

Figure 3.10

Run it to see if it "hisses" again. Let's spoil the code one more time. Remove one letter from the word `print`. Run the code by pressing F5 (Figure 3.10). What happens now? As you can see, Python is not able to recognize the instruction.

You may have noticed that the error message generated for the previous error is quite different from the first one (Figure 3.11).

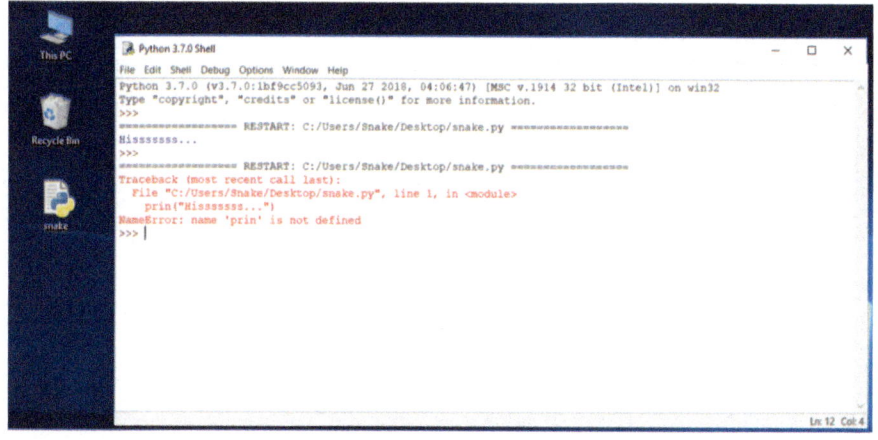

Figure 3.11

Downloading And Installing Python   23

This is because the nature of the error is different and the error is discovered at a different stage of interpretation. The editor window will not provide any useful information regarding the error, but the console windows might. In the subsequent lines, the message in red shows the following information:

- the traceback (which is the path that the code traverses through different parts of the program – you can ignore it for now, as it is empty in such a simple code);
- the location of the error (the name of the file containing the error, line number and module name); note: the number may be misleading, as Python usually shows the place where it first notices the effects of the error, not necessarily the error itself;
- the content of the erroneous line; note: IDLE's editor window doesn't show line numbers, but it displays the current cursor location at the bottom-right corner; use it to locate the erroneous line in a long source code;
- the name of the error and a short explanation.

Experiment with creating new files and running your code. Try to output a different message to the screen, e.g. `roar!`, `meow`, or even maybe an `oink!`. Try to spoil and fix your code — see what happens.

PART 2

PYTHON DATA TYPES, VARIABLES, OPERATORS, AND BASIC I/O OPERATIONS

FOUR
THE "HELLO, WORLD!" PROGRAM

It's time to start writing some real, working Python code. It'll be very simple for the time being. As we're going to show you some fundamental concepts and terms, these snippets of code won't be all that serious or complex. Run the following code. If everything goes okay here, you'll see the line of text in the console window.

```
1   print("Hello, world!")
2
```

Alternatively, launch IDLE, create a new Python source file, fill it with this code, name the file and save it. Now run it. If everything goes okay, you'll see the text contained within the quotation marks in the IDLE console window. The code you have run should look familiar. You saw something very similar when we led you through the setting up of the IDLE environment. Now we'll spend some time showing and explaining to you what you're actually seeing, and why it looks like this.

As you can see, this first program consists of the following parts: the word `print`; an opening parenthesis; a quotation mark; a line of text: `Hello, World!`; another quotation mark; a closing parenthesis. Each of these plays a very important role in the code.

The `print()` function

Look at this line of code:

```
1   print("Hello, World!")
2
```

The word *print* that you can see here is a function name. That doesn't mean that wherever the word appears it is always a function name. The meaning of the word comes from the context in which the word has been used. You've probably encountered the term *function* many times before, during math classes. You can probably also list several names of mathematical functions, like *sine* or *log*. Python functions, however, are more flexible, and can contain more content than their mathematical siblings.

A function in this context is a separate part of the computer code able to: cause some effect, evaluate a value, and return the value as the function's result; this is what makes Python functions the relatives of mathematical concepts. The effect can be something like sending text to the terminal, creating a file, drawing an image, playing a sound, etc. This is something completely unheard of in the world of mathematics. The value that it evaluates can be, for example, the square root of a value or the length of a given text. Moreover, many Python functions can do these two things together.

Where do functions come from?

Functions can come from Python itself. The print function is one of this kind. Such a function is an added value received together with Python and its environment. It is built-in, which means you don't have to do anything special if you want to make use of it. Functions may come from one or more of Python's add-ons named *modules*; some of the modules come with Python, while others may require separate installation – whatever the case, they all need to be explicitly connected with your code. Functions can also come from your own code. You can write them yourself, placing as many functions as you want and need inside your program to make it simpler, clearer and more elegant.

The name of the function should be significant — the name of the print function is self-evident. Of course, if you're going to make use of any already existing function, you have no influence on its name, but when you start writing your own functions, you should consider carefully your choice of names.

Function arguments

As we said before, a function may have an effect and a result. There's also a third, very important, function component — the argument(s). Mathematical functions usually take one argument. For example, $\sin(x)$ takes an x, which is the measure of an angle. Python functions, on the other hand, are more versatile. Depending on the individual needs, they may accept any number of arguments — as many as necessary to perform their tasks.

NOTE When we said *any number*, that includes zero – some Python functions don't need any argument.

```
print("Hello, World!")
```

In spite of the number of needed/provided arguments, Python functions strongly demand the presence of a pair of parentheses — opening and closing ones, respectively. If you want to deliver one or more arguments to a function, you place them inside the parentheses. If you're going to use a function which doesn't take any argument, you still have to have the parentheses.

> **NOTE** To distinguish ordinary words from function names, place a pair of empty parentheses after their names, even if the corresponding function wants one or more arguments. This is a standard convention.

The function we're talking about here is `print()`. Does the `print()` function in our example have any arguments? Of course it does, but what are they?

A string as an argument of the `print()` function

The only argument delivered to the `print()` function in this example is a string:

```
print("Hello, World!")
```

As you can see, the string is delimited with quotes — in fact, the quotes make the string — they cut out a part of the code and assign a different meaning to it. You can imagine that the quotes say something like: the text between us is not code. It isn't intended to be executed, and you should take it as is. Almost anything you put inside the quotes will be taken literally, not as code, but as data. Try to play with this particular string. Modify it, enter some new content, delete some of the existing content. There's more than one way to specify a string inside Python's code, but for now, though, this one is enough.

So far, you have learned about two important parts of the code: the function and the string. We've talked about them in terms of syntax, but now it's time to discuss them in terms of semantics.

Function invocation

The function name (`print` in this case) along with the parentheses and argument(s), forms the function invocation.

```
1  print("Hello, World!")
2
```

We'll discuss this in more depth soon, but let's just shed a little light on it right now.

What happens when Python encounters an invocation like this one?

```
function_name(argument)
```

First, Python checks if the name specified is legal. It browses its internal data in order to find an existing function of the name; if this search fails, Python aborts the code. Second, Python checks if the function's requirements for the number of arguments allows you to invoke the function in this way. For example, if a specific function demands exactly two arguments, any invocation delivering only one argument will be considered erroneous, and will abort the code's execution. Third, Python leaves your code for a moment and jumps into the function you want to invoke. Of course, it takes your argument(s) too and passes it/them to the function. Fourth, the function executes its code, causes the desired effect, if any, evaluates the desired result(s), if any, and finishes its task. Finally, Python returns to your code, to the place just after the invocation, and resumes its execution.

LAB: Working with the `print()` function

The `print()` command, which is one of the easiest directives in Python, simply prints out a line to the screen.

In your first lab:

- Use the `print()` function to print the line `Hello, Python!` to the screen. Use double quotes around the string.
- Having done that, use the `print()` function again, but this time print your first name.
- Remove the double quotes and run your code. Watch Python's reaction. What kind of error is thrown?
- Then, remove the parentheses, put back the double quotes, and run your code again. What kind of error is thrown this time?
- Experiment as much as you can. Change double quotes to single quotes, use multiple `print()` functions on the same line, and then on different lines. See what happens.

The `print()` function and its effect, arguments, and values returned

Three important questions have to be answered as soon as possible. The first is: what effect does the `print()` function cause? The effect is very useful and very spectacular. The function takes its arguments, converts them into human-readable form if needed, and sends the resulting data to the output device, usually the console; in other words, anything you put into the `print()` function will appear on your screen. Remember that a function may accept more than one argument and may also accept less than one argument. It is not always necessary to convert the arguments. For example, strings don't require this action, as the string is already readable. No wonder then, that from now on, you'll utilize `print()` very intensively to see the results of your operations and evaluations.

The second question to answer is: what arguments does `print()` expect? The answer is any. We'll show you soon that `print()` is able to operate with virtually all types of data offered by Python. Strings, numbers, characters, logical values, objects — any of these may be successfully passed to `print()`.

The third question to answer is: what value does the `print()` function return? The answer is none. Its effect is enough.

Instructions

You have already seen a computer program that contains one function invocation. A function invocation is one of many possible kinds of Python instruction.cOf course, any complex program usually contains many more instructions than one. The question is: how do you couple more than one instruction into the Python code? Python's syntax is quite specific in this area. Unlike most programming languages, Python requires that there cannot be more than one instruction in a line. A line can be empty, that is, it may contain no instruction at all, but it must not contain two, three or more instructions. This is strictly prohibited.

NOTE Python makes one exception to this rule — it allows one instruction to spread across more than one line, which may be helpful when your code contains complex constructions.

Let's expand the code a bit. Run it and note what you see.

```
1  print("The itsy bitsy spider climbed up the waterspout.")
2  print("Down came the rain and washed the spider out.")
3
```

Your Python console should now look like this:

```
The itsy bitsy spider climbed up the waterspout.
Down came the rain and washed the spider out.
```

This is a good opportunity to make some observations. The program invokes the `print()` function twice, and you can see two separate lines in the console — this means that `print()` begins its output from a new line each time it starts its execution; you can change this behavior, but you can also use it to your advantage. Each `print()` invocation contains a different string as its argument, and the console content reflects it — this means that the instructions in the code are executed in the same order in which they have been placed in the source file; no subsequent instruction is executed until the previous one is completed. There are some exceptions to this rule, but you can ignore them for now.

We've changed the example a bit — we've added one empty `print()` function invocation. We call it empty because we haven't delivered any arguments to the function. You can see it here. Run the code. What happens?

```
1  print("The itsy bitsy spider climbed up the waterspout.")
2  print()
3  print("Down came the rain and washed the spider out.")
4
```

If everything goes right, you should see something like this:

```
The itsy bitsy spider climbed up the waterspout.

Down came the rain and washed the spider out.
```

As you can see, the empty `print()` invocation is not as empty as you may have expected — it does output an empty line, or — and this interpretation is also correct — it outputs a newline. This is not the only way to produce a newline in the output console. We're now going to show you another way.

Python escape and newline characters

We've modified the code again. Look at it carefully. There are two very subtle changes — we've inserted a strange pair of characters inside the rhyme. They look like this: \n.

```
1  print("The itsy bitsy spider\nclimbed up the waterspout.")
2  print()
3  print("Down came the rain\nand washed the spider out.")
4
```

Interestingly, while you can see two characters, Python sees one. The backslash (\) has a very special meaning when used inside strings — this is called the escape character. The word *escape* should be understood specifically — it means that the series of characters in the string escapes for the moment, a very short moment, to introduce a special inclusion. In other words, the backslash doesn't mean anything in itself, but is only a kind of announcement that the next character after the backslash has a different meaning too.

The letter n placed after the backslash comes from the word *newline*. Both the backslash and the n form a special symbol named a newline character, which urges the console to start a new output line. Run the code. Your console should now look like this:

```
The itsy bitsy spider
climbed up the waterspout.

Down came the rain
and washed the spider out.
```

As you can see, two newlines appear in the nursery rhyme, in the places where the \n have been used. This convention has two important consequences. The first is that if you want to put just one backslash inside a string, don't forget its escaping nature — you have to double it. For example, an invocation like this will cause an error:

```
print("\")
```

While this one won't:

```
print("\\")
```

The second consequence is that not all escape pairs, that is, the backslash coupled with another character, mean something. Experiment with your code, run it, and see what happens.

```
1   print("The itsy bitsy spider\nclimbed up the waterspout.")
2   print()
3   print("Down came the rain\nand washed the spider out.")
4
```

Using multiple arguments

So far we have tested the `print()` function behavior with no arguments, and with one argument. It's also worth trying to feed the `print()` function with more than one argument. This is what we're going to test now:

```
1   print("The itsy bitsy spider" , "climbed up" , "the
    waterspout.")
2
```

There is one `print()` function invocation, but it contains three arguments. All of them are strings. The arguments are separated by commas. We've surrounded them with spaces to make them more visible, but it's not really necessary, and we won't be doing it anymore. In this case, the commas separating the arguments play a completely different role than the comma inside the string. The former is a part of Python's syntax, while the latter is intended to be shown in the console.

If you look at the code again, you'll see that there are no spaces inside the strings. Run the code and see what happens. The console should now be showing the following text:

```
The itsy bitsy spider climbed up the waterspout.
```

The spaces, removed from the strings, have appeared again. Can you explain why? Two conclusions emerge from this example: a `print()` function invoked with more than one argument outputs them all on one line; and the `print()` function puts a space between the outputted arguments on its own initiative.

Positional arguments

Now that you know a bit about `print()` function customs, we're going to show you how to change them. You should be able to predict the output without running the code.

```
1   print("My name is", "Python.")
2   print("Monty Python.")
3
```

The way in which we are passing the arguments into the `print()` function is the most common in Python, and is called the positional way. This name comes from the fact that the meaning of the argument is dictated by its position; for example, the second argument will be outputted after the first, not the other way round. Run the code and check if the output matches your predictions.

Keyword arguments

Python offers another mechanism for the passing of arguments, which can be helpful when you want to convince the `print()` function to change its behavior a bit. We aren't going to explain it in depth right now. We plan to do this when we talk about functions. For now, we simply want to show you how it works. Feel free to use it in your own programs. The mechanism is called keyword arguments. The name stems from the fact that the meaning of these arguments is taken not from its location (position) but from the special word (keyword) used to identify them. The `print()` function has two keyword arguments that you can use for your purposes. The first is called `end`. Here's a very simple example how to use a keyword argument.

```
1  print("My name is", "Python.", end=" ")
2  print("Monty Python.")
3
```

In order to use it, it is necessary to know some rules: a keyword argument consists of three elements: a keyword identifying the argument (`end` here); an equal sign (`=`); and a value assigned to that argument. Any keyword arguments have to be put after the last positional argument. This is very important. In our example, we have made use of the `end` keyword argument, and set it to a string containing one space. Run the code to see how it works. The console should now be showing the following text:

```
My name is Python. Monty Python.
```

As you can see, the `end` keyword argument determines the characters the `print()` function sends to the output once it reaches the end of its positional arguments. The default behavior reflects the situation where the `end` keyword argument is implicitly used in the following way: `end="\n"`. And now it's time to try something more difficult. If you look carefully, you'll see that we've used the `end` argument, but the string assigned to it is empty (it contains no characters at all). What will happen now? Run the program to find out.

```
1  print("My name is ", end="")
2  print("Monty Python.")
3
```

As the `end` argument has been set to nothing, the `print()` function outputs nothing too, once its positional arguments have been exhausted. The console should now be showing the following text:

```
My name is Monty Python.
```

No newlines have been sent to the output. The string assigned to the **end** keyword argument can be of any length. Experiment with it if you want. We said previously that the **print()** function separates its outputted arguments with spaces. This behavior can be changed, too. The keyword argument that can do this is named **sep** (as in *separator*). Look at the following code and run it.

```
1  print("My", "name", "is", "Monty", "Python.", sep="-")
2
```

The **sep** argument delivers the following results:

```
My-name-is-Monty-Python.
```

The **print()** function now uses a dash, instead of a space, to separate the outputted arguments.

NOTE The **sep** argument's value may be an empty string, too. Try it for yourself.

Both keyword arguments may be mixed in one invocation, just like here.

```
1  print("My", "name", "is", sep="_", end="*")
2  print("Monty", "Python.", sep="*", end="*\n")
3
```

The example doesn't make much sense, but it visibly presents the interactions between **end** and **sep**. Can you predict the output? Run the code and see if it matches your predictions.

Now that you understand the **print()** function, you're ready to consider how to store and process data in Python. Without **print()**, you wouldn't be able to see any results.

LAB: The print() function and its arguments

Modify the first line of code, using the **sep** and **end** keywords, to match the expected output. Use the two **print()** functions. Don't change anything in the second **print()** invocation.

EXPECTED OUTPUT
```
Programming***Essentials***in...Python
```

CODE
```
1  print("Programming","Essentials","in")
2  print("Python")
3
```

LAB: Formatting the output

We strongly encourage you to play with the code we've written for you, and make some, maybe even destructive, amendments. Feel free to modify any part of the code, but there is one condition — learn from your mistakes and draw your own conclusions.

Try to:

- minimize the number of `print()` function invocations by inserting the `\n` sequence into the strings;
- make the arrow twice as large, but keep the proportions;
- duplicate the arrow, placing both arrows side by side; note: a string may be multiplied by using the following trick: `"string"*2` will produce `"stringstring"` (we'll tell you more about it soon)
- remove any of the quotes, and look carefully at Python's response; pay attention to where Python sees an error — is this the place where the error really exists?
- do the same with some of the parentheses;
- change any of the `print` words into something else, differing only in case (e.g. `Print`) — what happens now?
- replace some of the quotes with apostrophes; watch what happens carefully.

CODE

```
 1
 2
 3   print("    *")
 4   print("   * *")
 5   print("  *   *")
 6   print(" *     *")
 7   print("***   ***")
 8   print("  *   *")
 9   print("  *   *")
10   print("  *****")
11
```

Summary

1. The `print()` function is a built-in function. It prints/outputs a specified message to the screen/console window.

2. Built-in functions, contrary to user-defined functions, are always available and don't have to be imported. Python 3.8 comes with 69 built-in functions. You can find their full list provided in alphabetical order in the Python Standard Library.

3. To call a function, you need to use the function name followed by parentheses. This process is known as function invocation or function call. You can pass arguments into a function by placing them inside the parentheses. You must separate arguments with a comma. For example,

`print("Hello,","world!")`. An "empty" `print()` function outputs an empty line to the screen.

4. Python strings are delimited with quotes, such as `"I am a string"` (double quotes), or `'I am a string, too'` (single quotes).

5. Computer programs are collections of instructions. An instruction is a command to perform a specific task when executed, for example, to print a certain message to the screen.

6. In Python strings the backslash (\) is a special character which announces that the next character has a different meaning. For example, \n (the newline character) starts a new output line.

7. Positional arguments are the ones whose meaning is dictated by their position, for example, the second argument is outputted after the first, the third is outputted after the second, etc.

8. Keyword arguments are the ones whose meaning is not dictated by their location, but by a special word (keyword) used to identify them.

9. The `end` and `sep` parameters can be used for formatting the output of the `print()` function. The `sep` parameter specifies the separator between the outputted arguments, for example, `print("H","E","L","L","O",sep="-")`, whereas the `end` parameter specifies what to print at the end of the print statement.

Quiz

QUESTION 1: What is the output of the following program?

```
1    print("My\nname\nis\nBond.", end=" ")
2    print("James Bond.")
3
```

QUESTION 2: What is the output of the following program?

```
1    print(sep="&", "fish", "chips")
2
```

QUESTION 3: Which of the following `print()` function invocations will cause a `SyntaxError`?

```
1    print('Greg\'s book.')
2    print("'Greg's book.'")
3    print('"Greg\'s book."')
4    print("Greg\'s book.")
5    print('"Greg's book."')
```

FIVE
PYTHON LITERALS

Now that you have a little knowledge of some of the powerful features offered by the `print()` function, it's time to learn about some new issues, and one important new term — the literal. A literal is data whose values are determined by the literal itself. As this is a difficult concept to understand, a good example may be helpful. Take a look at the following set of digits:

    123

Can you guess what value it represents? Of course you can — it's *one hundred twenty three*. But what about this:

    c

Does it represent any value? Maybe. It can be the symbol of the speed of light, for example. It can also be the constant of integration. Or even the length of a hypotenuse in the sense of a Pythagorean theorem. There are many possibilities. You cannot choose the right one without some additional knowledge. And this is the clue: `123` is a literal, and `c` is not. You use literals to encode data and to put them into your code. We're now going to show you some conventions you have to obey when using Python. Let's start with a simple experiment — take a look at the following snippet.

```
1   print("2")
2   print(2)
3
```

The first line looks familiar. The second seems to be erroneous due to the visible lack of quotes. Try to run it. If everything goes okay, you'll now see two identical lines. What happened? What does it mean?

Through this example, you encounter two different types of literals: a string, which you already know; and an integer number, something completely new. The `print()` function presents them in exactly the same way — this example is obvious, as their human-readable representation is also the same. Internally, in the computer's memory, these two values are stored in completely different ways — the string exists as just a string — a series of letters. The number is converted into machine representation (a set of bits). The `print()` function is able to show them both in a form readable to humans. We're now going to be spending some time discussing numeric literals and their internal life.

Integers

You may already know a little about how computers perform calculations on numbers. Perhaps you've heard of the binary system, and know that it's the system computers use for storing numbers, and that those computers can perform any operation upon them. We won't explore the intricacies of positional numeric systems here, but we will say that the numbers handled by modern computers are of two types: integers, that is, those which are devoid of the fractional part; and floating-point numbers (or simply floats), that contain, or are able to contain, the fractional part. This definition is not entirely accurate, but quite sufficient for now. The distinction is very important, and the boundary between these two types of numbers is very strict. Both of these kinds of numbers differ significantly in how they're stored in a computer memory and in the range of acceptable values.

The characteristic of the numeric value which determines its kind, range, and application, is called the type. If you encode a literal and place it inside Python code, the form of the literal determines the representation or type Python will use to store it in the memory.

We'll come back to floating-point numbers soon, but for now, let's leave them aside and consider the question of how Python recognizes integers. The process is almost like how you would write them with a pencil on paper — it's simply a string of digits that make up the number. But there's a reservation — you must not interject any characters that are not digits inside the number.

Take, for example, the number *eleven million one hundred eleven thousand one hundred eleven*. If you took a pencil in your hand right now, you would write the number like this: `11,111,111`, or like this: `11.111.111`, or even like this: `11111111`. It's clear that this provision makes it easier to read, especially when the number consists of many digits. However, Python doesn't accept things like these. It's prohibited. What Python does allow, though, is the use of underscores in numeric literals. Therefore, you can write this number either like this: `11111111`, or like this: `11_111_111`.

> **NOTE** Python 3.6 has introduced underscores in numeric literals, allowing for the placement of single underscores between digits and after base specifiers for improved readability. This feature is not available in older versions of Python.

And how do we code negative numbers in Python? As usual — by adding a minus. You can write: `-11111111`, or `-11_111_111`. Positive numbers do not need to be preceded by the plus sign, but it's permissible, if you wish to do it. The following lines describe the same number: `+11111111` and `11111111`.

Octal and hexadecimal numbers

There are two additional conventions in Python that are unknown to the world of mathematics. The first allows us to use numbers in an octal representation. If an integer number is preceded by an `0O` or `0o` prefix (zero-o), it will be treated as an octal value. This means that the number must contain digits taken from the [0..7] range only. `0o123` is an octal number with a (decimal) value equal to `83`. The `print()` function does the conversion automatically. Try this:

```
1  print(0o123)
2
```

The second convention allows us to use hexadecimal numbers. Such numbers should be preceded by the prefix `0x` or `0X` (zero-x). `0x123` is a hexadecimal number with a (decimal) value equal to `291`. The `print()` function can manage these values too. Try this:

```
1  print(0x123)
2
```

Floats

Now it's time to talk about another type, which is designed to represent and to store the numbers that, as a mathematician would say, have a non-empty decimal fraction. They are the numbers that have, or may have, a fractional part after the decimal point, and although such a definition is very poor, it's certainly sufficient for what we wish to discuss. Whenever we use a term like *two and a half* or *minus zero point four*, we think of numbers which the computer considers floating-point numbers:

```
2.5
-0.4
```

> **NOTE** *Two and a half* looks normal when you write it in a program, although if your native language prefers to use a comma instead of a point in the number, you should ensure that your number doesn't contain any commas at all.

Python will not accept commas, or in very rare but possible cases, may misunderstand your intentions, as the comma itself has its own reserved meaning in Python.

If you want to use just a value of two and a half, you should write it as shown previously. Note once again: there is a point between 2 and 5, not a comma. As you can probably imagine, the value of zero point four could be written in Python as:

```
0.4
```

But don't forget this simple rule: you can omit zero when it is the only digit in front of or after the decimal point. In essence, you can write the value 0.4 as:

```
.4
```

For example: the value of 4.0 could be written as:

```
4.
```

This will change neither its type nor its value.

Ints vs. floats

The decimal point is essential for recognizing floating-point numbers in Python. Look at these two numbers:

```
4
4.0
```

You may think that they are exactly the same, but Python sees them in a completely different way. `4` is an integer number, whereas `4.0` is a floating-point number. The point is what makes a float. On the other hand, it's not only points that make a float. You can also use the letter `e`.

When you want to use any numbers that are very large or very small, you can use scientific notation. Take, for example, the speed of light, expressed in *meters per second*. Written directly it would look like this: 300000000. To avoid writing out so many zeros, physics textbooks use an abbreviated form, which you have probably already seen: 3×10^8. It reads: three times ten to the power of eight. In Python, the same effect is achieved in a slightly different way — take a look:

```
3E8
```

The letter `E` (you can also use the lower-case letter `e` — it comes from the word exponent) is a concise record of the phrase *times ten to the power of*.

NOTE: The exponent (the value after the *E*) has to be an integer; the base (the value in front of the *E*) may be either an integer or a float.

Coding floats

Let's see how this convention is used to record numbers that are very small, in the sense of their absolute value, which is close to zero. A physical constant called *Planck's constant* (and denoted as *h*), according to the textbooks, has the value of: 6.62607 x 10-34. If you would like to use it in a program, you should write it this way:

```
6.62607E-34
```

NOTE The fact that you've chosen one of the possible forms of coding float values doesn't mean that Python will present it the same way. Python may sometimes choose different notation than you.

For example, let's say you've decided to use the following float literal:

```
0.00000000000000000000001
```

When you run this literal through Python:

```
1  print(0.00000000000000000000001)
2
```

This is the result:

```
1e-22
```

Python always chooses the more economical form of the number's presentation, and you should take this into consideration when creating literals.

Strings

Strings are used when you need to process text, like names of all kinds, addresses, novels, etc., not numbers. You already know a bit about them, for example, that strings need quotes the way floats need points.

This is a very typical string: `"I am a string."` However, there is a catch. The catch is how to encode a quote inside a string which is already delimited by quotes. Let's assume that we want to print a very simple message saying:

```
I like "Monty Python"
```

How do we do it without generating an error? There are two possible solutions. The first is based on the concept we already know of the escape character, which you should remember is played by the backslash. The backslash can escape quotes too. A quote preceded by a backslash changes its meaning — it's not a delimiter, but just a quote. This will work as intended:

```
1  print("I like \"Monty Python\"")
2
```

> **NOTE** There are two escaped quotes inside the string — can you see them both?

The second solution may be a bit surprising. Python can use an apostrophe instead of a quote. Either of these characters may delimit strings, but you must be consistent. If you open a string with a quote, you have to close it with a quote. If you start a string with an apostrophe, you have to end it with an apostrophe. This example will work too:

```
1  print('I like "Monty Python"')
2
```

> **NOTE** You don't need to do any escaping here.

Coding strings

Now, the next question is: how do you embed an apostrophe into a string placed between apostrophes? You should already know the answer, or to be precise, two possible answers. Try to print out a string containing the following message:

```
I'm Monty Python.
```

Do you know how to do it? Check in the answers section to see if you were right.

As you can see, the backslash is a very powerful tool — it can escape not only quotes, but also apostrophes. We've shown it already, but we want to emphasize this phenomenon once more: a string can be empty — it may contain no characters at all. An empty string still remains a string:

```
''
""
```

Boolean values

To conclude with Python's literals, there are two additional ones. They're not as obvious as any of the previous ones, as they're used to represent a very abstract value — truthfulness. Each time you ask Python if one number is greater than another, the question results in the creation of some specific data — a Boolean value.

The name comes from George Boole (1815-1864), the author of the fundamental work, *The Laws of Thought*, which contains the definition of Boolean algebra — a part of algebra which makes use of only two distinct values: `True` and `False`, denoted as `1` and `0`. A programmer writes a program, and the program asks questions. Python executes the program, and provides the answers. The program must be able to react according to the received answers. Fortunately, computers know only two kinds of answers: Yes, this is true; or No, this is false. You'll never get a response like: I don't know or Probably yes, but I don't know for sure. Python, then, is a binary reptile.

These two Boolean values have strict denotations in Python:

```
True
False
```

You cannot change anything — you have to take these symbols as they are, including case-sensitivity. Here's a challenge: What will be the output of the following snippet of code?

```
1    print(True > False)
2    print(True < False)
3
```

Run the code to check. Can you explain the result?

LAB: Python literals — strings

Write a one-line piece of code, using the `print()` function, as well as the newline and escape characters, to match the expected result outputted on three lines.

EXPECTED OUTPUT
```
"I'm"
""learning""
"""Python"""
```

Summary

1. Literals are notations for representing some fixed values in code. Python has various types of literals — for example, a literal can be a number (numeric literals, e.g. `123`), or a string (string literals, e.g. "I am a literal.").

2. The binary system is a system of numbers that employs 2 as the base. Therefore, a binary number is made up of 0s and 1s only, e.g. `1010` is *10* in decimal. Octal and hexadecimal numeration systems, similarly, employ *8* and *16* as their bases respectively. The hexadecimal system uses the decimal numbers and six extra letters.

3. Integers, or simply ints, are one of the numerical types supported by Python. They are numbers written without a fractional component, for example, `256` or `-1` (negative integers).

4. Floating-point numbers, or simply floats, are another one of the numerical types supported by Python. They are numbers that contain, or are able to contain, a fractional component, e.g. `1.27`.

5. To encode an apostrophe or a quote inside a string, you can either use the escape character (e.g. `'I\'m happy.'`) or open and close the string using an opposite set of symbols to the ones you wish to encode, (e.g. `"I'm happy."`) to encode an apostrophe, and `'He said "Python", not "typhoon"'` to encode a quote.

6. Boolean values are the two constant objects `True` and `False` used to represent truth values, In numeric contexts, `1` is `True`, while `0` is `False`.

EXTRA There is one more, special literal that is used in Python: the `None` literal. This literal is a `NoneType` object, and it is used to represent the absence of a value. We'll tell you more about it soon.

Quiz

QUESTION 1: What types of literals are the following two examples?

```
"Hello ", "007"
```

QUESTION 2: What types of literals are the following four examples?

```
"1.5", 2.0, 528, False
```

QUESTION 3: What is the decimal value of the following binary number?

```
1011
```

SIX
OPERATORS: DATA MANIPULATION TOOLS

Now, we're going to show you a completely new side of the `print()` function. You already know that the function is able to show you the values of the literals passed to it by arguments. Run the following code. Can you guess the output?

```
1    print(2+2)
2
```

You should see the number four. Feel free to experiment with other operators. Without taking this too seriously, you've just discovered that Python can be used as a calculator. Not a very handy one, and definitely not a pocket one, but a calculator nonetheless. Taking it more seriously, we are now entering the province of operators and expressions.

Basic operators

An operator is a symbol of the programming language, which is able to operate on the values. For example, just as in arithmetic, the + (plus) sign is the operator which is able to add two numbers, giving the result of the addition. Not all Python operators are as obvious as the plus sign, though, so let's go through some of the operators available in Python, and we'll explain which rules govern their use, and how to interpret the operations they perform. We'll begin with the operators which are associated with the most widely recognizable arithmetic operations.

They are:

+

-

*

/

//

%

**

The order of their appearance is not accidental. We'll talk more about it once we've gone through them all.

> **NOTE** Data and operators when connected together form expressions. The simplest expression is a literal itself.

Exponentiation

Look at the following example:

```
1  print(2 ** 3)
2  print(2 ** 3.)
3  print(2. ** 3)
4  print(2. ** 3.)
5
```

We've surrounded the double asterisks with spaces in our examples. It's not compulsory, but it improves the readability of the code. The examples show a very important feature of virtually all Python numerical operators. Run the code and look carefully at the results it produces. Can you see any regularity here? It's possible to formulate the following rules based on this result: when both ** arguments are integers, the result is an integer, too; and when at least one ** argument is a float, the result is a float, too. This is an important distinction to remember.

Multiplication

An * (asterisk) sign is a multiplication operator. Run the following code and check if our *integer vs. float* rule is still working.

```
1  print(2 * 3)
2  print(2 * 3.)
3  print(2. * 3)
4  print(2. * 3.)
5
```

Division

A / (slash) sign is a division operator. The value in front of the slash is a dividend, the value behind the slash, a divisor. Run the following code and analyze the results.

```
1    print(6 / 3)
2    print(6 / 3.)
3    print(6. / 3)
4    print(6. / 3.)
5
```

You should see that there is an exception to the rule. The result produced by the division operator is always a float, regardless of whether or not the result seems to be a float at first glance: **1/2**, or if it looks like a pure integer: **2/1**. Is this a problem? Yes, it is. It happens sometimes that you really need a division that provides an integer value, not a float. Fortunately, Python can help you with that.

Integer division (floor division)

A // (double slash) sign is an integer division operator. It differs from the standard / operator in two details: its result lacks the fractional part — it's absent (for integers), or is always equal to zero (for floats); this means that the results are always rounded; and it conforms to the *integer vs. float rule*. Run the following example and see the results:

```
1    print(6 // 3)
2    print(6 // 3.)
3    print(6. // 3)
4    print(6. // 3.)
5
```

As you can see, *integer by integer division* gives an integer result. All other cases produce floats. Let's do some more advanced tests. Look at the following snippet:

```
1    print(6 // 4)
2    print(6. // 4)
3
```

Imagine that we used / instead of // — could you predict the results? Yes, it would be **1.5** in both cases. That's clear. But what results should we expect with // division? Run the code and see for yourself. What we get is two ones — one integer and one float. The result of integer division is always rounded to the nearest integer value that is less than the real (not rounded) result. This is very important: rounding always goes to the lesser integer. Look at the following code and try to predict the results once again:

```
1    print(-6 // 4)
2    print(6. // -4)
3
```

Operators: Data Manipulation Tools   49

Note that some of the values are negative. This will obviously affect the result. But how? The result is two negative twos. The real (not rounded) result is `-1.5` in both cases. However, the results are the subjects of rounding. The rounding goes toward the lesser integer value, and the lesser integer value is -2, hence: `-2` and `-2.0`.

NOTE Integer division can also be called floor division. You will definitely come across this term in the future.

Remainder (modulo)

The next operator is quite a peculiar one, because it has no equivalent among traditional arithmetic operators. Its graphical representation in Python is the `%` (percent) sign, which may look a bit confusing. Try to think of it as a slash (division operator) accompanied by two funny little circles. The result of the operator is a remainder left after the integer division. In other words, it's the value left over after dividing one value by another to produce an integer quotient.

NOTE The operator is sometimes called modulo in other programming languages.

Take a look at the snippet — try to predict its result and then run it:

```
1   print(14 % 4)
2
```

As you can see, the result is two. This is why: `14//4` gives `3` — this is the integer quotient; `3*4` gives `12` — as a result of quotient and divisor multiplication; `14-12` gives `2` — this is the remainder. This following example is somewhat more complicated:

```
1   print(12 % 4.5)
2
```

What is the result? Check the answers section to see if you are right.

How not to divide

As you probably know, division by zero doesn't work. Do not try to perform a division by zero, perform an integer division by zero or find a remainder of a division by zero.

Addition

The addition operator is the + (plus) sign, which is fully in line with mathematical standards. Again, take a look at the snippet of the following program. The result should be nothing surprising. Run the code to check it.

```
1   print(-4 + 4)
2   print(-4. + 8)
3
```

The subtraction operator, unary and binary operators

The subtraction operator is obviously the - (minus) sign, although you should note that this operator also has another meaning: it can change the sign of a number.

This is a great opportunity to present a very important distinction between unary and binary operators. In subtracting applications, the minus operator expects two arguments: the left, a minuend in arithmetical terms, and right, a subtrahend. For this reason, the subtraction operator is considered to be one of the binary operators, just like the addition, multiplication and division operators. But the minus operator may be used in a different, unary way — take a look at line three of the following snippet:

```
1   print(-4 - 4)
2   print(4. - 8)
3   print(-1.1)
4
```

By the way, there is also a unary + operator. You can use it like this:

```
1   print(+2)
2
```

The operator preserves the sign of its only argument — the right one. Although such a construction is syntactically correct, using it doesn't make much sense, and it would be hard to find a good rationale for doing so. Take a look at the previous snippet — can you guess its output?

Operators and their priorities

So far, we've treated each operator as if it had no connection with the others. Obviously, such an ideal and simple situation is a rarity in real programming. Also, you will very often find more than one operator in one expression, and then things are no longer so simple. Consider the following expression:

```
2 + 3 * 5
```

You probably remember from school that multiplications precede additions. You surely remember that you should first multiply 3 by 5 and, keeping the 15 in your memory, then add it to 2, thus getting the result of 17. The phenomenon that causes some operators to act before others is known as the hierarchy of priorities.

Python precisely defines the priorities of all operators, and assumes that operators of a higher priority perform their operations before the operators of a lower priority. So, if you know that * has a higher priority than +, the computation of the final result should be obvious.

Operators and their bindings

The binding of the operator determines the order of computations performed by some operators with equal priority, put side by side in one expression. Most of Python's operators have left-sided binding, which means that the calculation of the expression is conducted from left to right.

```
1   print(9 % 6 % 2)
2
```

There are two possible ways of evaluating this expression: from left to right — first 9%6 gives 3, and then 3%2 gives 1; or rom right to left — first 6%2 gives 0, and then 9%0 causes a fatal error. Run the example and see what you get.

```
1   print(9 % 6 % 2)
2
```

The result should be 1. This operator has left-sided binding. But there's one interesting exception. Repeat the experiment, but now with exponentiation. Use this snippet of code:

```
1   print(2 ** 2 ** 3)
2
```

The two possible results are:

- 2**2, which is 4; 4**3, which is 64
- 2**3, which is 8; 2**8, which is 256

Run the code. What do you see? The result clearly shows that the exponentiation operator uses right-sided binding. This has an interesting effect. If the exponentiation operator uses right-sided binding, can you guess the output of the following snippet? Check the answers section to see if you're right.

```
1   print(-3 ** 2)
2   print(-2 ** 3)
3   print(-(3 ** 2))
4
```

List of priorities

Since you're new to Python operators, we don't want to present the complete list of operator priorities right now. Instead, we'll show you a truncated form, and we'll expand it consistently as we introduce new operators. Look at the following table. Note that we've enumerated the operators in order from the highest (1) to the lowest (4) priorities. Try to work through the following expression:

```
1   print(2 * 3 % 5)
2
```

Priority	Operator	
1	**	
2	+, – (note: unary operators located next to the right of the power operator bind more strongly)	unary
3	*, /, //, %	
4	+, –	binary

Both operators (* and %) have the same priority, so the result can be guessed only when you know the binding direction. What do you think? What is the result? Check the answers section to see if you're right.

Operators and parentheses

Of course, you're always allowed to use parentheses, which can change the natural order of a calculation. In accordance with the arithmetic rules, subexpressions in parentheses are always calculated first. You can use as many parentheses as you need, and they're often used to improve the readability of an expression, even if they don't change the order of the operations. An example of an expression with multiple parentheses is here:

```
1  print((5 * ((25 % 13) + 100) / (2 * 13)) // 2)
2
```

Try to compute the value that's printed to the console. What's the result of the `print()` function? Check the answers section to see if you're right.

Summary

Key takeaways

1. An expression is a combination of values or variables, operators, calls to functions, which evaluates to a certain value, e.g. 1+2.

2. Operators are special symbols or keywords which are able to operate on the values and perform mathematical operations. For example, the * operator multiplies two values: x*y.

3. Arithmetic operators in Python: + (addition), – (subtraction), * (multiplication), / (classic division – always returns a float), % (modulus – divides left operand by right operand and returns the remainder of the operation, e.g.5%2=1), ** (exponentiation – left operand raised to the power of right operand, e.g. 2**3=2*2*2=8), // (floor/integer

division — returns a number resulting from division, but rounded down to the nearest whole number, e.g. `3//2.0=1.0`).

4. A unary operator is an operator with only one operand, e.g. `-1`, or `+3`.

5. A binary operator is an operator with two operands, e.g. `4+5`, or `12%5`.

6. Some operators act before others — the hierarchy of priorities:

- the `**` operator (exponentiation) has the highest priority;
- then the unary `+` and `-` (note: a unary operator to the right of the exponentiation operator binds more strongly, for example `4**-1` equals `0.25`)
- then: `*`, `/`, and `%`,
- and finally, the lowest priority: binary `+` and `-`.

7. Subexpressions in parentheses are always calculated first, e.g. `15-1*(5*(1+2))=0`.

8. The exponentiation operator uses right-sided binding, e.g. `2**2**3=256`.

Quiz

QUESTION 1: What is the expected output of the following snippet?

```
1  print((2 ** 4), (2 * 4.), (2 * 4))
2
```

QUESTION 2: What is the expected output of the following snippet?

```
1  print((-2 / 4), (2 / 4), (2 // 4), (-2 // 4))
2
```

QUESTION 3: What is the expected output of the following snippet?

```
1  print((2 % -4), (2 % 4), (2 ** 3 ** 2))
2
```

SEVEN
VARIABLES

It seems fairly obvious that Python should allow you to encode literals carrying number and text values. You already know that you can do some arithmetic operations with these numbers: add, subtract, etc. You'll be doing that many times. But it's quite a normal question to ask how to store the results of these operations, in order to use them in other operations, and so on. How do you save the intermediate results, and use them again to produce subsequent ones?

Python will help you with that. It offers special "boxes" or "containers" as we may call them for that purpose, and these boxes are called variables — the name itself suggests that the content of these containers can be varied in almost any way. Every Python variable has a name and a value, which is the content of the container.

Let's start with the issues related to a variable's name. Variables do not appear in a program automatically. As a developer, you must decide how many and which variables to use in your programs. You must also name them.

Figure 7.1

Variable names

If you want to give a name to a variable, you must follow some strict rules:

- the name of the variable must be composed of upper-case or lower-case letters, digits, and the character _ (underscore)
- the name of the variable must begin with a letter;
- the underscore character is a letter;
- upper- and lower-case letters are treated as different (a little differently than in the real world – *Alice* and *ALICE* are the same first names, but in Python they are two different variable names, and consequently, two different variables);
- the name of the variable must not be any of Python's reserved words (the keywords – we'll explain more about this soon).

Note that the same restrictions apply to function names. Python does not impose restrictions on the length of variable names, but that doesn't mean that a long variable name is always better than a short one. Here are some correct, but not always convenient variable names:

- `MyVariable`
- `i`
- `l`
- `t34`
- `Exchange_Rate`
- `counter`
- `days_to_christmas`
- `TheNameIsTooLongAndHardlyReadable`
- `_`

These variable names are also correct:

- `Adiós_Señora`
- `sûr_la_mer`
- `Einbahnstraße`
- `переменная`

Python lets you use not only Latin letters but also characters specific to languages that use other alphabets.

And now for some incorrect names:

- `10t` — does not begin with a letter
- `!important` — does not begin with a letter
- `exchange rate` — contains a space

> **NOTE** The PEP 8 -- Style Guide for Python Code recommends the following naming convention for variables and functions in Python:
>
> - variable names should be lowercase, with words separated by underscores to improve readability (e.g. `var`, `my_variable`)
> - function names follow the same convention as variable names (e.g. `fun`, `my_function`)
> - it's also possible to use mixed case (e.g. `myVariable`), but only in contexts where that's already the prevailing style, to retain backward compatibility with the adopted convention.

Keywords

Take a look at the list of words that play a very special role in every Python program.

```
['False', 'None', 'True', 'and', 'as', 'assert', 'break',
'class', 'continue', 'def', 'del', 'elif', 'else', 'except',
'finally', 'for', 'from', 'global', 'if', 'import', 'in', 'is',
'lambda', 'nonlocal', 'not', 'or', 'pass', 'raise', 'return',
'try', 'while', 'with', 'yield']
```

They are called keywords, or more precisely, reserved keywords. They are reserved because you mustn't use them as names: neither for your variables, nor functions, nor any other named entities you want to create. The meaning of the reserved word is predefined, and mustn't be changed in any way. Fortunately, due to the fact that Python is case-sensitive, you can modify any of these words by changing the case of any letter, thus creating a new word, which is not reserved anymore. For example — you can't name your variable like this:

```
import
```

You mustn't have a variable named in such a way — it is prohibited. But you can do this instead:

```
Import
```

These words might be a mystery to you now, but you'll soon learn the meaning of them.

How to create a variable

What can you put inside a variable? Anything. You can use a variable to store any value of any of the already presented kinds, and many more of the ones we haven't shown you yet. The value of a variable is what you have put into it. It can vary as often as you need or want. It can be an integer one moment, and a float a moment later, eventually becoming a string. Let's talk now about two important things — how variables are created, and how to put values inside them, or rather, how to give or pass values to them.

NOTE A variable comes into existence as a result of assigning a value to it. Unlike in other languages, you don't need to declare it in any special way. If you assign any value to a non-existent variable, the variable will be automatically created. You don't need to do anything else.

The creation — in other words, its syntax — is extremely simple: just use the name of the desired variable, then the equal sign (=) and the value you want to put into the variable. Take a look at the following snippet:

```
1   var = 1
2   print(var)
3
```

It consists of two simple instructions: the first of them creates a variable named `var`, and assigns a literal with an integer value equal to 1; the second prints the value of the newly created variable to the console. As you can see, `print()` has yet another side to it — it can handle variables too. Do you know what the output of the snippet will be? Run the code to check.

How to use a variable

You're allowed to use as many variable declarations as you need to achieve your goal, like this:

```
1   var = 1
2   account_balance = 1000.0
3   client_name = 'John Doe'
4   print(var, account_balance, client_name)
5   print(var)
6
```

However, you're not allowed to use a variable which doesn't exist. In other words, you cannot use a variable that was not assigned a value. This example will cause an error:

```
1   var = 1
2   print(Var)
3
```

Do you know why? We've tried to use a variable named `Var`, which doesn't have any value, because `var` and `Var` are different entities, and have nothing in common as far as Python's concerned.

NOTE You can use the `print()` function and combine text and variables using the + operator to output strings and variables. For example:

```
1   var = "3.8.5"
2   print("Python version: " + var)
3
```

Can you guess the output of the snippet? Check in the answers section to see if you're right.

How to assign a new value to an already existing variable

How do you assign a new value to a variable that already exists? In the same way. You just need to use the equal sign. The equal sign is in fact an assignment operator. Although this may sound strange, the operator has a simple syntax and unambiguous interpretation. It assigns the value of its right argument to the left, while the right argument may be an arbitrarily complex expression involving literals, operators and already defined variables. Look at the code:

```
1   var = 1
2   print(var)
3   var = var + 1
4   print(var)
5
```

The code sends two lines to the console:

```
1
2
```

The first line of the snippet creates a new variable named `var` and assigns 1 to it. The statement reads: assign a value of 1 to a variable named `var`. We can say it shorter: assign 1 to `var`. Some prefer to read such a statement as: `var` becomes 1. The third line assigns the same variable with the new value taken from the variable itself, summed with 1. Seeing a record like that, a mathematician would probably protest — no value may be equal to itself plus one. This is a contradiction. But Python treats the sign = not as *equal to*, but as *assign a value*.

So how do you read such a record in the program? Take the current value of the variable `var`, add 1 to it and store the result in the variable `var`. In effect, the value of variable `var` has been incremented by one, which has nothing to do with comparing the variable with any value. Do you know what the output of the following snippet will be? Check in the answers section to see if you're right.

```
1   var = 100
2   var = 200 + 300
3   print(var)
4
```

Solving simple mathematical problems

Now you should be able to construct a short program solving simple mathematical problems such as the Pythagorean theorem: *the square of the hypotenuse is equal to the sum of the squares of the other two sides*. The following code evaluates the length of the hypotenuse (i.e. the longest side of a right-angled triangle, the one opposite of the right angle) using the Pythagorean theorem.

```
1    a = 3.0
2    b = 4.0
3    c = (a ** 2 + b ** 2) ** 0.5
4    print("c =", c)
5
```

NOTE we need to make use of the `**` operator to evaluate the square root as:

$$\sqrt{x} = x^{(1/2)}$$

and

$$c = \sqrt{a^2 + b^2}$$

Can you guess the output of the code? Check the answers section to see if you're right.

LAB: Variables

Here is a short story: once upon a time in Appleland, John had three apples, Mary had five apples, and Adam had six apples. They were all very happy and lived for a long time. End of story.

Your task is to:

- create the variables: `john`, `mary`, and `adam`;
- assign values to the variables. The values must be equal to the numbers of fruit possessed by John, Mary, and Adam respectively;
- having stored the numbers in the variables, print the variables on one line, and separate each of them with a comma;
- now create a new variable named `total_apples` equal to the addition of the three previous variables;
- print the value stored in `total_apples` to the console;
- experiment with your code: create new variables, assign different values to them, and perform various arithmetic operations on them (e.g. +, -, *, /, //, etc.). Try to print a string and an integer together on one line, e.g. `"Total number of apples:"` and `total_apples`.

Shortcut operators

It's time for the next set of operators that make a developer's life easier. Very often, we want to use one and the same variable both to the right and left sides of the = operator. For example, if we need to calculate a series of successive values of powers of 2, we may use a piece like this:

```
1    x = x * 2
2
```

You may use an expression like this if you can't fall asleep and you're trying to deal with it using some good, old-fashioned methods:

```
1    sheep = sheep + 1
2
```

Python offers you a shortened way of writing operations like these, which can be coded as follows:

```
1    x *= 2
2    sheep += 1
3
```

Let's try to present a general description for these operations. Imagine that op is a two-argument operator (this is a very important condition) and the operator is used in the following context:

```
variable = variable op expression
```

It can be simplified and shown as follows:

```
variable op= expression
```

Take a look at the following examples. Make sure you understand them all.

Expression	Shortcut operator
i=i+2*j	i+=2*j
var=var/2	var/=2
rem=rem%10	rem%=10
j=j-(i+var+rem)	j-=(i+var+rem)
x=x**2	x**=2

Variables   61

LAB: Variables − a simple converter

Miles and kilometers are units of length or distance. Bearing in mind that 1 mile is equal to approximately 1.61 kilometers, complete the program so that it converts:

- miles to kilometers;
- kilometers to miles.

Do not change anything in the existing code. Write your code in the places indicated by ###. Test your program with the data we've provided in the source code. Pay particular attention to what is going on inside the `print()` function. Analyze how we provide multiple arguments to the function, and how we output the expected data. Note that some of the arguments inside the `print()` function are strings (e.g. `"miles is"`, whereas some other are variables (e.g. `miles`).

TIP

There's one more interesting thing happening there. Can you see another function inside the `print()` function? It's the `round()` function. Its job is to round the outputted result to the number of decimal places specified in the parentheses, and return a float. Inside the `round()` function you can find the variable name, a comma, and the number of decimal places we're aiming for. We're going to talk about functions very soon, so don't worry that everything may not be fully clear yet. We just want to spark your curiosity.

After completing the lab, experiment some more. Try to write different converters, for example, a USD to EUR converter, a temperature converter, etc. Let your imagination fly! Try to output the results by combining strings and variables. Try to use and experiment with the `round()` function to round your results to one, two, or three decimal places. Check out what happens if you don't provide any number of digits. Remember to test your programs. Experiment, draw conclusions, and learn. Be curious.

EXPECTED OUTPUT

```
7.38 miles is 11.88 kilometers
12.25 kilometers is 7.61 miles
```

CODE

```
1   kilometers = 12.25
2   miles = 7.38
3
4   miles_to_kilometers = ###
5   kilometers_to_miles = ###
6
7   print(miles, "miles is", round(miles_to_kilometers, 2), "kilometers")
8   print(kilometers, "kilometers is", round(kilometers_to_miles, 2), "miles")
9
```

LAB: Operators and expressions

Take a look at the following code: it reads a float value, puts it into a variable named x, and prints the value of a variable named y. Your task is to complete the code in order to evaluate the following expression:

$3x^3 - 2x^2 + 3x - 1$

The result should be assigned to y.

Remember that classical algebraic notation likes to omit the multiplication operator — you need to use it explicitly. Note how we change data type to make sure that x is of type float. Keep your code clean and readable, and test it using the data we've provided, each time assigning it to the x variable by hardcoding it. Don't be discouraged by any initial failures. Be persistent and inquisitive.

SAMPLE INPUT
```
x = 0
x = 1
x = -1
```

SAMPLE OUTPUT
```
y = -1.0
y = 3.0
y = -9.0
```

CODE
```
1   x =     # Hardcode your test data here.
2   x = float(x)
3   # Write your code here.
4   print("y =", y)
5
```

Summary

A variable is a named location reserved to store values in the memory. A variable is created or initialized automatically when you assign a value to it for the first time.

Each variable must have a unique name — an identifier. A legal identifier name must be a non-empty sequence of characters, must begin with the underscore(_), or a letter, and it cannot be a Python keyword. The first character may be followed by underscores, letters, and digits. Identifiers in Python are case-sensitive.

Python is a dynamically-typed language, which means you don't need to *declare* variables in it. To assign values to variables, you can use a simple assignment operator in the form of the equal (=) sign, for example, var=1.

You can also use compound assignment operators (shortcut operators) to modify values assigned to variables, for example: `var+=1`, or `var/=5*2`.

You can assign new values to already existing variables using the assignment operator or one of the compound operators, for example:

```
1   var = 2
2   print(var)
3
4   var = 3
5   print(var)
6
7   var += 1
8   print(var)
9
```

You can combine text and variables using the + operator, and use the `print()` function to output strings and variables, for example:

```
1   var = "007"
2   print("Agent " + var)
3
```

Quiz

QUESTION 1: What is the output of the following code?

```
1   var = 2
2   var = 3
3   print(var)
4
```

- 3
- 2
- 5

QUESTION 2: Which of the following variable names are illegal in Python? (Select three answers)

- `my_var`
- `m`
- `101`
- `averylongVariablename`
- `m101`
- `m 101`
- `Del`
- `del`

64   Chapter 7

QUESTION 3: What is the output of the following snippet?

```
1  a = '1'
2  b = "1"
3  print(a + b)
4
```

- 1
- 11
- 2

QUESTION 4: What is the output of the following snippet?

```
1  a = 6
2  b = 3
3  a /= 2 * b
4  print(a)
5
```

- 1.0
- 1
- 9
- 6
- 6.0

EIGHT
COMMENTS

You may want to put in a few words addressed not to Python but to humans, usually to explain to other readers of the code how the tricks used in the code work, or the meanings of the variables, and eventually, in order to keep stored information on who the author is and when the program was written. A remark inserted into the program, which is omitted at runtime, is called a comment.

How do you leave this kind of comment in the source code? It has to be done in a way that won't force Python to interpret it as part of the code. Whenever Python encounters a comment in your program, the comment is completely transparent to it — from Python's point of view, this is only one space, regardless of how long the real comment is. In Python, a comment is a piece of text that begins with a # (hash) sign and extends to the end of the line. If you want a comment that spans several lines, you have to put a hash in front of them all. Just like here:

```
1   # This program evaluates the hypotenuse c.
2   # a and b are the lengths of the legs.
3   a = 3.0
4   b = 4.0
5   c = (a ** 2 + b ** 2) ** 0.5    # We use ** instead of a
    square root.
6   print("c =", c)
7
```

Responsible developers describe each important piece of code, for example, by explaining the role of the variables. Although it must be stated that the best way of commenting variables is to name them in an unambiguous manner.

For example, if a particular variable is designed to store an area of some unique square, the name `square_area` will obviously be better than `aunt_jane`. We say that the first name is self-commenting.

Marking fragments of code

Comments may be useful in another respect — you can use them to mark a piece of code that currently isn't needed for whatever reason. Look at the following example. If you uncomment the highlighted line, this will affect the output of the code. This is often done during the testing of a program, in order to isolate the place where an error might be hidden.

```
1  # This is a test program.
2  x = 1
3  y = 2
4  # y = y + x
5  print(x + y)
6
```

TIP If you'd like to quickly comment or uncomment multiple lines of code, select the line(s) you wish to modify and use the following keyboard shortcut: CTRL + / (Windows) or CMD + / (Mac OS). It's a very useful trick, isn't it? Now experiment with the following code.

```
1  # uncomment_me = 1
2  # uncomment_me_too = 3
3  # uncomment_me_also = 5
4
5  print(uncomment_me, uncomment_me_too, uncomment_me_also,
       sep="\n")
6
```

LAB: Comments

The code contains comments. Try to improve it. Add or remove comments where you find it appropriate: yes, sometimes removing a comment can make the code more readable. Change variable names where you think this will improve code comprehension.

NOTE Comments are very important. They are used not only to make your programs easier to understand, but also to disable those pieces of code that are currently not needed, such as when you need to test some parts of your code only, and ignore others. Good programmers describe each important piece of code, and give self-commenting names to variables, as sometimes it is simply much better to leave information in the code.

It's good to use readable variable names, and sometimes it's better to divide your code into named pieces (e.g. functions). In some situations, it's a good idea to write the steps of computations in a clearer way. One more thing: it may happen that a comment contains a wrong or incorrect piece of information — you should never do that on purpose!

CODE

```
1   #this program computes the number of seconds in a given
    number of hours
2   # this program was written two days ago
3
4   a = 2 # number of hours
5   seconds = 3600 # number of seconds in 1 hour
6
7   print("Hours: ", a) #printing the number of hours
8   # print("Seconds in Hours: ", a * seconds) # printing the
    number of seconds in a given number of hours
9
10  #here we should also print "Goodbye", but a programmer
    didn't have time to write any code
11  #this is the end of the program that computes the number of
    seconds in 3 hours
12
```

Summary

Comments can be used to leave additional information in code. They are omitted at runtime. The information left in the source code is addressed to human readers. In Python, a comment is a piece of text that begins with #. The comment extends to the end of the line.

If you want to place a comment that spans several lines, you need to place # in front of them all. Moreover, you can use a comment to mark a piece of code that is not needed at the moment. See the last line of the following snippet, for example.

```
1   # This program prints
2   # an introduction to the screen.
3   print("Hello!")  # Invoking the print() function
4   # print("I'm Python.")
5
```

Whenever possible and justified, you should give self-commenting names to variables. For example, if you're using two variables to store the length and width of something, the variable names `length` and `width` may be a better choice than `myvar1` and `myvar2`.

It's important to use comments to make programs easier to understand, and to use readable and meaningful variable names in code. However, it's equally important not to use variable names that are confusing, or leave comments that contain wrong or incorrect information!

Comments can be important when you are reading your own code after some time — trust us, developers do forget what their own code does — and when others are reading your code. They can help them understand more quickly what your programs do and how they do it.

Quiz

QUESTION 1: What is the output of the following snippet?

```
1    # print("String #1")
2    print("String #2")
3
```

QUESTION 2: What will happen when you run the following code?

```
1    # This is
2    a multiline
3    comment. #
4
5    print("Hello!")
6
```

NINE
INTERACTION WITH THE USER

We're now going to introduce you to a completely new function, which seems to be a mirror reflection of the good old `print()` function. Why? Well, `print()` sends data to the console. The new function gets data from it. `print()` has no usable result. The meaning of the new function is to return a very usable result.

The function is named `input()`. The name of the function says everything. The `input()` function is able to read data entered by the user and to return the same data to the running program. The program can manipulate the data, making the code truly interactive. Virtually all programs read and process data. A program which doesn't get a user's input is a deaf program. Take a look at our example:

```
1   print("Tell me anything...")
2   anything = input()
3   print("Hmm...", anything, "... Really?")
4
```

It shows a very simple case of using the `input()` function. The program prompts the user to input some data from the console, most likely using a keyboard, although it is also possible to input data using voice or image. The `input()` function is invoked without arguments — this is the simplest way of using the function; the function will switch the console to input mode; you'll see a blinking cursor, and you'll be able to input some keystrokes, finishing off by hitting the *Enter* key; all the inputted data will be sent to your program through the function's result. You need to assign the result to a variable; this is crucial — missing out this step will cause the entered data to be lost. Then we use the `print()` function to output the data we get, with some additional remarks.

Run the code and let the function show you what it can do for you.

```
1   print("Tell me anything...")
2   anything = input()
3   print("Hmm...", anything, "... Really?")
4
```

The `input()` function with an argument

The `input()` function can do something else: it can prompt the user without any help from `print()`. We've modified our example a bit, look at the code:

```
1   anything = input("Tell me anything...")
2   print("Hmm...", anything, "...Really?")
3
```

NOTE The `input()` function is invoked with one argument — it's a string containing a message. The message will be displayed on the console before the user is given an opportunity to enter anything. `input()` will then do its job.

This variant of the `input()` invocation simplifies the code and makes it clearer.

The result of the `input()` function

We've said it already, but it must be unambiguously stated once again: the result of the `input()` function is a string, a string containing all the characters the user enters from the keyboard. It is not an integer or a float. This means that you mustn't use it as an argument of any arithmetic operation. For example, you can't use this data to square it, divide it by anything, or divide anything by it.

```
1   anything = input("Enter a number: ")
2   something = anything ** 2.0
3   print(anything, "to the power of 2 is", something)
4
```

The `input()` function - prohibited operations

Look at the following code. Run it, enter any number, and press *Enter*.

```
1   # Testing a TypeError message.
2
3   anything = input("Enter a number: ")
4   something = anything ** 2.0
5   print(anything, "to the power of 2 is", something)
6
```

What happens? Python should have given you the following output:

```
Traceback (most recent call last):
File ".main.py", line 4, in <module>
something = anything ** 2.0
TypeError: unsupported operand type(s) for ** or pow(): 'str' and
'float'
```

The last line of the sentence explains everything — you tried to apply the ** operator to 'str' (string) accompanied with 'float'. This is prohibited. This should be obvious — can you predict the value of "to be or not to be" raised to the power of 2? We can't. Python can't, either. Have we fallen into a deadlock? Is there a solution to this issue? Of course there is.

Type casting, or type conversion

Python offers two simple functions to specify a type of data and solve this problem — here they are: int() and float(). Their names are self-commenting: the int() function takes one argument (e.g. a string: int(string)) and tries to convert it into an integer; if it fails, the whole program will fail too — there is a workaround for this situation, but we'll show you this a little later; the float() function takes one argument (e.g. a string: float(string)) and tries to convert it into a float. The rest is the same. This is very simple and very effective. Moreover, you can invoke any of the functions by passing the input() results directly to them. There's no need to use any variable as an intermediate storage.

We've implemented the idea — take a look at the following code. Can you imagine how the string entered by the user flows from input() into print()? Try to run the modified code. Don't forget to enter a valid number. Check some different values, small and big, negative and positive. Zero is a good input, too.

```
1    anything = float(input("Enter a number: "))
2    something = anything ** 2.0
3    print(anything, "to the power of 2 is", something)
4
```

More about input() and type casting

Having a team consisting of the trio input() — int() — float() opens up lots of new possibilities. You'll eventually be able to write complete programs, accepting data in the form of numbers, processing them and displaying the results. Of course, these programs will be very primitive and not very usable, as they cannot make decisions, and consequently are not able to react differently to different situations. This is not really a problem, though; we'll show you how to overcome it soon.

Our next example refers to the earlier program to find the length of a hypotenuse. Let's run it and make it able to read the lengths of the legs from the console. Check out the code — this is what it looks like now:

```
1  leg_a = float(input("Input first leg length: "))
2  leg_b = float(input("Input second leg length: "))
3  hypo = (leg_a**2 + leg_b**2) ** .5
4  print("Hypotenuse length is", hypo)
5
```

The program asks the user for the lengths of both legs, evaluates the hypotenuse and prints the result. Run it and try to input some negative values. The program, unfortunately, doesn't react to this obvious error. Let's ignore this weakness for now. We'll come back to it soon.

Note that in the program that you can see, the `hypo` variable is used for only one purpose — to save the calculated value between the execution of the adjoining line of code. As the `print()` function accepts an expression as its argument, you can remove the variable from the code. Just like this:

```
1  leg_a = float(input("Input first leg length: "))
2  leg_b = float(input("Input second leg length: "))
3  print("Hypotenuse length is", (leg_a**2 + leg_b**2) ** .5)
4
```

String operators

It's time to return to these two arithmetic operators: + and *. We want to show you that they have a second function. They are able to do something more than just add and multiply. We've seen them in action where their arguments are numbers — floats or integers, it doesn't matter. Now we're going to show you that they can handle strings, too, albeit in a very specific way.

The + (plus) sign, when applied to two strings, becomes a concatenation operator:

```
1  string + string
2
```

It simply concatenates (glues) two strings into one. Of course, like its arithmetic sibling, it can be used more than once in one expression, and in such a context it behaves according to left-sided binding. In contrast to its arithmetic sibling, the concatenation operator is not commutative. In other words, `"ab"+"ba"` is not the same as `"ba"+"ab"`.

Don't forget — if you want the + sign to be a concatenator, not an adder, you must ensure that both its arguments are strings. You cannot mix types here. This simple program shows the + sign in its second use:

```
1  fnam = input("May I have your first name, please? ")
2  lnam = input("May I have your last name, please? ")
3  print("Thank you.")
4  print("\nYour name is " + fnam + " " + lnam + ".")
5
```

> **NOTE** Using + to concatenate strings lets you construct the output in a more precise way than with a pure `print()` function, even if enriched with the `end=` and `sep=` keyword arguments.

Run the code and see if the output matches your predictions.

Replication

The * (asterisk) sign, when applied to a string and number — or a number and string, as it remains commutative in this position — becomes a replication operator:

```
1    string * number
2    number * string
3
```

It replicates the string the same number of times specified by the number. For example:

- `"James"*3` gives `"JamesJamesJames"`
- `3*"an"` gives `"ananan"`
- `5*"2"(or"2"*5)` gives `"22222"` (not 10!)

Remember that a number less than or equal to zero produces an empty string. This simple program "draws" a rectangle, making use of an old operator (+) in a new role:

```
1    print("+" + 10 * "-" + "+")
2    print(("|" + " " * 10 + "|\n") * 5, end="")
3    print("+" + 10 * "-" + "+")
4
```

Note the way in which we've used the parentheses in the second line of the code. Try practicing to create other shapes or your own artwork!

Type conversion once again
str()

You already know how to use the `int()` and `float()` functions to convert a string into a number. This form of conversion is not a one-way street. You can also convert a number into a string, which is way easier and safer — this kind of operation is always possible.

A function capable of doing that is called `str()`:

```
1    str(number)
2
```

To be honest, it can do much more than just transform numbers into strings, but that can wait for later.

The right-angle triangle again

Here is our "right-angle triangle" program again:

```
1  leg_a = float(input("Input first leg length: "))
2  leg_b = float(input("Input second leg length: "))
3  print("Hypotenuse length is " + str((leg_a**2 + leg_b**2) ** .5))
4
```

We've modified it a bit to show you how the `str()` function works. Thanks to this, we can pass the whole result to the `print()` function as one string, forgetting about the commas.

You've made some serious strides on your way to Python programming. You already know the basic data types, and a set of fundamental operators. You know how to organize the output and how to get data from the user. These are very strong foundations for Part 3. But before we move on to the next part, let's do a few labs, and recap all that you've learned in this section.

LAB: Simple input and output

Your task is to complete the code in order to evaluate the results of four basic arithmetic operations. The results have to be printed to the console. You may not be able to protect the code from a user who wants to divide by zero. That's okay, don't worry about it for now. Test your code — does it produce the results you expect? We won't show you any test data — that would be too simple.

CODE

```
1   # input a float value for variable a here
2   # input a float value for variable b here
3
4   # output the result of addition here
5   # output the result of subtraction here
6   # output the result of multiplication here
7   # output the result of division here
8
9   print("\nThat's all, folks!")
10
```

LAB: Operators and expressions

Your task is to complete the code in order to evaluate the following expression:

$$x + \cfrac{1}{x + \cfrac{1}{x + \cfrac{1}{x + \cfrac{1}{x}}}}$$

The result should be assigned to y. Be careful — watch the operators and keep their priorities in mind. Don't hesitate to use as many parentheses as you need. You can use additional variables to shorten the expression, but it's not necessary. Test your code carefully.

SAMPLE INPUT:
```
1
```

EXPECTED OUTPUT:
```
y = 0.6000000000000001
```

SAMPLE INPUT:
```
10
```

EXPECTED OUTPUT:
```
y = 0.09901951266867294
```

SAMPLE INPUT:
```
100
```

EXPECTED OUTPUT:
```
y = 0.009999000199950014
```

SAMPLE INPUT:
```
-5
```

EXPECTED OUTPUT:
```
y = -0.19258202567760344
```

CODE
```
1   x = float(input("Enter value for x: "))
2
3   # Write your code here.
4
5   print("y =", y)
6
```

LAB: Operators and expressions 2

Your task is to prepare a simple code able to evaluate the end time of a period of time, given as a number of minutes (it could be arbitrarily large). The start time is given as a pair of hours (0..23) and minutes (0..59). The result has to be printed to the console. For example, if an event starts at 12:17 and lasts 59 minutes, it will end at 13:16. Don't worry about any imperfections in your code — it's okay if it accepts an invalid time — the most important thing is that the code produces valid results for valid input data. Test your code carefully.

HINT Using the % operator may be the key to success.

SAMPLE INPUT:
```
12
17
59
```

EXPECTED OUTPUT:
```
13:16
```

SAMPLE INPUT:
```
23
58
642
```

EXPECTED OUTPUT:
```
10:40
```

SAMPLE INPUT:
```
0
1
2939
```

EXPECTED OUTPUT:
```
1:0
```

CODE
```
1  hour = int(input("Starting time (hours): "))
2  mins = int(input("Starting time (minutes): "))
3  dura = int(input("Event duration (minutes): "))
4
5  # Write your code here.
6
```

Summary

The `print()` function sends data to the console, while the `input()` function gets data from the console.

The `input()` function comes with an optional parameter: the prompt string. It allows you to write a message before the user input, as in the following code:

```
1  name = input("Enter your name: ")
2  print("Hello, " + name + ". Nice to meet you!")
3
```

When the `input()` function is called, the program's flow is stopped, the prompt symbol keeps blinking (it prompts the user to take action when the console is switched to input mode) until the user has entered an input and/or pressed the *Enter* key.

NOTE You can test the functionality of the `input()` function in its full scope locally on your machine.

> **TIP**
>
> This feature of the `input()` function can be used to prompt the user to end a program. Look at the following code:

```
1   name = input("Enter your name: ")
2   print("Hello, " + name + ". Nice to meet you!")
3   print("\nPress Enter to end the program.")
4   input()
5   print("THE END.")
6
```

The result of the `input()` function is a string. You can add strings to each other using the concatenation (+) operator. Check out this code:

```
1   num_1 = input("Enter the first number: ") # Enter 12
2   num_2 = input("Enter the second number: ") # Enter 21
3   print(num_1 + num_2) # the program returns 1221
4
```

You can also multiply (* — replication) strings, e.g.:

```
1   my_input = input("Enter something: ") # Example input: hello
2   print(my_input * 3) # Expected output: hellohellohello
3
```

Quiz

QUESTION 1: What is the output of the following snippet?

```
1   x = int(input("Enter a number: ")) # The user enters 2
2   print(x * "5")
3
```

QUESTION 2: What is the expected output of the following snippet?

```
1   x = input("Enter a number: ") # The user enters 2
2   print(type(x))
3
```

Interaction With The User   79

PART 3

BOOLEAN VALUES, CONDITIONAL EXECUTION, LOOPS, LISTS AND LIST PROCESSING, LOGICAL AND BITWISE OPERATIONS

TEN
MAKING DECISIONS IN PYTHON

A programmer writes a program and the program asks questions. A computer executes the program and provides the answers. The program must be able to react according to the received answers. Fortunately, computers know only two kinds of answers: yes, this is true; or no, this is false. You will never get a response like *Let me think....., I don't know,* or *Probably yes, but I don't know for sure.* To ask questions, Python uses a set of very special operators. Let's go through them one after another, illustrating their effects on some simple examples.

Comparison: equality operator

Question: are two values equal? To ask this question, you use the == (equal equal) operator. Don't forget this important distinction: = is an assignment operator, e.g. a=b assigns a with the value of b; == is the question *are these values equal?* so a==b compares a and b. It is a binary operator with left-sided binding. It needs two arguments and checks if they are equal.

Exercises

Now let's ask a few questions. Try to guess the answers.

QUESTION 1: What is the result of the following comparison?

    2 == 2

QUESTION 2: What is the result of the following comparison?

    2 == 2.

QUESTION 3: What is the result of the following comparison?

```
1 == 2
```

Check the answers section to see if you're right.

Operators

Equality: the equal to operator (==)

The == (equal to) operator compares the values of two operands. If they are equal, the result of the comparison is True. If they are not equal, the result of the comparison is False. Look at the equality following comparison — what is the result of this operation?

```
var == 0
```

Note that we cannot find the answer if we do not know what value is currently stored in the variable var. If the variable has been changed many times during the execution of your program, or its initial value is entered from the console, the answer to this question can be given only by Python and only at runtime. Now imagine a programmer who suffers from insomnia, and has to count black and white sheep separately as long as there are exactly twice as many black sheep as white ones. The question will be as follows:

```
black_sheep == 2 * white_sheep
```

Due to the low priority of the == operator, the question shall be treated as equivalent to this one:

```
black_sheep == (2 * white_sheep)
```

So, let's practice your understanding of the == operator now — can you guess the output of the code? Run the code and check if you're right.

```
1  var = 0    # Assigning 0 to var
2  print(var == 0)
3
4  var = 1    # Assigning 1 to var
5  print(var == 0)
6
```

Inequality: the not equal to operator (!=)

The != (not equal to) operator compares the values of two operands, too. Here is the difference: if they are equal, the result of the comparison is False. If they are not equal, the result of the comparison is True. Now take a look at the following inequality comparison — can you guess the result of this operation?

```
1    var = 0    # Assigning 0 to var
2    print(var != 0)
3
4    var = 1    # Assigning 1 to var
5    print(var != 0)
6
```

Run the code and check if you're right.

Comparison operators: greater than

You can also ask a comparison question using the > (greater than) operator. If you want to know if there are more black sheep than white ones, you can write it as follows:

```
1    black_sheep > white_sheep   # Greater than
2
```

`True` confirms it; `False` denies it.

Comparison operators: greater than or equal to

The *greater than* operator has another special, non-strict variant, but it's denoted differently than in classical arithmetic notation: >= (greater than or equal to). There are two subsequent signs, not one. Both of these operators (strict and non-strict), as well as the two others discussed next, are binary operators with left-sided binding, and their priority is greater than that shown by == and !=. If we want to find out whether or not we have to wear a warm hat, we ask the following question:

```
1    centigrade_outside >= 0.0 # Greater than or equal to
2
```

Comparison operators: less than/less than or equal to

As you've probably already guessed, the operators used in this case are: the < (less than) operator and its non-strict sibling: <= (less than or equal to). Look at this simple example:

```
1    current_velocity_mph < 85    # Less than
2    current_velocity_mph <= 85   # Less than or equal to
3
```

We're going to check if there's a risk of being fined by the highway police. The first question is strict, the second isn't.

Making use of the answers

What can you do with the answer (i.e. the result of a comparison operation) you get from the computer? There are at least two possibilities: first, you can memorize it (store it in a variable) and make use of it later. How do you do that? Well, you use an arbitrary variable like this:

```
answer = number_of_lions >= number_of_lionesses
```

The content of the variable will tell you the answer to the question asked. The second possibility is more convenient and far more common: you can use the answer you get to make a decision about the future of the program. You need a special instruction for this purpose, and we'll discuss it very soon. Now we need to update our priority table, and put all the new operators into it. It now looks as follows:

Priority	Operator	
1	+, -	unary
2	**	
3	*, /, //, %	
4	+, -	binary
5	<, <=, >, >=	
6	==, !=	

LAB: Variables — Questions and answers

Using one of the comparison operators in Python, write a simple two-line program that takes the parameter n as input, which is an integer, and prints False if n is less than 100, and True if n is greater than or equal to 100. Don't create any if blocks. We're going to talk about them very soon. Test your code using the data we've provided for you.

SAMPLE INPUT:
    55

EXPECTED OUTPUT:
    False

SAMPLE INPUT:
    99

EXPECTED OUTPUT:
    False

SAMPLE INPUT:
    100

EXPECTED OUTPUT:
```
True
```

SAMPLE INPUT:
```
101
```

EXPECTED OUTPUT:
```
True
```

SAMPLE INPUT:
```
-5
```

EXPECTED OUTPUT:
```
False
```

SAMPLE INPUT:
```
+123
```

EXPECTED OUTPUT:
```
True
```

1   1

Conditions and conditional execution

You already know how to ask Python questions, but you still don't know how to make reasonable use of the answers. You have to have a mechanism which will allow you to do something if a condition is met, and not do it if it isn't. It's just like in real life: you do certain things or you don't when a specific condition is met or not, e.g. you go for a walk if the weather is good, or stay home if it's wet and cold.

To make such decisions, Python offers a special instruction. Due to its nature and its application, it's called a conditional instruction or conditional statement. There are several variants of it. We'll start with the simplest, increasing the difficulty slowly. The first form of a conditional statement is written very informally but figuratively:

```
if true_or_not:
    do_this_if_true
```

This conditional statement consists of the following, strictly necessary, elements in this and this order only: the `if` keyword; one or more white spaces; an expression, either a question or an answer, whose value will be interpreted solely in terms of `True` when its value is non-zero and `False` when it is equal to zero; a colon followed by a newline; an indented instruction or set of instructions — at least one instruction is absolutely required

The instruction indentation may be achieved in two ways: by inserting a particular number of spaces — the recommendation is to use four spaces of indentation — or by using the *tab* character. Note that if there is more than one instruction in the indented part, the indentation should be the same in all lines; even though it may look the same if you use tabs mixed with spaces, it's important to make all indentations exactly the same — Python 3 does not allow the mixing of spaces and tabs for indentation.

How does that statement work? If the `true_or_not` expression represents the truth (i.e. its value is not equal to zero), the indented statement(s) will be executed; if the `true_or_not` expression does not represent the truth (i.e. its value is equal to zero), the indented statement(s) will be omitted, that is, ignored, and the next executed instruction will be the one after the original indentation level.

In real life, we often express a desire:

*If the weather is good, we'll go for a walk,
then we'll have lunch.*

As you can see, having lunch is not a conditional activity and doesn't depend on the weather. Knowing what conditions influence our behavior, and assuming that we have the parameterless functions `go_for_a_walk()` and `have_lunch()`, we can write the following snippet:

```
1  if the_weather_is_good:
2      go_for_a_walk()
3  have_lunch()
4
```

Conditional execution: the `if` statement

If a certain sleepless Python developer falls asleep when he or she counts 120 sheep, and the sleep-inducing procedure may be implemented as a special function named `sleep_and_dream()`, the whole code takes the following shape:

```
1  if sheep_counter >= 120: # Evaluate a test expression
2      sleep_and_dream() # Execute if test expression is True
3
```

You can read it as: if `sheep_counter` is greater than or equal to 120, then fall asleep and dream (i.e. execute the `sleep_and_dream` function.)

We've said that conditionally executed statements have to be indented. This creates a very legible structure, clearly demonstrating all possible execution paths in the code. Take a look at the following code:

```
1  if sheep_counter >= 120:
2      make_a_bed()
3      take_a_shower()
4      sleep_and_dream()
5  feed_the_sheepdogs()
6
```

As you can see, making a bed, taking a shower and falling asleep and dreaming are all executed conditionally — when `sheep_counter` reaches the desired limit. Feeding the sheepdogs, however, is always done (i.e. the `feed_the_sheepdogs()` function is not indented and does not belong to the `if` block, which means it is always executed.)

Now we're going to discuss another variant of the conditional statement, which also allows you to perform an additional action when the condition is not met.

Conditional execution: the `if-else` statement

We started out with a simple phrase which read: *If the weather is good, we will go for a walk.* Note that there is not a word about what will happen if the weather is bad. We only know that we won't go outdoors, but what we could do instead is not known. We may want to plan something in case of bad weather, too.

We can say, for example: *If the weather is good, we will go for a walk, otherwise we will go to a theater.* Now we know what we'll do if the conditions are met, and we know what we'll do if not everything goes our way. In other words, we have a "Plan B". Python allows us to express such alternative plans. This is done with a second, slightly more complex form of the conditional statement, the `if-else` statement:

```
1    if true_or_false_condition:
2        perform_if_condition_true
3    else:
4        perform_if_condition_false
5
```

Thus, there is a new word: `else` — this is a keyword. The part of the code which begins with `else` says what to do if the condition specified for the `if` is not met (note the colon after the word). The `if-else` execution goes as follows: if the condition evaluates to True (its value is not equal to zero), the `perform_if_condition_true` statement is executed, and the conditional statement comes to an end; if the condition evaluates to False (it is equal to zero), the `perform_if_condition_false` statement is executed, and the conditional statement comes to an end.

The `if-else` statement: more conditional execution

By using this form of conditional statement, we can describe our plans as follows:

```
1    if the_weather_is_good:
2        go_for_a_walk()
3    else:
4        go_to_a_theater()
5    have_lunch()
6
```

Making Decisions In Python

If the weather is good, we'll go for a walk. Otherwise, we'll go to a theater. No matter if the weather is good or bad, we'll have lunch afterwards, either after the walk or after going to the theater. Everything we've said about indentation works in the same manner inside the `else` branch:

```
1  if the_weather_is_good:
2      go_for_a_walk()
3      have_fun()
4  else:
5      go_to_a_theater()
6      enjoy_the_movie()
7  have_lunch()
8
```

Nested `if-else` statements

Now let's discuss two special cases of the conditional statement. First, consider the case where the instruction placed after the `if` is another `if`. Read what we have planned for this Sunday. If the weather is fine, we'll go for a walk. If we find a nice restaurant, we'll have lunch there. Otherwise, we'll eat a sandwich. If the weather is poor, we'll go to the theater. If there are no tickets, we'll go shopping in the nearest mall. Let's write the same in Python. Consider carefully the code here:

```
1   if the_weather_is_good:
2       if nice_restaurant_is_found:
3           have_lunch()
4       else:
5           eat_a_sandwich()
6   else:
7       if tickets_are_available:
8           go_to_the_theater()
9       else:
10          go_shopping()
11
```

Here are two important points: this use of the `if` statement is known as nesting — remember that every `else` refers to the `if` which lies at the same indentation level and you need to know this to determine how the `if`s and `else`s pair up; consider how the indentation improves readability, and makes the code easier to understand and trace.

The `elif` statement

The second special case introduces another new Python keyword: `elif`. As you probably suspect, it's a shorter form of else if. `elif` is used to check more than just one condition, and to stop when the first statement which is true is found. Our next example resembles nesting, but the similarities are very slight. Again, we'll change our plans and express them as follows: If the weather is fine, we'll go for a walk, otherwise if we get tickets, we'll go to the theater, otherwise if there are free tables at the restaurant, we'll go for lunch; if all else fails, we'll stay home and play chess. Have you noticed how many times we've used the word *otherwise*? This is the stage where the `elif` keyword plays its role. Let's write the same scenario using Python:

```python
if the_weather_is_good:
    go_for_a_walk()
elif tickets_are_available:
    go_to_the_theater()
elif table_is_available:
    go_for_lunch()
else:
    play_chess_at_home()
```

The way to assemble subsequent `if-elif-else` statements is sometimes called a cascade. Notice again how the indentation improves the readability of the code. Some additional attention has to be paid in this case. You mustn't use `else` without a preceding `if`. `else` is always the last branch of the cascade, regardless of whether you've used `elif` or not. `else` is an optional part of the cascade, and may be omitted. If there is an `else` branch in the cascade, only one of all the branches is executed. If there is no `else` branch, it's possible that none of the available branches is executed. This may sound a little puzzling, but hopefully some simple examples will help shed more light.

Analyzing code samples

Now we're going to show you some simple yet complete programs. We won't explain them in detail, because we consider the comments and the variable names inside the code to be sufficient guides. All the programs solve the same problem — they find the largest of several numbers and print it out.

EXAMPLE 1

We'll start with the simplest case — how to identify the larger of two numbers:

```python
# Read two numbers
number1 = int(input("Enter the first number: "))
number2 = int(input("Enter the second number: "))

# Choose the larger number
if number1 > number2:
    larger_number = number1
else:
    larger_number = number2

# Print the result
print("The larger number is:", larger_number)
```

This snippet should be clear — it reads two integer values, compares them, and finds which is the larger.

Example 2
Now we're going to show you one intriguing fact. Python has an interesting feature — look at the following code:

```python
# Read two numbers
number1 = int(input("Enter the first number: "))
number2 = int(input("Enter the second number: "))

# Choose the larger number
if number1 > number2: larger_number = number1
else: larger_number = number2

# Print the result
print("The larger number is:", larger_number)

```

NOTE If any of the `if-elif-else` branches contains just one instruction, you may code it in a more comprehensive form. You don't need to make an indented line after the keyword, but just continue the line after the colon. This style, however, may be misleading, and we're not going to use it in our future programs, but it's definitely worth knowing if you want to read and understand someone else's programs. There are no other differences in the code.

Example 3
It's time to complicate the code — let's find the largest of three numbers. Will it enlarge the code? A bit. We assume that the first value is the largest. Then we verify this hypothesis with the two remaining values. Look at the following code:

```python
# Read three numbers
number1 = int(input("Enter the first number: "))
number2 = int(input("Enter the second number: "))
number3 = int(input("Enter the third number: "))

# We temporarily assume that the first number
# is the largest one.
# We will verify this soon.
largest_number = number1

# We check if the second number is larger than the current largest_number
# and update the largest_number if needed.
if number2 > largest_number:
    largest_number = number2

# We check if the third number is larger than the current largest_number
# and update the largest_number if needed.
```

```
18  if number3 > largest_number:
19      largest_number = number3
20
21  # Print the result
22  print("The largest number is:", largest_number)
23
```

This method is significantly simpler than trying to find the largest number all at once, by comparing all possible pairs of numbers, that is, first with second, second with third, third with first. Try to rebuild the code for yourself.

Pseudocode and introduction to loops

You should now be able to write a program which finds the largest of four, five, six, or even ten numbers. You already know the scheme, so extending the size of the problem will not be particularly complex. But what happens if we ask you to write a program that finds the largest of two hundred numbers? Can you imagine the code? You'll need two hundred variables. If two hundred variables isn't bad enough, try to imagine searching for the largest of a million numbers.

Imagine a code that contains 199 conditional statements and two hundred invocations of the `input()` function. Luckily, you don't need to deal with that. There's a simpler approach. We'll ignore the requirements of Python syntax for now, and try to analyze the problem without thinking about the real programming. In other words, we'll try to write the algorithm, and when we're happy with it, we'll implement it.

In this case, we'll use a kind of notation which is not an actual programming language (it can be neither compiled nor executed), but it is formalized, concise and readable. It's called pseudocode.

Let's look at our pseudocode:

```
1   largest_number = -999999999
2   number = int(input())
3   if number == -1:
4       print(largest_number)
5       exit()
6   if number > largest_number:
7       largest_number = number
8   # Go to line 02
9
```

What's happening in it? Firstly, we can simplify the program if, at the very beginning of the code, we assign the variable `largest_number` with a value which will be smaller than any of the entered numbers. We'll use -999999999 for that purpose. Secondly, we assume that our algorithm will not know in advance how many numbers will be delivered to the program. We expect that the user will enter as many numbers as she/he wants — the algorithm will work well with one hundred and with one thousand numbers. How do we do that? We make a deal with the user: when the value `-1` is entered, it will be a sign that there are no more data and the program should end its work. Otherwise, if the entered value is not equal to -1, the program will read another number, and so on. The trick is based on the assumption that any part of the code can be performed more than once — precisely, as many times as needed.

Performing a certain part of the code more than once is called a loop. The meaning of this term is probably obvious to you. Lines `02` through `08` make a loop. We'll pass through them as many times as needed to review all the entered values. Can you use a similar structure in a program written in Python? Yes, you can.

EXTRA Python often comes with a lot of built-in functions that will do the work for you. For example, to find the largest number of all, you can use a Python built-in function called `max()`. You can use it with multiple arguments. Analyze the following code:

```
1   # Read three numbers.
2   number1 = int(input("Enter the first number: "))
3   number2 = int(input("Enter the second number: "))
4   number3 = int(input("Enter the third number: "))
5
6   # Check which one of the numbers is the greatest
7   # and pass it to the largest_number variable.
8
9   largest_number = max(number1, number2, number3)
10
11  # Print the result.
12  print("The largest number is:", largest_number)
13
```

By the same fashion, you can use the `min()` function to return the lowest number. You can rebuild this code and experiment with it in the Sandbox.

We're going to talk about these and many other functions soon. For the time being, our focus will be on conditional execution and loops to let you gain more confidence in programming and teach you the skills that will let you fully understand and apply the two concepts in your code. So, for now, we're not taking any shortcuts.

LAB: Comparison operators and conditional execution

Spathiphyllum, more commonly known as a peace lily or white sail plant, is one of the most popular indoor houseplants that filters out harmful toxins from the air. Some of the toxins that it neutralizes include benzene, formaldehyde, and ammonia. Imagine that your computer program loves these plants. Whenever it receives an input in the form of the word `Spathiphyllum`, it involuntarily shouts to the console the following string: `"Spathiphyllum is the best plant ever!"`

Write a program that utilizes the concept of conditional execution, takes a string as input, and:

- prints the sentence `"Yes-Spathiphyllum is the best plant ever!"` to the screen if the inputted string is `"Spathiphyllum"` (upper-case)
- prints `"No,I want a big Spathiphyllum!"` if the inputted string is `"spathiphyllum"` (lower-case)
- prints `"Spathiphyllum! Not[input]!"` otherwise. Note: `[input]` is the string taken as input.

Test your code using the data we've provided for you. And get yourself a Spathiphyllum, too!

SAMPLE INPUT:
```
spathiphyllum
```

EXPECTED OUTPUT:
```
No, I want a big Spathiphyllum!
```

SAMPLE INPUT:
```
pelargonium
```

EXPECTED OUTPUT:
```
Spathiphyllum! Not pelargonium!
```

SAMPLE INPUT:
```
Spathiphyllum
```

EXPECTED OUTPUT:
```
Yes - Spathiphyllum is the best plant ever!
```

LAB: Essentials of the `if-else` statement

Once upon a time there was a land — a land of milk and honey, inhabited by happy and prosperous people. The people paid taxes, of course — their happiness had limits. The most important tax, called the *Personal Income Tax* (*PIT* for short) had to be paid once a year, and was evaluated using the following rule:

- if the citizen's income was not higher than 85,528 thalers, the tax was equal to 18% of the income minus 556 thalers and 2 cents (this was what they called *tax relief*)
- if the income was higher than this amount, the tax was equal to 14,839 thalers and 2 cents, plus 32% of the surplus over 85,528 thalers.

Your task is to write a tax calculator. It should accept one floating-point value: the income. Next, it should print the calculated tax, rounded to full thalers. There's a function named `round()` which will do the rounding for you – you'll find it in the following skeleton code.

Note that this happy country never returns any money to its citizens. If the calculated tax was less than zero, it would only mean no tax at all, that the tax was equal to zero. Take this into consideration during your calculations. Look at the code — it only reads one input value and outputs a result, so you need to complete it with some smart calculations. Test your code using the data we've provided.

SAMPLE INPUT:
```
10000
```

EXPECTED OUTPUT:
```
The tax is: 1244.0 thalers
```

SAMPLE INPUT:
```
100000
```

EXPECTED OUTPUT:
```
The tax is: 19470.0 thalers
```

SAMPLE INPUT:
```
1000
```

EXPECTED OUTPUT:
```
The tax is: 0.0 thalers
```

SAMPLE INPUT:
```
-100
```

EXPECTED OUTPUT:
```
The tax is: 0.0 thalers
```

CODE
```
1   income = float(input("Enter the annual income: "))
2
3   if income < 85528:
4    tax = income * 0.18 - 556.02
5   # Write the rest of your code here.
6
7   tax = round(tax, 0)
8   print("The tax is:", tax, "thalers")
9
```

LAB: Essentials of the `if-elif-else` statement

As you surely know, due to some astronomical reasons, years may be *leap* or *common*. The former are 366 days long, while the latter are 365 days long. Since the introduction of the Gregorian calendar in 1582) the following rule is used to determine the kind of year:

- if the year number isn't divisible by four, it's a *common year*;
- otherwise, if the year number isn't divisible by 100, it's a *leap year*;
- otherwise, if the year number isn't divisible by 400, it's a *common year*;
- otherwise, it's a *leap year*.

Look at the following code — it only reads a year number, and needs to be completed with the instructions implementing the test we've just described. The code should output one of two possible messages, which are `Leap year` or `Common year`, depending on the value entered. It would be good to verify if the entered year falls into the Gregorian era, and output a warning otherwise: `Not within the Gregorian calendar period`. Tip: use the `!=` and `%` operators. Test your code using the data we've provided.

SAMPLE INPUT:
```
2000
```

EXPECTED OUTPUT:
```
Leap year
```

SAMPLE INPUT:
```
2015
```

EXPECTED OUTPUT:
```
Common year
```

SAMPLE INPUT:
```
1999
```

EXPECTED OUTPUT:
```
Common year
```

SAMPLE INPUT:
```
1996
```

EXPECTED OUTPUT:
```
Leap year
```

SAMPLE INPUT:
```
1580
```

EXPECTED OUTPUT:
```
Not within the Gregorian calendar period
```

CODE

```
1  year = int(input("Enter a year: "))
2
3  if year < 1582:
4      print("Not within the Gregorian calendar period")
5  else:
6      # Write the if-elif-elif-else block here.
7
```

Summary

1. The comparison (otherwise known as *relational*) operators are used to compare values. The following table illustrates how the comparison operators work, assuming that `x=0`, `y=1`, and `z=0`.

Operator	Description	Example
==	returns `True` if operands' values are equal, and `False` otherwise	`x==y#False` `x==z#True`
!=	returns `True` if operands' values are not equal, and `False` otherwise	`x!=y#True` `x!=z#False`
>	`True` if the left operand's value is greater than the right operand's value, and `False` otherwise	`x>y#False` `y>z#True`
<	`True` if the left operand's value is less than the right operand's value, and `False` otherwise	`x<y#True` `y<z#False`

>=	`True` if the left operand's value is greater than or equal to the right operand's value, and `False` otherwise	`x>=y#False`
		`x>=z#True`
		`y>=z#True`

<=	`True` if the left operand's value is less than or equal to the right operand's value, and `False` otherwise	`x<=y#True`
		`x<=z#True`
		`y<=z#False`

2. When you want to execute some code only if a certain condition is met, you can use a conditional statement:

- A single `if` statement, e.g.:

```
1  x = 10
2
3  if x == 10:  # condition
4      print("x is equal to 10")   # Executed if the condition is True.
5
```

- A series of `if` statements, e.g.:

```
1   x = 10
2
3   if x > 5: # condition one
4       print("x is greater than 5")   # Executed if condition one is True.
5
6   if x < 10: # condition two
7       print("x is less than 10")   # Executed if condition two is True.
8
9   if x == 10: # condition three
10      print("x is equal to 10")   # Executed if condition three is True.
11
```

Each `if` statement is tested separately.

- An `if-else` statement, e.g.:

```
1   x = 10
2
3   if x < 10: # condition     print("x is less than 10")   # Executed if the condition is True.
4
5   else:
6       print("x is greater than or equal to 10")   # Executed if the condition is False.
7
```

- A series of `if` statements followed by an `else`, e.g.:

```
1   x = 10
2
3   if x > 5: # condition one
4       print("x is greater than 5")   # Executed if condition one is True.
5
6   if x < 10: # condition two
7       print("x is less than 10")   # Executed if condition two is True.
8
9   if x == 10: # condition three
10      print("x is equal to 10")   # Executed if condition three is True.
11
```

Each `if` is tested separately. `else` is executed if the last `if` is `False`.

- The `if-elif-else` statement, e.g.:

```
1   x = 10
2
3   if x == 10: # True
4       print("x == 10")
5
6   if x > 15: # False
7       print("x > 15")
8
9   elif x > 10: # False
10      print("x > 10")
11
12  elif x > 5: # True
13      print("x > 5")
14
15  else:
16      print("else will not be executed")
17
```

If the condition for `if` is `False`, the program checks the conditions of the subsequent `elif` blocks — the first `elif` block that is `True` is executed. If all the conditions are `False`, the `else` block will be executed.

- Nested conditional statements, e.g.:

```
1   x = 10
2
3   if x > 5: # True
4       if x == 6: # False
5           print("nested: x == 6")
6       elif x == 10: # True
7           print("nested: x == 10")
8       else:
9           print("nested: else")
10  else:
11      print("else")
12
```

Quiz

QUESTION 1: What is the output of the following snippet?

```
x = 5
y = 10
z = 8

print(x > y)
print(y > z)
```

QUESTION 2: What is the output of the following snippet?

```
x, y, z = 5, 10, 8

print(x > z)
print((y - 5) == x)
```

QUESTION 3: What is the output of the following snippet?

```
x, y, z = 5, 10, 8
x, y, z = z, y, x

print(x > z)
print((y - 5) == x)
```

QUESTION 4: What is the output of the following snippet?

```
x = 10

if x == 10:
    print(x == 10)
if x > 5:
    print(x > 5)
if x < 10:
    print(x < 10)
else:
    print("else")
```

Making Decisions In Python

QUESTION 5: What is the output of the following snippet?

```
x = "1"

if x == 1:
    print("one")
elif x == "1":
    if int(x) > 1:
        print("two")
    elif int(x) < 1:
        print("three")
    else:
        print("four")
if int(x) == 1:
    print("five")
else:
    print("six")
```

QUESTION 6: What is the output of the following snippet?

```
x = 1
y = 1.0
z = "1"

if x == y:
    print("one")
if y == int(z):
    print("two")
elif x == y:
    print("three")
else:
    print("four")
```

ELEVEN
LOOPS IN PYTHON

Do you agree with the following statement?

```
while there is something to do
    do it
```

Note that this record also declares that if there is nothing to do, nothing at all will happen. In general, in Python, a loop can be represented as follows:

```
while
    instruction
```

If you notice some similarities to the `if` instruction, that's quite all right. Indeed, the syntactic difference is only one: you use the word `while` instead of the word `if`. The semantic difference is more important: when the condition is met, `if` performs its statements only once; `while` repeats the execution as long as the condition evaluates to `True`.

NOTE All the rules regarding indentation are applicable here, too. We'll show you this soon.

Look at the following algorithm:

```
while conditional_expression:
    instruction_one
    instruction_two
    instruction_three
    :
    :
    instruction_n
```

It is now important to remember that if you want to execute more than one statement inside one `while` loop, you must, as with `if`, indent all the instructions in the same way. An instruction or set of instructions executed inside the `while` loop is called the loop's body. If the condition is `False` (equal to zero) as early as when it is tested for the first time, the body is not executed even once — note the analogy of not having to do anything if there is nothing to do. The body should be able to change the condition's value, because if the condition is `True` at the beginning, the body might run continuously to infinity — notice that doing a thing usually decreases the number of things to do.

An infinite loop

An infinite loop, also called an endless loop, is a sequence of instructions in a program which repeat indefinitely, or loop endlessly. Here's an example of a loop that is not able to finish its execution:

```
1  while True:
2      print("I'm stuck inside a loop.")
3
```

This loop will infinitely print `"I'm stuck inside a loop."` on the screen.

NOTE If you want to get the best learning experience from seeing how an infinite loop behaves, launch IDLE, create a *New File*, copy-paste the previous code, save your file, and run the program. What you will see is the never-ending sequence of `"I'm stuck inside a loop."` strings printed to the Python console window. To terminate your program, just press *Ctrl-C* (or *Ctrl-Break* on some computers). This will cause a `KeyboardInterrupt` exception and let your program get out of the loop. We'll talk about it later in the course.

Let's go back to the sketch of the algorithm we showed you recently. We're going to show you how to use this newly learned loop to find the largest number from a large set of entered data. Analyze the program carefully. See where the loop starts (line 8). Locate the loop's body and find out how the body is exited. Check how this code implements the algorithm we showed you earlier.

```
1  # Store the current largest number here.
2  largest_number = -999999999
3
4  # Input the first value.
5  number = int(input("Enter a number or type -1 to stop: "))
6
7  # If the number is not equal to -1, continue.
8  while number != -1:
9      # Is number larger than largest_number?
10     if number > largest_number:
11         # Yes, update largest_number.
12         largest_number = number
```

```
13      # Input the next number.
14      number = int(input("Enter a number or type -1 to stop: "))
15
16  # Print the largest number.
17  print("The largest number is:", largest_number)
18
```

The while loop: more examples

Let's look at another example employing the while loop. Follow the comments to find out the idea and the solution.

```
1   # A program that reads a sequence of numbers
2   # and counts how many numbers are even and how many are odd.
3   # The program terminates when zero is entered.
4
5   odd_numbers = 0
6   even_numbers = 0
7
8   # Read the first number.
9   number = int(input("Enter a number or type 0 to stop: "))
10
11  # 0 terminates execution.
12  while number != 0:
13      # Check if the number is odd.
14      if number % 2 == 1:
15          # Increase the odd_numbers counter.
16          odd_numbers += 1
17      else:
18          # Increase the even_numbers counter.
19          even_numbers += 1
20      # Read the next number.
21      number = int(input("Enter a number or type 0 to stop: "))
22
23  # Print results.
24  print("Odd numbers count:", odd_numbers)
25  print("Even numbers count:", even_numbers)
26
```

Certain expressions can be simplified without changing the program's behavior. Try to recall how Python interprets the truth of a condition, and note that these two forms are equivalent:

While number!=0: and while number:

The condition that checks if a number is odd can be coded in these equivalent forms, too:

If number % 2==1: and if number % 2:

Loops In Python   105

Using a `counter` variable to exit a loop

Look at the following snippet:

```
1   counter = 5
2   while counter != 0:
3       print("Inside the loop.", counter)
4       counter -= 1
5   print("Outside the loop.", counter)
6
```

This code is intended to print the string `"Inside the loop."` and the value stored in the `counter` variable during a given loop exactly five times. Once the condition has not been met (the `counter` variable has reached `0`), the loop is exited, and the message `"Outside the loop."` as well as the value stored in `counter` is printed. But there's one thing that can be written more compactly — the condition of the `while` loop. Can you see the difference?

```
1   counter = 5
2   while counter:
3       print("Inside the loop.", counter)
4       counter -= 1
5   print("Outside the loop.", counter)
6
```

Is it more compact than previously? A bit. Is it more legible? That's disputable.

NOTE Don't feel obliged to code your programs in a way that is always the shortest and the most compact. Readability may be a more important factor. Keep your code ready for a new programmer.

LAB: Guess the secret number

A junior magician has picked a secret number. He has hidden it in a variable named `secret_number`. He wants everyone who runs his program to play the *Guess the secret number* game, and guess what number he has picked for them. Those who don't guess the number will be stuck in an endless loop forever! Unfortunately, he does not know how to complete the code.

Your task is to help the magician complete the code in such a way so that the code:

- will ask the user to enter an integer number;
- will use a `while` loop;
- will check whether the number entered by the user is the same as the number picked by the magician. If the number chosen by the user is different than the magician's secret number, the user should see the message `"Haha! You're stuck in my loop!"` and be prompted to enter a number again. If the number

entered by the user matches the number picked by the magician, the number should be printed to the screen, and the magician should say the following words: `"Well done, muggle! You are free now."`

The magician is counting on you! Don't disappoint him.

NOTE Look at the `print()` function. The way we've used it here is called *multi-line printing*. You can use triple quotes to print strings on multiple lines in order to make text easier to read, or create a special text-based design. Experiment with it.

CODE

```
1   secret_number = 777
2
3   print(
4   """
5   +==================================+
6   | Welcome to my game, muggle!      |
7   | Enter an integer number          |
8   | and guess what number I've       |
9   | picked for you.                  |
10  | So, what is the secret number?   |
11  +==================================+
12  """)
13
```

Looping your code with `for`

Another kind of loop available in Python comes from the observation that sometimes it's more important to count the "turns" of the loop than to check the conditions. Imagine that a loop's body needs to be executed exactly one hundred times. If you would like to use the `while` loop to do it, it may look like this:

```
1   i = 0
2   while i < 100:
3       # do_something()
4       i += 1
5
```

It would be nice if somebody could do this boring counting for you. Is that possible? Of course it is — there's a special loop for these kinds of tasks, and it is named `for`. Actually, the `for` loop is designed to do more complicated tasks — it can "browse" large collections of data item by item. We'll show you how to do that soon, but right now we're going to present a simpler variant of its application. Take a look at the snippet:

```
1   for i in range(100):
2       # do_something()
3       pass
4
```

Loops In Python   107

There are some new elements. The `for` keyword opens the `for` loop; note — there's no condition after it; you don't have to think about conditions, as they're checked internally, without any intervention. Any variable after the `for` keyword is the control variable of the loop; it counts the loop's turns, and does it automatically. The `in` keyword introduces a syntax element describing the range of possible values being assigned to the control variable. The `range()` function is a very special function and is responsible for generating all the desired values of the control variable; in our example, the function will create subsequent values from the following set: 0, 1, 2 .. 97, 98, 99 — we can also say that it will feed the loop with these values. Note that in this case, the `range()` function starts its job from 0 and finishes it one step or integer number before the value of its argument. Observe the `pass` keyword inside the loop body — it does nothing at all; it's an empty instruction — we put it here because the `for` loop's syntax demands at least one instruction inside the body. By the way, `if`, `elif`, `else`, and `while` express the same thing.

Our next examples will be a bit more modest in the number of loop repetitions. Take a look at the following snippet. Can you predict its output? Run the code to check if you were right.

```
1   for i in range(10):
2       print("The value of i is currently", i)
3
```

NOTE The loop has been executed ten times. It's the `range()` function's argument. The last control variable's value is `9`, not `10`, as it starts from `0`, not from `1`.

The `range()` function invocation may be equipped with two arguments, not just one:

```
1   for i in range(2, 8):
2       print("The value of i is currently", i)
3
```

In this case, the first argument determines the initial (first) value of the control variable. The last argument shows the first value the control variable will not be assigned. The `range()` function accepts only integers as its arguments, and generates sequences of integers. Can you guess the output of the program? Run it to check if you were right now, too. The first value shown is `2`, taken from the `range()`'s first argument. The last is `7` (although the `range()`'s second argument is `8`).

Chapter 11

More about the `for` loop and the `range()` function with three arguments

The `range()` function may also accept three arguments — take a look at the following code.

```
1   for i in range(2, 8, 3):
2       print("The value of i is currently", i)
3
```

The third argument is an increment — it's a value added to control the variable at every loop turn. As you may suspect, the default value of the increment is 1. Can you tell us how many lines will appear in the console and what values they will contain? Run the program to find out if you're right. You should be able to see the following lines in the console window:

```
The value of i is currently 2
The value of i is currently 5
```

Do you know why? The first argument passed to the `range()` function tells us what the starting number of the sequence is, hence 2 in the output. The second argument tells the function where to stop the sequence. The function generates numbers up to the number indicated by the second argument, but doesn't include it. Finally, the third argument indicates the step, which means the difference between each number in the sequence of numbers generated by the function. 2 (starting number) to 5 (2 incremented by 3 equals 5 — the number is within the range from 2 to 8) to 8 (5 incremented by 3 equals 8 — the number is not within the range from 2 to 8, because the stop parameter is not included in the sequence of numbers generated by the function).

NOTE If the set generated by the `range()` function is empty, the loop won't execute its body at all. Just like here — there will be no output:

```
1   for i in range(1, 1):
2       print("The value of i is currently", i)
3
```

The set generated by the `range()` has to be sorted in ascending order. There's no way to force the `range()` to create a set in a different form when the `range()` function accepts exactly two arguments. This means that the `range()`'s second argument must be greater than the first. Thus, there will be no output here, either:

```
1   for i in range(2, 1):
2       print("The value of i is currently", i)
3
```

Let's have a look at a short program whose task is to write some of the first powers of two:

```
1  power = 1
2  for expo in range(16):
3      print("2 to the power of", expo, "is", power)
4      power *= 2
5
```

The `expo` variable is used as a control variable for the loop, and indicates the current value of the *exponent*. The exponentiation itself is replaced by multiplying by two. Since 20 is equal to 1, then 2 × 1 is equal to 21, 2 × 21 is equal to 22, and so on. What is the greatest exponent for which our program still prints the result? Run the code and check if the output matches your expectations.

LAB: Essentials of the `for` loop – counting mississippily

Do you know what Mississippi is? It's the name of one of the states and rivers in the United States. The Mississippi River is about 2,340 miles long, which makes it the second longest river in the United States, the longest being the Missouri River. It's so long that a single drop of water needs 90 days to travel its entire length. The word *Mississippi* is also used for a slightly different purpose: to *count mississippily*. If you're not familiar with the phrase, we're here to explain to you what it means: it's used to count seconds. The idea behind it is that adding the word *Mississippi* to a number when counting seconds aloud makes them sound closer to clock-time, and therefore "one Mississippi, two Mississippi, three Mississippi" will take approximately three seconds of time! It's often used by children playing hide-and-seek to make sure the seeker does an honest count.

Your task is very simple here: write a program that uses a `for` loop to "count mississippily" to five. Having counted to five, the program should print to the screen the final message `"Ready or not, here I come!"` Use the skeleton we've provided for you.

NOTE The code contains two elements which may be unclear to you at this moment: the `import time` statement, and the `sleep()` method. We're going to talk about them soon. For now, just know that we've imported the time module and used the `sleep()` method to suspend the execution of each subsequent `print()` function inside the `for` loop for one second, so that the message outputted to the console resembles an actual counting.

EXPECTED OUTPUT:
```
1 Mississippi
2 Mississippi
3 Mississippi
4 Mississippi
5 Mississippi
```

CODE

```
1   import time
2
3   # Write a for loop that counts to five.
4       # Body of the loop - print the loop iteration number and the word "Mississippi".
5       # Body of the loop - use: time.sleep(1)
6
7   # Write a print function with the final message.
8
```

The break and continue statements

So far, we've treated the body of the loop as an indivisible and inseparable sequence of instructions that are performed completely at every turn of the loop. However, as a developer, you could be faced with the following choices: it appears that it's unnecessary to continue the loop as a whole and you should refrain from further execution of the loop's body and go further; or it appears that you need to start the next turn of the loop without completing the execution of the current turn.

Python provides two special instructions for the implementation of both these tasks. Let's say for the sake of accuracy that their existence in the language is not necessary — an experienced programmer is able to code any algorithm without these instructions. Such additions, which don't improve the language's expressive power, but only simplify the developer's work, are sometimes called syntactic candy, or syntactic sugar. The first of these two instructions are **break**, which exits the loop immediately and unconditionally ends the loop's operation; the program begins to execute the nearest instruction after the loop's body. The second is **continue**, which behaves as if the program has suddenly reached the end of the body; the next turn is started and the condition expression is tested immediately. Both these words are keywords.

Now we'll show you two simple examples to illustrate how the two instructions work. Look at the following code. Run the program and analyze the output. Modify the code and experiment.

```
1   # break - example
2
3   print("The break instruction:")
4   for i in range(1, 6):
5       if i == 3:
6           break
7       print("Inside the loop.", i)
8   print("Outside the loop.")
9
10
11  # continue - example
12
13  print("\nThe continue instruction:")
14  for i in range(1, 6):
15      if i == 3:
```

```
16          continue
17      print("Inside the loop.", i)
18  print("Outside the loop.")
19
```

The `break` and `continue` statements: more examples

Let's return to our program that recognizes the largest among the entered numbers. We'll convert it twice, using the `break` and `continue` instructions. Analyze the code, and judge whether and how you would use either of them.

The `break` variant goes here. Run it, test it, and experiment with it.

```
1   largest_number = -99999999
2   counter = 0
3
4   while True:
5       number = int(input("Enter a number or type -1 to end the program: "))
6       if number == -1:
7           break
8       counter += 1
9       if number > largest_number:
10          largest_number = number
11
12  if counter != 0:
13      print("The largest number is", largest_number)
14  else:
15      print("You haven't entered any number.")
16
```

And now the `continue` variant:

```
1   largest_number = -99999999
2   counter = 0
3
4   number = int(input("Enter a number or type -1 to end program: "))
5
6   while number != -1:
7       if number == -1:
8           continue
9       counter += 1
10
11      if number > largest_number:
12          largest_number = number
13      number = int(input("Enter a number or type -1 to end the program: "))
14
```

Chapter 11

```
15  if counter:
16      print("The largest number is", largest_number)
17  else:
18      print("You haven't entered any number.")
19
```

Look carefully, the user enters the first number before the program enters the `while` loop. The subsequent number is entered when the program is already in the loop. Again — run the program, test it, and experiment with it.

LAB: The `break` statement — Stuck in a loop

The `break` statement is used to exit/terminate a loop.

Design a program that uses a `while` loop and continuously asks the user to enter a word unless the user enters `"chupacabra"` as the secret exit word, in which case the message `"You've successfully left the loop."` should be printed to the screen, and the loop should terminate. Don't print any of the words entered by the user. Use the concept of conditional execution and the `break` statement.

LAB: The `continue` statement — the Ugly Vowel Eater

The `continue` statement is used to skip the current block and move ahead to the next iteration, without executing the statements inside the loop. It can be used with both the `while` and `for` loops.

Your task here is very special: you must design a vowel eater! Write a program that uses a `for` loop, the concept of conditional execution (`if-elif-else`), and the `continue` statement. Your program must:

- ask the user to enter a word;
- use `user_word=user_word.upper()` to convert the word entered by the user to upper case; we'll talk about string methods and the `upper()` method very soon – don't worry;
- use conditional execution and the `continue` statement to "eat" the following vowels A, E, I, O, U from the inputted word;
- print the uneaten letters to the screen, each one of them on a separate line.

Test your program with the data we've provided for you.

SAMPLE INPUT:
```
Gregory
```

EXPECTED OUTPUT:
```
G
R
G
R
Y
```

Loops In Python

SAMPLE INPUT:
```
abstemious
```

EXPECTED OUTPUT:
```
B
S
T
M
S
```

SAMPLE INPUT:
```
IOUEA
```

EXPECTED OUTPUT:

CODE
```
1  # Prompt the user to enter a word
2  # and assign it to the user_word variable.
3
4  for letter in user_word:
5      # Complete the body of the for loop.
6
```

LAB: The continue statement – the Pretty Vowel Eater

Your task here is even more special than before: you must redesign the ugly vowel eater from the previous lab and create a better, upgraded pretty vowel eater. Write a program that uses a `for` loop, the concept of conditional execution (`if-elif-else`), and the `continue` statement. Your program must:

- ask the user to enter a word;
- use `user_word=user_word.upper()` to convert the word entered by the user to upper case; we'll talk about string methods and the `upper()` method very soon – don't worry;
- use conditional execution and the `continue` statement to "eat" the following vowels A, E, I, O, U from the inputted word;
- assign the uneaten letters to the `word_without_vowels` variable and print the variable to the screen.

Look at the following code. We've created `word_without_vowels` and assigned an empty string to it. Use concatenation operation to ask Python to combine selected letters into a longer string during subsequent loop turns, and assign it to the `word_without_vowels` variable. Test your program with the data we've provided for you.

SAMPLE INPUT:
```
Gregory
```

EXPECTED OUTPUT:
```
GRGRY
```

SAMPLE INPUT:
```
abstemious
```

EXPECTED OUTPUT:
```
BSTMS
```

SAMPLE INPUT:
```
IOUEA
```

EXPECTED OUTPUT:

CODE
```
1   word_without_vowels = ""
2
3   # Prompt the user to enter a word
4   # and assign it to the user_word variable.
5
6
7   for letter in user_word:
8       # Complete the body of the loop.
9
10  # Print the word assigned to word_without_vowels.
11
```

The `while` loop and the `else` branch

Both loops, `while` and `for`, have one interesting and rarely used feature. We'll show you how it works — try to judge for yourself if it's usable and whether you can live without it or not. In other words, try to convince yourself if the feature is valuable and useful, or is just syntactic sugar. Take a look at the following snippet. There's something strange at the end — the `else` keyword. As you may have suspected, loops may have the `else` branch too, like `if`s. The loop's `else` branch is always executed once, regardless of whether the loop has entered its body or not. Can you guess the output? Run the program to check if you were right.

```
1   i = 1
2   while i < 5:
3       print(i)
4       i += 1
5   else:
6       print("else:", i)
7
```

Modify the snippet a bit so that the loop has no chance to execute its body even once: The `while`'s condition is `False` at the beginning — can you see it? Run and test the program, and check whether the `else` branch has been executed or not.

The `for` loop and the `else` branch

`for` loops behave a bit differently — take a look at the following snippet and run it.

```
1   for i in range(5):
2       print(i)
3   else:
4       print("else:", i)
5
```

The output may be a bit surprising. The `i` variable retains its last value. Modify the code a bit to carry out one more experiment.

```
1   i = 111
2   for i in range(2, 1):
3       print(i)
4   else:
5       print("else:", i)
6
```

Can you guess the output? The loop's body won't be executed here at all. Note that we've assigned the `i` variable before the loop. Run the program and check its output. When the loop's body isn't executed, the control variable retains the value it had before the loop.

NOTE If the control variable doesn't exist before the loop starts, it won't exist when the execution reaches the `else` branch.

How do you feel about this variant of `else`? Soon we'll tell you about some other kinds of variables. Our current variables can only store one value at a time, but there are variables that can do much more — they can store as many values as you want. But let's do some labs, first.

LAB: Essentials of the `while` loop

Listen to this story: a boy and his father, a computer programmer, are playing with wooden blocks. They are building a pyramid. Their pyramid is a bit weird, as it is actually a pyramid-shaped wall — it's flat. The pyramid is stacked according to one simple principle: each lower layer contains one block more than the layer above. Figure 11.1 illustrates the rule used by the builders.

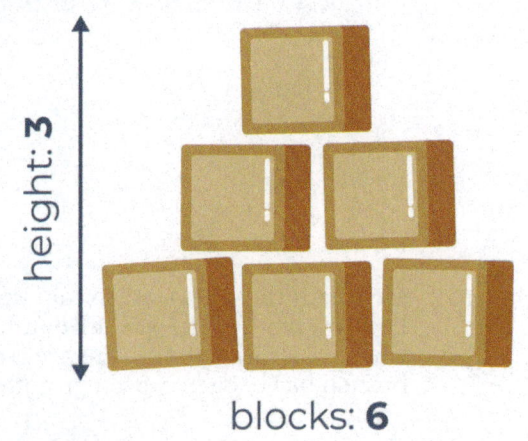

Figure 11.1

Your task is to write a program which reads the number of blocks the builders have, and outputs the height of the pyramid that can be built using these blocks.

Note that the height is measured by the number of fully completed layers — if the builders don't have a sufficient number of blocks and cannot complete the next layer, they finish their work immediately. Test your code using the data we've provided.

SAMPLE INPUT:
```
6
```

EXPECTED OUTPUT:
```
The height of the pyramid: 3
```

SAMPLE INPUT:
```
20
```

EXPECTED OUTPUT:
```
The height of the pyramid: 3
```

SAMPLE INPUT:
```
1000
```

EXPECTED OUTPUT:
```
The height of the pyramid: 44
```

SAMPLE INPUT:
```
2
```

EXPECTED OUTPUT:
```
The height of the pyramid: 1
```

CODE
```
1    blocks = int(input("Enter the number of blocks: "))
2
3    #
4    # Write your code here.
5    #
6
7    print("The height of the pyramid:", height)
8
```

LAB: Collatz's hypothesis

In 1937, a German mathematician named Lothar Collatz formulated an intriguing, still unproven hypothesis which can be described in the following way:

- take any non-negative and non-zero integer number and name it c_0;
- if it's even, evaluate a new c_0 as $c_0 \div 2$;

- otherwise, if it's odd, evaluate a new `c0` as `3×c0+1`;
- if `c0≠1`, go back to point 2.

The hypothesis says that regardless of the initial value of `c0`, it will always go to 1. Of course, it's an extremely complex task to use a computer in order to prove the hypothesis for any natural number, but you can use Python to check some individual numbers. Maybe you'll even find the one which would disprove the hypothesis.

Write a program which reads one natural number and executes these steps as long as `c0` remains different from 1. We also want you to count the steps needed to achieve the goal. Your code should output all the intermediate values of `c0`, too.

HINT The most important part of the problem is how to transform Collatz's idea into a `while` loop — this is the key to success. Test your code using the data we've provided.

SAMPLE INPUT:
```
15
```

EXPECTED OUTPUT:
```
46
46
70
35
106
53
160
80
40
20
10
5
16
8
4
2
1
steps = 17
```

SAMPLE INPUT:
```
16
```

EXPECTED OUTPUT:
```
8
4
2
1
steps = 4
```

SAMPLE INPUT:
1023

EXPECTED OUTPUT:
3070
1535
4606
2303
6910
3455
10366
5183
15550
7775
23326
11663
34990
17495
52486
26243
78730
39365
118096
59048
29524
14762
7381
22144
11072
5536
2768
1384
692
346
173
173
260
130
65
196
98
49
148
74
37
37
56
28
14
7
22
11

```
34
17
52
26
13
40
20
10
5
16
8
4
2
1
2
```

Summary

1. There are two types of loops in Python: `while` and `for`.

   - The `while` loop executes a statement or a set of statements as long as a specified boolean condition is true, e.g.:

     ```
     1  # Example 1
     2  while True:
     3      print("Stuck in an infinite loop.")
     4
     5  # Example 2
     6  counter = 5
     7  while counter > 2:
     8      print(counter)
     9      counter -= 1
     10
     ```

   - The `for` loop executes a set of statements many times; it's used to iterate over a sequence (e.g. a list, a dictionary, a tuple, or a set — you will learn about them soon) or other iterable objects (e.g. strings). You can use the `for` loop to iterate over a sequence of numbers using the built-in range function. Look at the following examples:

     ```
     1  # Example 1
     2  word = "Python"
     3  for letter in word:
     4      print(letter, end="*")
     5
     6  # Example 2
     7  for i in range(1, 10):
     8      if i % 2 == 0:
     9          print(i)
     10
     ```

2. You can use the `break` and `continue` statements to change the flow of a loop.

- You use `break` to exit a loop, e.g.:

```
1  text = "OpenEDG Python Institute"
2  for letter in text:
3      if letter == "P":
4          break
5      print(letter, end="")
6
```

- You use `continue` to skip the current iteration, and continue with the next iteration, e.g.:

```
1  text = "pyxpyxpyx"
2  for letter in text:
3      if letter == "x":
4          continue
5      print(letter, end="")
6
```

3. The `while` and `for` loops can also have an `else` clause in Python. The `else` clause executes after the loop finishes its execution as long as it has not been terminated by `break`, e.g.:

```
1   n = 0
2
3   while n != 3:
4       print(n)
5       n += 1
6   else:
7       print(n, "else")
8
9   print()
10
11  for i in range(0, 3):
12      print(i)
13  else:
14      print(i, "else")
15
```

4. The `range()` function generates a sequence of numbers. It accepts integers and returns range objects. The syntax of `range()` looks as follows: `range(start, stop, step)`, where:

- `start` is an optional parameter specifying the starting number of the sequence (0 by default)
- `stop` is an optional parameter specifying the end of the sequence generated (it is not included)
- and `step` is an optional parameter specifying the difference between the numbers in the sequence (1 by default)

Example code:

```
1   for i in range(3):
2       print(i, end=" ")   # Outputs: 0 1 2
3
4   for i in range(6, 1, -2):
5       print(i, end=" ")   # Outputs: 6, 4, 2
6
```

Quiz

QUESTION 1: Create a `for` loop that counts from 0 to 10, and prints odd numbers to the screen. Use the following skeleton:

```
for i in range(0, 11):
    # Line of code.
        # Line of code.
```

QUESTION 2: Create a `while` loop that counts from 0 to 10, and prints odd numbers to the screen. Use the following skeleton:

```
x = 1
while x < 11:
    # Line of code.
        # Line of code.
    # Line of code.
```

QUESTION 3: Create a program with a `for` loop and a `break` statement. The program should iterate over characters in an email address, exit the loop when it reaches the @ symbol, and print the part before @ on one line. Use the following skeleton:

```
for ch in "john.smith@pythoninstitute.org":
    if ch == "@":
        # Line of code.
    # Line of code.
```

QUESTION 4: Create a program with a `for` loop and a `continue` statement. The program should iterate over a string of digits, replace each `0` with `x`, and print the modified string to the screen. Use the following skeleton:

```
for digit in "0165031806510":
    if digit == "0":
        # Line of code.
        # Line of code.
    # Line of code.
```

QUESTION 5: What is the output of the following code?

```
n = 3

while n > 0:
    print(n + 1)
    n -= 1
else:
    print(n)
```

QUESTION 6: What is the output of the following code?

```
n = range(4)

for num in n:
    print(num - 1)
else:
    print(num)
```

QUESTION 7: What is the output of the following code?

```
for i in range(0, 6, 3):
    print(i)
```

TWELVE
LOGIC AND BIT OPERATIONS IN PYTHON

Have you noticed that the conditions we've used so far have been very simple, not to say, quite primitive? The conditions we use in real life are much more complex. Let's look at this sentence: *If we have some free time, and the weather is good, we will go for a walk.* We've used the conjunction *and*, which means that going for a walk depends on the simultaneous fulfillment of these two conditions. In the language of logic, such a connection of conditions is called a conjunction.

And now another example: *If you are in the mall or I am in the mall, one of us will buy a gift for Mom.* The appearance of the word *or* means that the purchase depends on at least one of these conditions. In logic, such a compound is called a disjunction. It's clear that Python must have operators to build conjunctions and disjunctions. Without them, the expressive power of the language would be substantially weakened. They're called logical operators.

The **and** operator

One logical conjunction operator in Python is the word **and**. It's a binary operator with a priority that is lower than the one expressed by the comparison operators. It allows us to code complex conditions without the use of parentheses like this one:

```
1
2    counter > 0 and value == 100
3
```

The result provided by the and operator can be determined on the basis of the truth table. If we consider the conjunction of **A** and **B**, the set of possible values of arguments and corresponding values of the conjunction looks as follows:

Argument A	Argument B	A and B
False	False	False
False	True	False
True	False	False
True	True	True

The or operator

A disjunction operator is the word or. It's a binary operator with a lower priority than and. Its truth table is as follows:

Argument A	Argument B	A or B
False	False	False
False	True	True
True	False	True
True	True	True

The not operator

In addition, there's another operator that can be applied to the construction of conditions. It's a unary operator performing a logical negation. Its operation is simple: it turns truth into falsehood and falsehood into truth. This operator is written as the word not, and its priority is very high: the same as the unary + and -. Its truth table is simple:

Argument	not Argument
False	True
True	False

Logical expressions

Let's create a variable named `var` and assign 1 to it. The following conditions are pairwise equivalent:

```
1   # Example 1:
2   print(var > 0)
3   print(not (var <= 0))
4
5
6   # Example 2:
7   print(var != 0)
8   print(not (var == 0))
9
```

You may be familiar with De Morgan's laws. They say the negation of a conjunction is the disjunction of the negations. The negation of a disjunction is the conjunction of the negations. Let's rewrite it using Python:

```
1   not (p and q) == (not p) or  (not q)
2   not (p or  q) == (not p) and (not q)
3
```

Note how the parentheses have been used to code the expressions — we put them there to improve readability. We should add that none of these two-argument operators can be used in the abbreviated form known as op=. This exception is worth remembering.

Logical values vs. single bits

Logical operators take their arguments as a whole regardless of how many bits they contain. The operators are aware only of the value: zero means False, when all the bits are reset; and not zero means True, when at least one bit is set. The result of their operations is one of these values: `False` or `True`. This means that this snippet will assign the value `True` to the `j` variable if `i` is not zero; otherwise, it will be `False`.

```
1   i = 1
2   j = not not i
3
```

Bitwise operators

However, there are four operators that allow you to manipulate single bits of data. They are called bitwise operators. They cover all the operations we mentioned before in the logical context, and one additional operator. This is the xor (as in exclusive or) operator, and is denoted as ^ (caret). Here are all of them:

- & (ampersand) — bitwise conjunction;
- | (bar) — bitwise disjunction;
- ~ (tilde) — bitwise negation;
- ^ (caret) — bitwise exclusive or (xor).

Bitwise operations (&, |, and ^)

Argument A	Argument B	A&B	A|B	A^B
0	0	0	0	0
0	1	0	1	1
1	0	0	1	1
1	1	1	1	0

Bitwise operations (~)

Argument	~ Argument
0	1
1	0

Let's make it easier:

- & requires exactly two 1s to provide **1** as the result;
- | requires at least one 1 to provide **1** as the result;
- ^ requires exactly one 1 to provide **1** as the result.

Let us add an important remark: the arguments of these operators must be integers; we must not use floats here. The difference in the operation of the logical and bit operators is important: the logical operators do not penetrate into the bit level of its argument. They're only interested in the final integer value.

Bitwise operators are stricter: they deal with every bit separately. If we assume that the integer variable occupies 64 bits, which is common in modern computer systems) you can imagine the bitwise operation as a 64-fold evaluation of the logical operator for each pair of bits of the arguments. This analogy is obviously imperfect, as in the real world all these 64 operations are performed at the same time, in other words, simultaneously.

Logical vs. bit operations

We'll now show you an example of the difference in operation between the logic and bit operations. Let's assume that the following assignments have been performed:

```
1   i = 15
2   j = 22
3
```

If we assume that the integers are stored with 32 bits, the bitwise image of the two variables will be as follows:

```
i: 00000000000000000000000000001111
j: 00000000000000000000000000010110
```

The assignment is given:

```
1   log = i and j
2
```

We are dealing with a logical conjunction here. Let's trace the course of the calculations. Both variables i and j are not zeros, so will be deemed to represent True. Consulting the truth table for the **and** operator, we can see that the result will be `True`. No other operations are performed.

```
1   log: True
2
```

Now the bitwise operation — here it is:

```
1   bit = i & j
2
```

The **&** operator will operate with each pair of corresponding bits separately, producing the values of the relevant bits of the result. Therefore, the result will be as follows:

i	00000000000000000000000000001111
j	00000000000000000000000000010110
bit=i&j	00000000000000000000000000000110

These bits correspond to the integer value of six. Let's look at the negation operators now. First the logical one:

```
1   logneg = not i
2
```

The `logneg` variable will be set to `False` — nothing more needs to be done. The bitwise negation goes like this:

```
1  bitneg = ~i
2
```

It may be a bit surprising: the `bitneg` variable value is `-16`. This may seem strange, but isn't at all. If you wish to learn more, you should check out the binary numeral system and the rules governing two's complement numbers.

i	00000000000000000000000000001111
bitneg=~i	11111111111111111111111111110000

Each of these two-argument operators can be used in abbreviated form. These are the examples of their equivalent notations:

x=x&y	x&=y
x=x|y	x|=y
x=x^y	x^=y

How do we deal with single bits?

We'll now show you what you can use bitwise operators for. Imagine that you're a developer obliged to write an important piece of an operating system. You've been told that you're allowed to use a variable assigned in the following way:

```
flag_register = 0x1234
```

The variable stores the information about various aspects of system operation. Each bit of the variable stores one yes/no value. You've also been told that only one of these bits is yours — the third (remember that bits are numbered from zero, and bit number zero is the lowest one, while the highest is number 31). The remaining bits are not allowed to change, because they're intended to store other data. Here's your bit marked with the letter x:

```
flag_register = 0000000000000000000000000000x000
```

You may be faced with the following tasks:

1. Check the state of your bit — you want to find out the value of your bit; comparing the whole variable to zero will not do anything, because the

remaining bits can have completely unpredictable values, but you can use the following conjunction property:

```
1    x & 1 = x
2    x & 0 = 0
3
```

If you apply the & operation to the flag_register variable along with the following bit image as the result (note the 1 at your bit's position):

00000000000000000000000000001000

you obtain one of the following bit strings:

00000000000000000000000000001000 if your bit was set to 1

00000000000000000000000000000000 if your bit was reset to 0

Such a sequence of zeros and ones, whose task is to grab the value or to change the selected bits, is called a bit mask. Let's build a bit mask to detect the state of your bit. It should point to the third bit. That bit has the weight of 23 = 8. A suitable mask could be created by the following declaration:

```
1    the_mask = 8
2
```

You can also make a sequence of instructions depending on the state of your bit. Here it is:

```
1    if flag_register & the_mask:
2        # My bit is set.
3    else:
4        # My bit is reset.
5
```

2. Reset your bit — you assign a zero to the bit while all the other bits must remain unchanged; let's use the same property of the conjunction as before, but let's use a slightly different mask — exactly as follows:

11111111111111111111111111110111

Note that the mask was created as a result of the negation of all the bits of the_mask variable. Resetting the bit is simple, and looks like this (choose the one you like more):

```
1    flag_register = flag_register & ~the_mask
2    flag_register &= ~the_mask
3
```

Logic And Bit Operations In Python   131

3. Set your bit — you assign a 1 to your bit, while all the remaining bits must remain unchanged; use the following disjunction property:

```
1   x | 1 = 1
2   x | 0 = x
3
```

You're now ready to set your bit with one of the following instructions:

```
1   flag_register = flag_register | the_mask
2   flag_register |= the_mask
3
```

4. Negate your bit — you replace a 1 with a 0 and a 0 with a 1. You can use an interesting property of the xor operator:

```
1   x ^ 1 = ~x
2   x ^ 0 = x
3
```

and negate your bit with the following instructions:

```
1   flag_register = flag_register ^ the_mask
2   flag_register ^= the_mask
3
```

Binary left shift and binary right shift

Python offers yet another operation relating to single bits: shifting. This is applied only to integer values, and you mustn't use floats as arguments for it. You already apply this operation very often and quite unconsciously. How do you multiply any number by ten? Take a look:

12345 × 10 = 123450

As you can see, multiplying by ten is in fact a shift of all the digits to the left and filling the resulting gap with zero. Division by ten? Take a look:

12340 ÷ 10 = 1234

Dividing by ten is nothing but shifting the digits to the right. The same kind of operation is performed by the computer, but with one difference: as two is the base for binary numbers (not 10), shifting a value one bit to the left thus corresponds to multiplying it by two; respectively, shifting one bit to the right is like dividing by two. Notice that the rightmost bit is lost. The shift operators in Python are a pair of digraphs: << and >>, clearly suggesting in which direction the shift will act.

```
value << bits
value >> bits
```

The left argument of these operators is an integer value whose bits are shifted. The right argument determines the size of the shift. It shows that this operation is certainly not commutative.

The priority of these operators is very high. You'll see them in the updated table of priorities, which we'll show you at the end of this section. Take a look at the shifts in the code.

```
1   var = 17
2   var_right = var >> 1
3   var_left = var << 2
4   print(var, var_left, var_right)
5
```

The final `print()` invocation produces the following output:

```
17 68 8
```

`17>>1` becomes `17//2` (17 floor-divided by 2 to the power of 1) becomes 8 (shifting to the right by one bit is the same as integer division by two). `17<<2` becomes `17*4` (17 multiplied by 2 to the power of 2) becomes 68 (shifting to the left by two bits is the same as integer multiplication by four). And here is the updated priority table, containing all the operators introduced so far:

Priority	Operator	
1	~, +, −	
2	**	unary
3	*, /, //, %	
4	+, −	
5	<<, >>	
6	<, <=, >, >=	
7	==, !=	binary
8	&	
9	|	
10	=, +=, −=, *=, /=, %=, &=, ^=, |=, >>=, <<=	

Logic And Bit Operations In Python   133

Summary

1. Python supports the following logical operators:

   - and if both operands are true, the condition is true, e.g. (True and True) is True
   - or if any of the operands are true, the condition is true, e.g. (True or False) is True
   - not returns false if the result is true, and returns true if the result is false, e.g. notTrue is False

2. You can use bitwise operators to manipulate single bits of data. The following sample data will be used to illustrate the meaning of bitwise operators in Python.

   - x=15, which is 00001111 in binary
   - y=16, which is 00010000 in binary

   Analyze the following examples:

   - & does a bitwise and, e.g. x&y=0, which is 00000000 in binary
   - | does a bitwise or, e.g. x|y=31, which is 00011111 in binary
   - ~ does a bitwise not, e.g. ~x=240*, which is 11110000 in binary
   - ^ does a bitwise xor, e.g. x^y=31, which is 00011111 in binary
   - >> does a bitwise right shift, e.g. y>>1=8, which is 0000 1000 in binary
   - << does a bitwise left shift, e.g. y<<3=, which is 10000000 in binary

* -16 (decimal from two's complement) -- read more about the two's complement operation at https://en.wikipedia.org/wiki/Two%27s_complement.

Quiz

QUESTION 1: What is the output of the following snippet?

```
1   x = 1
2   y = 0
3
4   z = ((x == y) and (x == y)) or not(x == y)
5   print(not(z))
6
```

QUESTION 2: What is the output of the following snippet?

```
1   x = 4
2   y = 1
3
4   a = x & y
5   b = x | y
6   c = ~x    # tricky!
7   d = x ^ 5
8   e = x >> 2
9   f = x << 2
10
11  print(a, b, c, d, e, f)
12
```

THIRTEEN
LISTS

Why do we need lists? It may happen that you have to read, store, process, and finally, print dozens, maybe hundreds, perhaps even thousands of numbers. What then? Do you need to create a separate variable for each value? Will you have to spend long hours writing statements like the following one?

```
var1 = int(input())
var2 = int(input())
var3 = int(input())
var4 = int(input())
var5 = int(input())
var6 = int(input())
:
:
```

If you don't think that this is a complicated task, then take a piece of paper and write a program that reads five numbers and then prints them in order from the smallest to the largest (NB, this kind of processing is called sorting). You should find that you don't even have enough paper to complete the task.

So far, you've learned how to declare variables that are able to store exactly one given value at a time. Such variables are sometimes called scalars by analogy with mathematics. All the variables you've used so far are actually scalars. Think of how convenient it would be to declare a variable that could store more than one value. For example, a hundred, or a thousand or even ten thousand. It would still be one and the same variable, but very wide and capacious. Sounds appealing? Perhaps, but how would it handle such a container full of different values? How would it choose just the one you need?

What if you could just number them? And then say: *give me the value number 2; assign the value number 15; increase the value number 10000*. We'll show you how to declare such multi-value variables. We'll do this with the example we just suggested. We'll write a program that sorts a sequence of numbers. We won't be particularly ambitious — we'll assume that there are exactly five numbers.

Let's create a variable called `numbers`; it's assigned with not just one number, but is filled with a list consisting of five values (note: the list starts with an open square bracket and ends with a closed square bracket; the space between the brackets is filled with five numbers separated by commas).

```
numbers = [10, 5, 7, 2, 1]
```

Let's say the same thing using adequate terminology: `numbers` is a list consisting of five values, all of them numbers. We can also say that this statement creates a list of length equal to five, as in there are five elements inside it.

The elements inside a list may have different types. Some of them may be integers, others floats, and yet others may be lists. Python has adopted a convention stating that the elements in a list are always numbered starting from zero. This means that the item stored at the beginning of the list will have the number zero. Since there are five elements in our list, the last of them is assigned the number four. Don't forget this. You'll soon get used to it, and it'll become second nature.

Before we go any further in our discussion, we have to state the following: our list is a collection of elements, but each element is a scalar.

Indexing lists

How do you change the value of a chosen element in the list? Let's assign a new value of 111 to the first element in the list. We do it this way:

```
1  numbers = [10, 5, 7, 2, 1]
2  print("Original list contents:", numbers)   # Printing
   original list contents.
3
4  numbers[0] = 111
5  print("New list contents: ", numbers)   # Current list
   contents.
6
```

And now we want the value of the fifth element to be copied to the second element — can you guess how to do it?

```
1  numbers = [10, 5, 7, 2, 1]
2  print("Original list contents:", numbers)   # Printing
   original list contents.
3
4  numbers[0] = 111
5  print("\nPrevious list contents:", numbers)   # Printing
   previous list contents.
6
7  numbers[1] = numbers[4]   # Copying value of the fifth element
   to the second.
8  print("New list contents:", numbers)   # Printing current
   list contents.
9
```

The value inside the brackets which selects one element of the list is called an index, while the operation of selecting an element from the list is known as indexing. We're going to use the `print()` function to print the list content each time we make the changes. This will help us follow each step more carefully and see what's going on after a particular list modification.

NOTE All the indices used so far are literals. Their values are fixed at runtime, but any expression can be the index, too. This opens up lots of possibilities.

Accessing list content

Each of the list's elements may be accessed separately. For example, it can be printed like this:

```
1  print(numbers[0])  # Accessing the list's first element.
2
```

Assuming that all of the previous operations have been completed successfully, the snippet will send 111 to the console.

```
1   numbers = [10, 5, 7, 2, 1]
2   print("Original list contents:", numbers)   # Printing
    original list contents.
3
4   numbers[0] = 111
5   print("\nPrevious list contents:", numbers)   # Printing
    previous list contents.
6
7   numbers[1] = numbers[4]   # Copying value of the fifth element
    to the second.
8   print("Previous list contents:", numbers)   # Printing
    previous list contents.
9
10  print("\nList length:", len(numbers))   # Printing the list's
    length.
11
```

Lists

As you can see, the list may also be printed as a whole — just like here:

```
1  print(numbers) # Printing the whole list.
2
```

As you've probably noticed before, Python decorates the output in a way that suggests that all the presented values form a list. The output from the example snippet looks like this:

```
[111, 1, 7, 2, 1]
```

The `len()` function

The length of a list may vary during execution. New elements may be added to the list, while others may be removed from it. This means that the list is a very dynamic entity. If you want to check the list's current length, you can use a function named `len()`. The name comes from *length*. The function takes the list's name as an argument, and returns the number of elements currently stored inside the list — in other words, the list's length. Look at the last line of the previous code, run the program and check what value it will print to the console. Can you guess?

Removing elements from a list

Any of the list's elements may be removed at any time — this is done with an instruction named `del` (delete). Note that it's an instruction, not a function. You have to point to the element to be removed — it'll vanish from the list, and the list's length will be reduced by one. Look at the following snippet. Can you guess what output it will produce? Run the program and check.

```
1  del numbers[1]
2  print(len(numbers))
3  print(numbers)
4
```

You can't access an element which doesn't exist — you can neither get its value nor assign it a value. Both of these instructions will cause runtime errors now:

```
1  print(numbers[4])
2  numbers[4] = 1
3
```

Add the previous snippet after the last line of code, run the program and check what happens.

```
1   numbers = [10, 5, 7, 2, 1]
2   print("Original list content:", numbers)   # Printing
    original list content.
3
4   numbers[0] = 111
5   print("\nPrevious list content:", numbers)  # Printing
    previous list content.
6
7   numbers[1] = numbers[4]   # Copying value of the fifth element
    to the second.
8   print("Previous list content:", numbers)   # Printing
    previous list content.
9
10  print("\nList's length:", len(numbers))   # Printing previous
    list length.
11
12  ###
13
14  del numbers[1]   # Removing the second element from the
    list.
15  print("New list's length:", len(numbers))   # Printing new
    list length.
16  print("\nNew list content:", numbers)   # Printing current
    list content.
17
18  ###
19
```

NOTE We've removed one of the list's elements — there are only four elements in the list now. This means that element number four doesn't exist.

Negative indices are legal

It may look strange, but negative indices are legal, and can be very useful. An element with an index equal to -1 is the last one in the list.

```
1   numbers = [111, 7, 2, 1]
2   print(numbers[-1])
3
```

The example snippet will output 1. Run the program and check. Similarly, the element with an index equal to -2 is the one before last in the list.

```
1   numbers = [111, 7, 2, 1]
2   print(numbers[-2])
3
```

The example snippet will output 2. The last accessible element in our list is numbers[-4] (the first one) — don't try to go any further!

LAB: The basics of lists

There once was a hat. The hat contained no rabbit, but a list of five numbers: 1, 2, 3, 4, and 5.

Your task is to:

- write a line of code that prompts the user to replace the middle number in the list with an integer number entered by the user (Step 1)
- write a line of code that removes the last element from the list (Step 2)
- write a line of code that prints the length of the existing list (Step 3).

Ready for this challenge?

CODE

```
1   hat_list = [1, 2, 3, 4, 5]   # This is an existing list of
    numbers hidden in the hat.
2
3   # Step 1: write a line of code that prompts the user
4   # to replace the middle number with an integer number
    entered by the user.
5
6   # Step 2: write a line of code that removes the last element
    from the list.
7
8   # Step 3: write a line of code that prints the length of the
    existing list.
9
10  print(hat_list)
11
```

Functions vs. methods

A method is a specific kind of function — it behaves like a function and looks like a function, but differs in the way in which it acts, and in its invocation style. A function doesn't belong to any data — it gets data, it may create new data and it generally produces a result.

A method does all these things, but is also able to change the state of a selected entity. A method is owned by the data it works for, while a function is owned by the whole code. This also means that invoking a method requires some specification of the data from which the method is invoked. It may sound puzzling here, but we'll deal with it in depth when we delve into object-oriented programming. In general, a typical function invocation may look like this:

```
result = function(arg)
```

The function takes an argument, does something, and returns a result. A typical method invocation usually looks like this:

```
result = data.method(arg)
```

NOTE The name of the method is preceded by the name of the data which owns the method. Next, you add a dot, followed by the method name, and a pair of parenthesis enclosing the arguments.

The method will behave like a function, but can do something more — it can change the internal state of the data from which it has been invoked. You may ask: why are we talking about methods, not about lists? This is an essential issue right now, as we're going to show you how to add new elements to an existing list. This can be done with methods owned by all the lists, not by functions.

Adding elements to a list: append() and insert()

A new element may be *glued* to the end of the existing list:

```
list.append(value)
```

Such an operation is performed by a method named `append()`. It takes its argument's value and puts it at the end of the list which owns the method. The list's length then increases by one. The `insert()` method is a bit smarter — it can add a new element at any place in the list, not only at the end.

```
list.insert(location, value)
```

It takes two arguments. The first shows the required location of the element to be inserted. All the existing elements that occupy locations to the right of the new element, including the one at the indicated position, are shifted to the right, in order to make space for the new element. The second argument is the element to be inserted.

Look at the following code. See how we use the `append()` and `insert()` methods. Pay attention to what happens after using `insert()`: the former first element is now the second, the second the third, and so on.

```
1   numbers = [111, 7, 2, 1]
2   print(len(numbers))
3   print(numbers)
4
5   ###
6
7   numbers.append(4)
8
9   print(len(numbers))
10  print(numbers)
11
12  ###
```

Lists   143

```
13
14  numbers.insert(0, 222)
15  print(len(numbers))
16  print(numbers)
17
18  #
19
```

Add the following snippet after the last line of code:

```
1  numbers.insert(1, 333)
2
```

Print the final list content to the screen and see what happens. This snippet inserts 333 into the list, making it the second element. The former second element becomes the third, the third the fourth, and so on. You can start a list's life by making it empty and then adding new elements to it as needed. You make it empty by adding an empty pair of square brackets Take a look at the following snippet. Try to guess its output after the **for** loop execution. Run the program to check if you were right.

```
1  my_list = []   # Creating an empty list.
2
3  for i in range(5):
4      my_list.append(i + 1)
5
6  print(my_list)
7
```

It'll be a sequence of consecutive integer numbers from **1** (you then add one to all the appended values) to **5**. We've modified the snippet a bit:

```
1  my_list = []   # Creating an empty list.
2
3  for i in range(5):
4      my_list.insert(0, i + 1)
5
6  print(my_list)
7
```

What happens now? Run the program and check if this time you're right, too. You should get the same sequence, but in reverse order. This is the merit of using the **insert()** method.

Making use of lists

The for loop has a special variant that can process lists very effectively — let's take a look at that.

```
1    my_list = [10, 1, 8, 3, 5]
2    total = 0
3
4    for i in range(len(my_list)):
5        total += my_list[i]
6
7    print(total)
8
```

Let's assume that you want to calculate the sum of all the values stored in the my_list list. You need a variable whose sum will be stored and initially assigned a value of 0 — its name will be total. Note that we're not going to name it sum as Python uses the same name for one of its built-in functions: sum(). Using the same name would generally be considered bad practice. Then you add to it all the elements of the list using the for loop. Take a look at the previous snippet.

Let's comment on this example. The list is assigned a sequence of five integer values. The i variable takes the values 0, 1, 2, 3, and 4, and then it indexes the list, selecting the subsequent elements: the first, second, third, fourth and fifth. Each of these elements is added together by the += operator to the total variable, giving the final result at the end of the loop. Note the way in which the len() function has been employed — it makes the code independent of any possible changes in the list's contents.

The second aspect of the for loop

The for loop can do much more. It can hide all the actions connected to the list's indexing, and deliver all the list's elements in a handy way. This modified snippet shows how it works:

```
1    my_list = [10, 1, 8, 3, 5]
2    total = 0
3
4    for i in my_list:
5        total += i
6
7    print(total)
8
```

What happens here? The for instruction specifies the variable used to browse the list (i here) followed by the in keyword and the name of the list being processed (my_list here). The i variable is assigned the values of all the subsequent list's elements, and the process occurs as many times as there are elements in the list. This means that you use the i variable as a copy of the elements' values, and you don't need to use indices. The len() function is not needed here, either.

Lists in action

Let's leave lists aside for a short moment and look at one intriguing issue. Imagine that you need to rearrange the elements of a list, that it, you need to reverse the order of the elements: the first and the fifth as well as the second and fourth elements will be swapped. The third one will remain untouched. How can you swap the values of two variables? Take a look at the following snippet.

```
1   variable_1 = 1
2   variable_2 = 2
3
4   variable_2 = variable_1
5   variable_1 = variable_2
6
```

If you do something like this, you would lose the value previously stored in `variable_2`. Changing the order of the assignments will not help. You need a third variable that serves as an auxiliary storage. This is how you can do it:

```
1   variable_1 = 1
2   variable_2 = 2
3
4   auxiliary = variable_1
5   variable_1 = variable_2
6   variable_2 = auxiliary
7
```

Python offers a more convenient way of doing the swap — take a look:

```
1   variable_1 = 1
2   variable_2 = 2
3
4   variable_1, variable_2 = variable_2, variable_1
5
```

Clear, effective and elegant — isn't it? Now you can easily swap the list's elements to reverse their order:

```
1   my_list = [10, 1, 8, 3, 5]
2
3   my_list[0], my_list[4] = my_list[4], my_list[0]
4   my_list[1], my_list[3] = my_list[3], my_list[1]
5
6   print(my_list)
7
```

Run the snippet. Its output should look like this:

```
[5, 3, 8, 1, 10]
```

It looks fine with five elements. Will it still be acceptable with a list containing 100 elements? No, it won't. Can you use the `for` loop to do the same thing automatically, irrespective of the list's length? Yes, you can. This is how we've done it:

```
1  for i in range(length // 2):
2      my_list[i], my_list[length - i - 1] = my_list[length - i - 1], my_list[i]
3
4  print(my_list)
5
```

NOTE We've assigned the `length` variable with the current list's length. This makes our code a bit clearer and shorter. We've launched the `for` loop to run through its body `length//2` times. This works well for lists with both even and odd lengths, because when the list contains an odd number of elements, the middle one remains untouched. We've swapped the ith element from the beginning of the list with the one with an index equal to (`length-i-1`) from the end of the list. In our example, for `i` equal to `0` the (`length-i-1`) gives 4; for `i` equal to 1 gives 3 — this is exactly what we need.

Lists are extremely useful, and you'll encounter them very often.

LAB: The basics of lists — the Beatles

The Beatles were one of the most popular music groups of the 1960s, and the best-selling band in history. Some people consider them to be the most influential act of the rock era. Indeed, they were included in *Time* magazine's compilation of the 20th Century's 100 most influential people. The band underwent many line-up changes, culminating in 1962 with the line-up of John Lennon, Paul McCartney, George Harrison, and Richard Starkey, better known as Ringo Starr.

Write a program that reflects these changes and lets you practice with the concept of lists. Your task is to:

- step 1: create an empty list named `beatles` ;
- step 2: use the `append()` method to add the following members of the band to the list: `John Lennon`, `Paul McCartney`, and `GeorgeHarrison`;
- step 3: use the `for` loop and the `append()` method to prompt the user to add the following members of the band to the list: `Stu Sutcliffe`, and `Pete Best`;
- step 4: use the `del` instruction to remove `Stu Sutcliffe` and `PeteBest` from the list;
- step 5: use the `insert()` method to add `Ringo Starr` to the beginning of the list.

By the way, are you a Beatles fan? The Beatles is one of Greg's favorite bands. But wait...who's Greg...?

CODE

```
1   # step 1
2   print("Step 1:", beatles)
3
4   # step 2
5   print("Step 2:", beatles)
6
7   # step 3
8   print("Step 3:", beatles)
9
10  # step 4
11  print("Step 4:", beatles)
12
13  # step 5
14  print("Step 5:", beatles)
15
16
17  # testing list length
18  print("The Fab", len(beatles))
19
```

Summary

1. The list is a type of data in Python used to store multiple objects. It is an ordered and mutable collection of comma-separated items between square brackets, e.g.:

```
1   my_list = [1, None, True, "I am a string", 256, 0]
2
```

2. Lists can be indexed and updated, e.g.:

```
1   my_list = [1, None, True, 'I am a string', 256, 0]
2   print(my_list[3])    # outputs: I am a string
3   print(my_list[-1])   # outputs: 0
4
5   my_list[1] = '?'
6   print(my_list)   # outputs: [1, '?', True, 'I am a string', 256, 0]
7
8   my_list.insert(0, "first")
9   my_list.append("last")
10  print(my_list)   # outputs: ['first', 1, '?', True, 'I am a string', 256, 0, 'last']
11
```

3. Lists can be nested, e.g.:

```
1   my_list = [1, 'a', ["list", 64, [0, 1], False]]
2
```

You will learn more about nesting soon — for the time being, we just want you to be aware that something like this is possible, too.

4. List elements and lists can be deleted, e.g.:

```
1   my_list = [1, 2, 3, 4]
2   del my_list[2]
3   print(my_list)   # outputs: [1, 2, 4]
4
5   del my_list   # deletes the whole list
6
```

Again, you will learn more about this soon — don't worry. For the time being just try to experiment with this code and check how changing it affects the output.

5. Lists can be iterated through using the `for` loop, e.g.:

```
1   my_list = ["white", "purple", "blue", "yellow", "green"]
2
3   for color in my_list:
4       print(color)
5
```

6. The `len()` function may be used to check the list's length, e.g.:

```
1   my_list = ["white", "purple", "blue", "yellow", "green"]
2   print(len(my_list))   # outputs 5
3
4   del my_list[2]
5   print(len(my_list))   # outputs 4
6
```

7. A typical function invocation looks as follows:
`result=function(arg)`, while a typical method invocation looks like this: `result=data.method(arg)`.

Lists   149

Quiz

QUESTION 1: What is the output of the following snippet?

```
1  lst = [1, 2, 3, 4, 5]
2  lst.insert(1, 6)
3  del lst[0]
4  lst.append(1)
5
6  print(lst)
7
```

QUESTION 2: What is the output of the following snippet?

```
1   lst = [1, 2, 3, 4, 5]
2   lst_2 = []
3   add = 0
4
5   for number in lst:
6       add += number
7       lst_2.append(add)
8
9   print(lst_2)
10
```

QUESTION 3: What is the output of the following snippet?

```
1  lst = []
2  del lst
3  print(lst)
4
```

QUESTION 4: What is the output of the following snippet?

```
1  lst = [1, [2, 3], 4]
2  print(lst[1])
3  print(len(lst))
4
```

150   Chapter 13

FOURTEEN

SORTING SIMPLE LISTS: THE BUBBLE SORT ALGORITHM

Now that you can effectively juggle the elements of lists, it's time to learn how to sort them. Many sorting algorithms have been invented so far, which differ a lot in speed, as well as in complexity. We are going to show you a very simple algorithm, easy to understand, but unfortunately not too efficient, either. It's used very rarely, and certainly not for large and extensive lists.

Let's say that a list can be sorted in two ways. The first is by increasing, or more precisely — non-decreasing — if in every pair of adjacent elements, the former element is not greater than the latter. The second is by decreasing, or more precisely — non-increasing — if in every pair of adjacent elements, the former element is not less than the latter. In the following sections, we'll sort the list in increasing order, so that the numbers will be ordered from the smallest to the largest. Here's the list:

| 8 | 10 | 6 | 2 | 4 |

We'll try to use the following approach: we'll take the first and the second elements and compare them; if we determine that they're in the wrong order (i.e. the first is greater than the second), we'll swap them round; if their order is valid, we'll do nothing. A glance at our list confirms the latter — the elements 01 and 02 are in the proper order, as in `8<10`. Now look at the second and the third elements. They're in the wrong positions. We have to swap them:

| 8 | 6 | 10 | 2 | 4 |

We go further, and look at the third and the fourth elements. Again, this is not what it's supposed to be like. We have to swap them:

8	6	2	10	4

Now we check the fourth and the fifth elements. Yes, they too are in the wrong positions. Another swap occurs:

8	6	2	4	10

10
4
2
6
8

The first pass through the list is already finished. We're still far from finishing our job, but something curious has happened in the meantime. The largest element, 10, has already gone to the end of the list. Note that this is the desired place for it. All the remaining elements form a picturesque mess, but this one is already in place. Now, for a moment, try to imagine the list in a slightly different way — namely, like the table on the left. Look — 10 is at the top. We could say that it floated up from the bottom to the surface, just like the bubble in a glass of champagne. The sorting method derives its name from the same observation — it's called a bubble sort.

Now we start with the second pass through the list. We look at the first and second elements — a swap is necessary:

6	8	2	4	10

Time for the second and third elements: we have to swap them too:

6	2	8	4	10

Now the third and fourth elements, and the second pass is finished, as 8 is already in place:

6	2	4	8	10

We start the next pass immediately. Watch the first and the second elements carefully — another swap is needed:

2	6	4	8	10

Now 6 needs to go into place. We swap the second and the third elements:

2	4	6	8	10

The list is already sorted. We have nothing more to do. This is exactly what we want. As you can see, the essence of this algorithm is simple: we compare the adjacent elements, and by swapping some of them, we achieve our goal. Let's code into Python all the actions performed during a single pass through the list, and then we'll consider how many passes we actually need in order to perform it. We haven't explained this so far, and we'll do that a little later.

Sorting a list

How many passes do we need to sort the entire list? We solve this issue in the following way: we introduce another variable; its task is to observe if any swap has been done during the pass or not; if there is no swap, then the list is already sorted, and nothing more has to be done. We create a variable named `swapped`, and we assign a value of `False` to it, to indicate that there are no swaps. Otherwise, it will be assigned `True`.

```
1  my_list = [8, 10, 6, 2, 4]  # list to sort
2
3  for i in range(len(my_list) - 1):  # we need (5 - 1) comparisons
4      if my_list[i] > my_list[i + 1]:  # compare adjacent elements
5          my_list[i], my_list[i + 1] = my_list[i + 1], my_list[i]   # If we end up here, we have to swap the elements.
6
```

You should be able to read and understand this program without any problems:

```
1   my_list = [8, 10, 6, 2, 4]  # list to sort
2   swapped = True  # It's a little fake, we need it to enter the while loop.
3
4   while swapped:
5       swapped = False  # no swaps so far
6       for i in range(len(my_list) - 1):
7           if my_list[i] > my_list[i + 1]:
8               swapped = True  # a swap occurred!
9               my_list[i], my_list[i + 1] = my_list[i + 1], my_list[i]
10
11  print(my_list)
12
```

Run the program and test it.

Sorting Simple Lists: The Bubble Sort Algorithm   153

The bubble sort — interactive version

Take a look at the following complete program, enriched by a conversation with the user, and allowing the user to enter and to print elements from the list: the bubble sort — final interactive version.

```
1   my_list = []
2   swapped = True
3   num = int(input("How many elements do you want to sort: "))
4
5   for i in range(num):
6       val = float(input("Enter a list element: "))
7       my_list.append(val)
8
9   while swapped:
10      swapped = False
11      for i in range(len(my_list) - 1):
12          if my_list[i] > my_list[i + 1]:
13              swapped = True
14              my_list[i], my_list[i + 1] = my_list[i + 1], my_list[i]
15
16  print("\nSorted:")
17  print(my_list)
18
```

Python, however, has its own sorting mechanisms. No one needs to write their own sorts, as there is a sufficient number of ready-to-use tools. We explained this sorting system to you because it's important to learn how to process a list's contents, and to show you how real sorting may work. If you want Python to sort your list, you can do it like this:

```
1   my_list = [8, 10, 6, 2, 4]
2   my_list.sort()
3   print(my_list)
4
```

It is as simple as that. The snippet's output is as follows:

```
[2, 4, 6, 8, 10]
```

As you can see, all the lists have a method named `sort()`, which sorts them as fast as possible. You've already learned about some of the list methods before, and you're going to learn more about others very soon.

Summary

1. You can use the `sort()` method to sort elements of a list, e.g.:

```
1    lst = [5, 3, 1, 2, 4]
2    print(lst)
3
4    lst.sort()
5    print(lst)   # outputs: [1, 2, 3, 4, 5]
6
```

2. There is also a list method called `reverse()`, which you can use to reverse the list, e.g.:

```
1    lst = [5, 3, 1, 2, 4]
2    print(lst)
3
4    lst.reverse()
5    print(lst)   # outputs: [4, 2, 1, 3, 5]
6
```

Quiz

QUESTION 1: What is the output of the following snippet?

```
1    lst = ["D", "F", "A", "Z"]
2    lst.sort()
3
4    print(lst)
5
```

QUESTION 2: What is the output of the following snippet?

```
1    a = 3
2    b = 1
3    c = 2
4
5    lst = [a, c, b]
6    lst.sort()
7
8    print(lst)
9
```

Question 3: What is the output of the following snippet?

```
1   a = "A"
2   b = "B"
3   c = "C"
4   d = " "
5
6   lst = [a, b, c, d]
7   lst.reverse()
8
9   print(lst)
10
```

FIFTEEN

OPERATIONS ON LISTS

Now we want to show you one important, and very surprising, feature of lists, which strongly distinguishes them from ordinary variables. We want you to memorize it — it may affect your future programs, and cause severe problems if forgotten or overlooked. Take a look at the following snippet.

```
1    list_1 = [1]
2    list_2 = list_1
3    list_1[0] = 2
4    print(list_2)
5
```

The program creates a one-element list named `list_1`, assigns it to a new list named `list_2`, changes the only element of `list_1`, and prints out `list_2`. The surprising part is the fact that the program will output: [2], not [1], which seems to be the obvious solution. Lists, and many other complex Python entities, are stored in different ways than ordinary, scalar variables.

You could say that the name of an ordinary variable is the name of its content, and the name of a list is the name of a memory location where the list is stored. Read these two lines once more — the difference is essential for understanding what we are going to talk about next.

The assignment: `list_2=list_1` copies the name of the array, not its contents. In effect, the two names (`list_1` and `list_2`) identify the same location in the computer memory. Modifying one of them affects the other, and vice versa. How do you cope with that?

Powerful slices

Fortunately, the solution is at your fingertips — it's called a slice. A slice is an element of Python syntax that allows you to make a brand new copy of a list, or parts of a list. It actually copies the list's contents, not the list's name. This is exactly what you need. Take a look:

```
1  list_1 = [1]
2  list_2 = list_1[:]
3  list_1[0] = 2
4  print(list_2)
5
```

Its output is [1]. The inconspicuous part of the code described as [:] is able to produce a brand new list. One of the most general forms of the slice looks as follows:

```
my_list[start:end-1]
```

As you can see, it resembles indexing, but the colon inside makes a big difference. A slice of this form makes a new (target) list, taking elements from the source list — the elements of the indices from start to end−1.

NOTE The elements of an index finish not at end, but end−1. An element with an index equal to end is the first element which does not take part in the slicing.

Using negative values for both start and end is possible, just like in indexing. Take a look at the snippet:

```
1  my_list = [10, 8, 6, 4, 2]
2  new_list = my_list[1:3]
3  print(new_list)
4
```

The new_list list will have end−start (3 − 1 = 2) elements — the ones with indices equal to 1 and 2 (but not 3). The snippet's output is: [8,6] Run the following code to see how Python copies the entire list, and some fragment of a list. Feel free to experiment!

```
1   # Copying the entire list.
2   list_1 = [1]
3   list_2 = list_1[:]
4   list_1[0] = 2
5   print(list_2)
6
7   # Copying some part of the list.
8   my_list = [10, 8, 6, 4, 2]
9   new_list = my_list[1:3]
10  print(new_list)
11
```

Chapter 15

Slices — negative indices

Look at the following snippet:

```
my_list[start:end]
```

To repeat: `start` is the index of the first element included in the slice; `end` is the index of the first element not included in the slice. This is how negative indices work with the slice:

```
1   my_list = [10, 8, 6, 4, 2]
2   new_list = my_list[1:-1]
3   print(new_list)
4
```

The snippet's output is:

```
[8, 6, 4]
```

If the `start` specifies an element lying further than the one described by the `end` (from the list's beginning), the slice will be empty:

```
my_list = [10, 8, 6, 4, 2]
new_list = my_list[-1:1]
print(new_list)
```

The snippet's output is:

```
[]
```

If you omit the `start` in your slice, it is assumed that you want to get a slice beginning at the element with index `0`. In other words, the slice of this form:

```
my_list[:end]
```

is a more compact equivalent of:

```
my_list[0:end]
```

Look at the following snippet:

```
1   my_list = [10, 8, 6, 4, 2]
2   new_list = my_list[:3]
3   print(new_list)
4
```

This is why its output is: `[10,8,6]`. Similarly, if you omit the `end` in your slice, it is assumed that you want the slice to end at the element with the index `len(my_list)`. In other words, the slice of this form:

```
my_list[start:]
```

Operations On Lists

is a more compact equivalent of:

```
my_list[start:len(my_list)]
```

Look at the following snippet:

```
1  my_list = [10, 8, 6, 4, 2]
2  new_list = my_list[3:]
3  print(new_list)
4
```

Its output is therefore: [4,2]. As we've said before, omitting both `start` and `end` makes a copy of the whole list:

```
1  my_list = [10, 8, 6, 4, 2]
2  new_list = my_list[:]
3  print(new_list)
4
```

The snippet's output is: [10,8,6,4,2].

More about the `del` instruction

The previously described `del` instruction is able to delete more than just a list's elements at once — it can delete slices too:

```
1  my_list = [10, 8, 6, 4, 2]
2  del my_list[1:3]
3  print(my_list)
4
```

NOTE In this case, the slice doesn't produce any new list!

The snippet's output is: [10,4,2]. Deleting all the elements at once is possible too:

```
1  my_list = [10, 8, 6, 4, 2]
2  del my_list[:]
3  print(my_list)
4
```

The list becomes empty, and the output is: []. Removing the slice from the code changes its meaning dramatically. Take a look:

```
1  my_list = [10, 8, 6, 4, 2]
2  del my_list
3  print(my_list)
4
```

The `del` instruction will delete the list itself, not its content. The `print()` function invocation from the last line of the code will then cause a runtime error.

The `in` and `not in` operators

Python offers two very powerful operators, able to look through the list in order to check whether a specific value is stored inside the list or not. These operators are:

```
1    elem in my_list
2    elem not in my_list
3
```

The first of them (`in`) checks if a given element, that is, its left argument, is currently stored somewhere inside the list, the right argument — the operator returns `True` in this case. The second (`not in`) checks if a given element, its left argument, is absent in a list — the operator returns `True` in this case. Look at the following code. The snippet shows both operators in action. Can you guess its output? Run the program to check if you were right.

```
1    my_list = [0, 3, 12, 8, 2]
2
3    print(5 in my_list)
4    print(5 not in my_list)
5    print(12 in my_list)
6
```

Lists — some simple programs

Now we want to show you some simple programs utilizing lists. The first of them tries to find the greater value in the list. Look at the following code.

```
1    my_list = [17, 3, 11, 5, 1, 9, 7, 15, 13]
2    largest = my_list[0]
3
4    for i in range(1, len(my_list)):
5        if my_list[i] > largest:
6            largest = my_list[i]
7
8    print(largest)
9
```

The concept is rather simple — we temporarily assume that the first element is the largest one, and check the hypothesis against all the remaining elements in the list. The code outputs **17**, as expected. The code may be rewritten to make use of the newly introduced form of the `for` loop:

```
1    my_list = [17, 3, 11, 5, 1, 9, 7, 15, 13]
2    largest = my_list[0]
3
4    for i in my_list:
5        if i > largest:
```

Operations On Lists

```
6        largest = i
7
8    print(largest)
9
```

This program performs one unnecessary comparison, when the first element is compared with itself, but this isn't a problem at all. The code outputs **17**, too, which is nothing unusual. If you need to save computer power, you can use a slice:

```
1    my_list = [17, 3, 11, 5, 1, 9, 7, 15, 13]
2    largest = my_list[0]
3
4    for i in my_list[1:]:
5        if i > largest:
6            largest = i
7
8    print(largest)
9
```

The question is: which of these two actions consumes more computer resources — just one comparison, or slicing almost all of a list's elements? Now let's find the location of a given element inside a list:

```
1    my_list = [1, 2, 3, 4, 5, 6, 7, 8, 9, 10]
2    to_find = 5
3    found = False
4
5    for i in range(len(my_list)):
6        found = my_list[i] == to_find
7        if found:
8            break
9
10   if found:
11       print("Element found at index", i)
12   else:
13       print("absent")
14
```

NOTE The target value is stored in the `to_find` variable. The current status of the search is stored in the `found` variable (`True`/`False`). When `found` becomes `True`, the `for` loop is exited.

Let's assume that you've chosen the following numbers in the lottery: 3, 7, 11, 42, 34, 49. The numbers that have been drawn are: 5, 11, 9, 42, 3, 49. The question is: how many numbers have you hit? This program will give you the answer:

```
1    drawn = [5, 11, 9, 42, 3, 49]
2    bets = [3, 7, 11, 42, 34, 49]
3    v
4
```

```
5    for number in bets:
6        if number in drawn:
7            hits += 1
8
9    print(hits)
10
```

> **NOTE** The `drawn` list stores all the drawn numbers. The `bets` list stores your bets. The `hits` variable counts your hits.

The program output is: 4.

LAB: Operating with lists — basics

Imagine a list — not very long, not very complicated, just a simple list containing some integer numbers. Some of these numbers may be repeated, and this is the clue. We don't want any repetitions. We want them to be removed.

Your task is to write a program which removes all the number repetitions from the list. The goal is to have a list in which all the numbers appear not more than once.

> **NOTE** Assume that the source list is hard-coded inside the code — you don't have to enter it from the keyboard. Of course, you can improve the code and add a part that can carry out a conversation with the user and obtain all the data from her/him.

> **HINT** We encourage you to create a new list as a temporary work area — you don't need to update the list in situ. We've provided no test data, as that would be too easy. You can use our skeleton instead.

CODE

```
1    my_list = [1, 2, 4, 4, 1, 4, 2, 6, 2, 9]
2    #
3    # Write your code here.
4    #
5    print("The list with unique elements only:")
6    print(my_list)
7
```

Summary

1. If you have a list `list_1`, then the following assignment: `list_2 = list_1` does not make a copy of the `list_1` list, but makes the variables `list_1` and `list_2` point to one and the same list in memory. For example:

```
1   vehicles_one = ['car', 'bicycle', 'motor']
2   print(vehicles_one) # outputs: ['car', 'bicycle', 'motor']
3
4   vehicles_two = vehicles_one
5   del vehicles_one[0] # deletes 'car'
6   print(vehicles_two) # outputs: ['bicycle', 'motor']
7
```

2. If you want to copy a list or part of the list, you can do it by performing slicing:

```
1   colors = ['red', 'green', 'orange']
2
3   copy_whole_colors = colors[:]    # copy the entire list
4   copy_part_colors = colors[0:2]   # copy part of the list
5
```

3. You can use negative indices to perform slices, too. For example:

```
1   sample_list = ["A", "B", "C", "D", "E"]
2   new_list = sample_list[2:-1]
3   print(new_list)  # outputs: ['C', 'D']
4
```

4. The `start` and `end` parameters are optional when performing a slice: `list[start:end]`, e.g.:

```
1   my_list = [1, 2, 3, 4, 5]
2   slice_one = my_list[2: ]
3   slice_two = my_list[ :2]
4   slice_three = my_list[-2: ]
5
6   print(slice_one)    # outputs: [3, 4, 5]
7   print(slice_two)    # outputs: [1, 2]
8   print(slice_three)  # outputs: [4, 5]
9
```

5. You can delete slices using the `del` instruction:

```
1   my_list = [1, 2, 3, 4, 5]
2   del my_list[0:2]
3   print(my_list)   # outputs: [3, 4, 5]
4
5   del my_list[:]
6   print(my_list)   # deletes the list content, outputs: []
7
```

6. You can test if some items exist in a list or not using the keywords in and not in, e.g.:

```
1   my_list = ["A", "B", 1, 2]
2
3   print("A" in my_list)       # outputs: True
4   print("C" not in my_list)   # outputs: True
5   print(2 not in my_list)     # outputs: False
6
```

Quiz

QUESTION 1: What is the output of the following snippet?

```
1   list_1 = ["A", "B", "C"]
2   list_2 = list_1
3   list_3 = list_2
4
5   del list_1[0]
6   del list_2[0]
7
8   print(list_3)
9
```

QUESTION 2: What is the output of the following snippet?

```
1   list_1 = ["A", "B", "C"]
2   list_2 = list_1
3   list_3 = list_2
4
5   del list_1[0]
6   del list_2
7
8   print(list_3)
9
```

QUESTION 3: What is the output of the following snippet?

```
1   list_1 = ["A", "B", "C"]
2   list_2 = list_1
3   list_3 = list_2
4
5   del list_1[0]
6   del list_2[:]
7
8   print(list_3)
9
```

QUESTION 4: What is the output of the following snippet?

```
1   list_1 = ["A", "B", "C"]
2   list_2 = list_1[:]
3   list_3 = list_2[:]
4
5   del list_1[0]
6   del list_2[0]
7
8   print(list_3)
9
```

QUESTION 5: Insert in or not in instead of ??? so that the code outputs the expected result.

```
1   my_list = [1, 2, "in", True, "ABC"]
2
3   print(1 ??? my_list)       # outputs True
4   print("A" ??? my_list)     # outputs True
5   print(3 ??? my_list)       # outputs True
6   print(False ??? my_list)   # outputs False
7
```

166   Chapter 15

SIXTEEN
LISTS IN ADVANCED APPLICATIONS

Lists can consist of scalars (namely numbers) and elements of a much more complex structure. You've already seen such examples as strings, booleans, or even other lists in the previous chapters. Let's have a closer look at the case where a list's elements are just lists. We often find such arrays in our lives. Probably the best example of this is a chessboard. A chessboard is composed of rows and columns. There are eight rows and eight columns. Each column is marked with the letters A through H. Each line is marked with a number from one to eight. The location of each field is identified by letter-digit pairs. Thus, we know that the bottom left corner of the board, the one with the white rook, is A1, while the opposite corner is H8. Let's assume that we're able to use the selected numbers to represent any chess piece. We can also assume that every row on the chessboard is a list. Look at the following code:

```
1  row = []
2
3  for i in range(8):
4      row.append("WHITE_PAWN")
5
```

It builds a list containing eight elements representing the second row of the chessboard — the one filled with pawns (assume that `WHITE_PAWN` is a predefined symbol representing a white pawn).

List comprehensions

The same effect may be achieved by means of a list comprehension, the special syntax used by Python in order to fill massive lists. A list comprehension is actually a list, but created on-the-fly during program execution, and is not described statically. Take a look at the snippet:

```
1    row = ["WHITE_PAWN" for i in range(8)]
2
```

The part of the code placed inside the brackets specifies the data to be used to fill the list (`WHITE_PAWN`) and the clause indicating how many times the data occurs inside the list (`for i in range(8)`). Take a look at some other list comprehension examples:

Example #1:

```
1    squares = [x ** 2 for x in range(10)]
2
```

The snippet produces a ten-element list filled with squares of ten integer numbers starting from zero (0, 1, 4, 9, 16, 25, 36, 49, 64, 81)

Example #2:

```
1    twos = [2 ** i for i in range(8)]
2
```

The snippet creates an eight-element array containing the first eight powers of two (1, 2, 4, 8, 16, 32, 64, 128)

Example #3:

```
1    odds = [x for x in squares if x % 2 != 0 ]
2
```

The snippet makes a list with only the odd elements of the `squares` list.

Two-dimensional arrays

Let's also assume that a predefined symbol named `EMPTY` designates an empty field on the chessboard. So, if we want to create a list of lists representing the whole chessboard, it may be done in the following way:

```
1    board = []
2
3    for i in range(8):
4        row = ["EMPTY" for i in range(8)]
5        board.append(row)
6
```

NOTE The inner part of the loop creates a row consisting of eight elements, each of them equal to `EMPTY`, and appends it to the `board` list. The outer part repeats it eight times. In total, the `board` list consists of 64 elements, all equal to `EMPTY`.

This model perfectly mimics a real chessboard, which is in fact an eight-element list of elements, all being single rows. We can summarize our observations by saying that the elements of the rows are fields, eight of them per row and the elements of the chessboard are rows, eight of them per chessboard. The `board` variable is now a two-dimensional array. It's also called, by analogy to algebraic terms, a matrix. As list comprehensions can be nested, we can shorten the board creation in the following way:

```
1   board = [["EMPTY" for i in range(8)] for j in range(8)]
2
```

The inner part creates a row, and the outer part builds a list of rows. Access to the selected field of the board requires two indices — the first selects the row; the second — the field number inside the row, which is de facto a column number. Take a look at the chessboard (Figure 16.1). Every field contains a pair of indices which should be given to access the field's contents. Glancing at the previous figure, let's set some chess pieces on the board. First, let's add all the rooks:

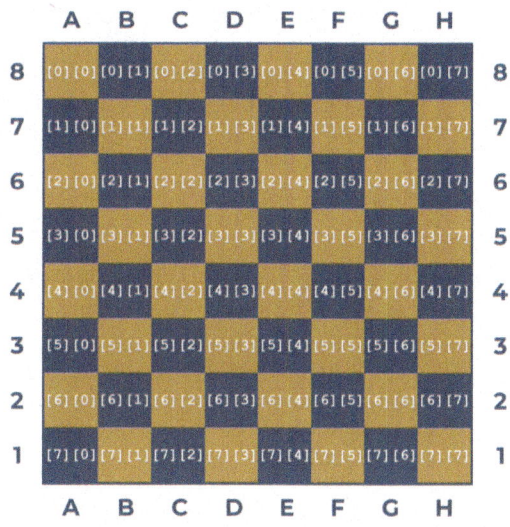

Figure 16.1

```
1   board[0][0] = ROOK
2   board[0][7] = ROOK
3   board[7][0] = ROOK
4   board[7][7] = ROOK
5
```

If you want to add a knight to C4, you do it as follows:

```
1   board[4][2] = KNIGHT
2
```

And now a pawn to E5:

```
1   board[3][4] = PAWN
2
```

And now — experiment with the code yourself.

Multidimensional nature of lists: advanced applications

Let's go deeper into the multidimensional nature of lists. To find any element of a two-dimensional list, you have to use two *coordinates*: a vertical one (row number) and a horizontal one (column number). Imagine that you're developing a piece of software for an automatic weather station. The device records the air temperature on an hourly basis and does it throughout the month. This gives you a total of 24 × 31 = 744 values. Let's try to design a list capable of storing all these results. First, you have to decide which data type would be adequate for this application. In this case, a `float` would be best, since this thermometer is able to measure the temperature with an accuracy of 0.1ºC. Then you take an arbitrary decision that the rows will record the readings every hour on the hour — so the row will have 24 elements — and each of the rows will be assigned to one day of the month. Let's assume that each month has 31 days, so you need 31 rows. Here's the appropriate pair of comprehensions — h is for hour and d for day:

```
1   temps = [[0.0 for h in range(24)] for d in range(31)]
2
```

The whole matrix is filled with zeros now. You can assume that it's updated automatically using special hardware agents. The thing you have to do is to wait for the matrix to be filled with measurements. Now it's time to determine the monthly average noon temperature. Add up all 31 readings recorded at noon and divide the sum by 31. You can assume that the midnight temperature is stored first. Here's the relevant code:

```
1   temps = [[0.0 for h in range(24)] for d in range(31)]
2   #
3   # The matrix is magically updated here.
4   #
5
6   total = 0.0
7
8   for day in temps:
9       total += day[11]
10
11  average = total / 31
12
13  print("Average temperature at noon:", average)
14
```

NOTE The `day` variable used by the `for` loop is not a scalar — each pass through the `temps` matrix assigns it with the subsequent rows of the matrix; hence, it's a list. It has to be indexed with `11` to access the temperature value measured at noon.

Now find the highest temperature during the whole month.

```
1   temps = [[0.0 for h in range(24)] for d in range(31)]
2   #
3   # The matrix is magically updated here.
4   #
5
6   highest = -100.0
7
8   for day in temps:
9       for temp in day:
10          if temp > highest:
11              highest = temp
12
13  print("The highest temperature was:", highest)
14
```

NOTE The **day** variable iterates through all the rows in the **temps** matrix and the **temp** variable iterates through all the measurements taken in one day.

Now count the days when the temperature at noon was at least 20°C:

```
1   temps = [[0.0 for h in range(24)] for d in range(31)]
2   #
3   # The matrix is magically updated here.
4   #
5
6   hot_days = 0
7
8   for day in temps:
9       if day[11] > 20.0:
10          hot_days += 1
11
12  print(hot_days, "days were hot.")
13
```

Python does not limit the depth of list-in-list inclusion. Here you can see an example of a three-dimensional array:

```
1   rooms = [[[False for r in range(20)] for f in range(15)] for t in range(3)]
2
```

Imagine a hotel. It's a huge hotel consisting of three buildings, 15 floors each. There are 20 rooms on each floor. For this, you need an array which can collect and process information on the occupied and free rooms. The first step is to decide the type of the array's elements. In this case, a Boolean value (**True/False**) would fit. The second step is a calm analysis of the situation. Summarize the available information: three buildings, 15 floors, 20 rooms. Now you can create the array.

```
1  rooms = [[[False for r in range(20)] for f in range(15)] for
   t in range(3)]
2
```

The first index (0 through 2) selects one of the buildings; the second (0 through 14) selects the floor, the third (0 through 19) selects the room number. All rooms are initially free. Now you can book a room for two newlyweds: in the second building, on the tenth floor, room 14:

```
1  rooms[1][9][13] = True
2
```

And you can release the second room on the fifth floor located in the first building:

```
1  rooms[0][4][1] = False
2
```

Check if there are any vacancies on the 15th floor of the third building:

```
1  vacancy = 0
2
3  for room_number in range(20):
4      if not rooms[2][14][room_number]:
5          vacancy += 1
6
```

The `vacancy` variable contains 0 if all the rooms are occupied, or the number of available rooms otherwise.

Summary

1. List comprehension allows you to create new lists from existing ones in a concise and elegant way. The syntax of a list comprehension looks as follows:

```
[expression for element in list if conditional]
```

which is actually an equivalent of the following code:

```
for element in list:
    if conditional:
        expression
```

Here's an example of a list comprehension — the code creates a five-element list filled with the first five natural numbers raised to the power of 3:

```
1  cubed = [num ** 3 for num in range(5)]
2  print(cubed)  # outputs: [0, 1, 8, 27, 64]
3
```

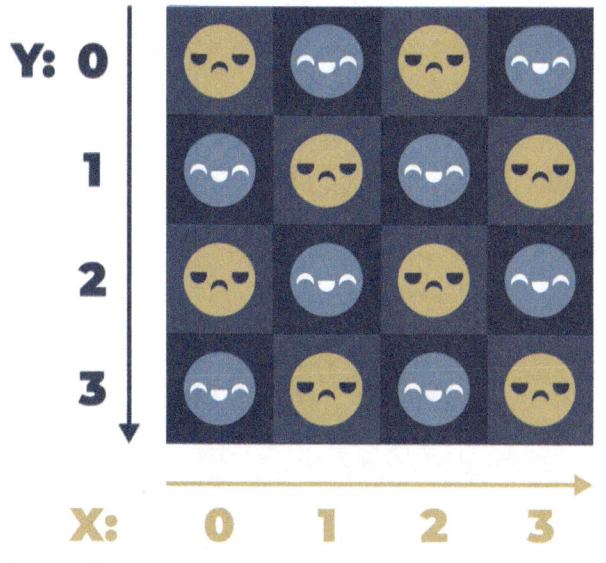

Figure 16.2

2. You can use nested lists in Python to create matrices (i.e. two-dimensional lists). For example, see Figure 16.2.

```python
# A four-column/four-row table - a two dimensional array (4x4)

table = [[":(", ":)", ":(", ":)"],
         [":)", ":(", ":)", ":)"],
         [":(", ":)", ":)", ":("],
         [":)", ":)", ":)", ":("]]

print(table)
print(table[0][0])   # outputs: ':('
print(table[0][3])   # outputs: ':)'
```

3. You can nest as many lists in lists as you want, thereby creating n-dimensional lists, e.g. three-, four- or even sixty-four-dimensional arrays (Figure 16.3).

```python
# Cube - a three-dimensional array (3x3x3)

cube = [[[':(', 'x', 'x'],
         [':)', 'x', 'x'],
         [':(', 'x', 'x']],

        [[':)', 'x', 'x'],
         [':(', 'x', 'x'],
         [':)', 'x', 'x']],

        [[':(', 'x', 'x'],
```

Lists In Advanced Applications

```
12              [':)', 'x', 'x'],
13              [':)', 'x', 'x']]]
14
15   print(cube)
16   print(cube[0][0][0])   # outputs: ':('
17   print(cube[2][2][0])   # outputs: ':)'
18
```

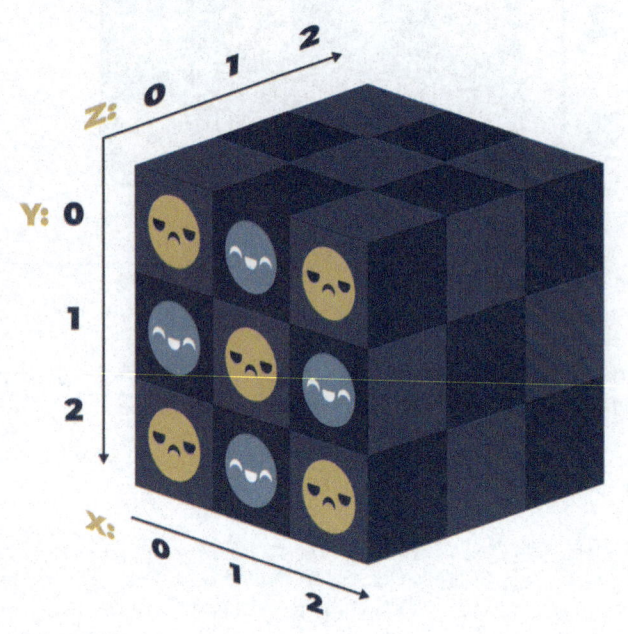

Figure 16.3

PART 4

FUNCTIONS, TUPLES, DICTIONARIES, EXCEPTIONS, AND DATA PROCESSING

SEVENTEEN
FUNCTIONS

You've come across functions many times so far, but the view on their merits that we have given you has been rather one-sided. You've only invoked functions by using them as tools to make life easier, and to simplify time-consuming and tedious tasks. When you want some data to be printed on the console, you use print(). When you want to read the value of a variable, you use input(), coupled with either int() or float(). You've also made use of some methods, which are in fact functions, but declared in a very specific way.

Now you'll learn how to write and use your own functions. We'll write several functions together, from the very simple to the rather complex, which will require your focus and attention. It often happens that a particular piece of code is repeated many times in your program. It's repeated either literally, or with only a few minor modifications, consisting of the use of other variables in the same algorithm. It also happens that a programmer cannot resist simplifying their work, and begins to clone such pieces of code using the clipboard and copy-paste operations. It could end up as greatly frustrating when suddenly it turns out that there was an error in the cloned code. The programmer will have a lot of drudgery to find all the places that need corrections. There's also a high risk of the corrections causing errors.

We can now define the first condition which can help you decide when to start writing your own functions: if a particular fragment of the code begins to appear in more than one place, consider the possibility of isolating it in the form of a function invoked from the points where the original code was placed before.

It may happen that the algorithm you're going to implement is so complex that your code begins to grow in an uncontrolled manner, and suddenly you notice that you're not able to navigate through it so easily anymore. You can try to cope with the issue by commenting the code extensively, but soon you find that this dramatically worsens your situation — too many comments make the code larger and harder to read. Some say that a well-written function should be viewed entirely in one glance.

A good, attentive developer divides the code — or more accurately, the problem — into well-isolated pieces, and encodes each of them in the form of a function. This considerably simplifies the work of the program, because each piece of code can be encoded separately, and tested separately. The process described here is often called decomposition.

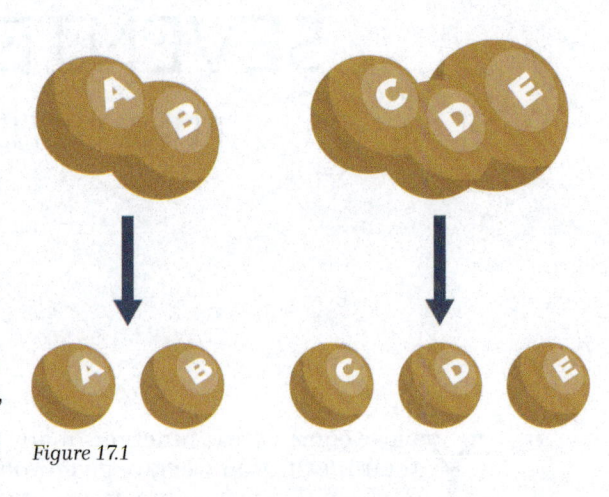

Figure 17.1

We can now state the second condition: if a piece of code becomes so large that reading and understating it may cause a problem, consider dividing it into separate, smaller problems, and implement each of them in the form of a separate function. This decomposition continues until you get a set of short functions, easy to understand and test.

Decomposition

It often happens that the problem is so large and complex that it cannot be assigned to a single developer, and a team of developers have to work on it. The problem must be split between several developers in a way that ensures their efficient and seamless cooperation. It seems inconceivable that more than one programmer should write the same piece of code at the same time, so the job has to be dispersed among all the team members. This kind of decomposition has a different purpose to the one described previously — it's not only about sharing the work, but also about sharing the responsibility among many developers. Each of them writes a clearly defined and described set of functions, which when combined into the module will give the final product. This leads us directly to the third condition: if you're going to divide the work among multiple programmers, decompose the problem to allow the product to be implemented as a set of separately written functions packed together in different modules.

Where do functions come from?

In general, functions come from at least three places:

1. From Python itself — numerous functions, like `print()`, are an integral part of Python, and are always available without any additional effort on behalf of the programmer; we call these functions built-in functions.

2. From Python's preinstalled modules — a lot of functions, very useful ones, but used significantly less often than built-in ones, are available in a number of modules installed together with Python; the use of these functions requires some additional steps from the programmer in order to make them fully accessible. We'll tell you about this in a while.

3. Directly from your code — you can write your own functions, place them inside your code, and use them freely.

4. There is one other possibility, but it's connected with classes, so we'll omit it for now.

Your first function

Take a look at the following snippet:

```
1   print("Enter a value: ")
2   a = int(input())
3
4   print("Enter a value: ")
5   b = int(input())
6
7   print("Enter a value: ")
8   c = int(input())
9
```

It's rather simple, but we only want it to be an example of transforming a repeating part of a code into a function. The messages sent to the console by the `print()` function are always the same. Of course, there's nothing really bad in such a code, but try to imagine what you would have to do if your boss asked you to change the message to make it more polite, e.g. to start it with the phrase `"Please"`.

It seems that you'd have to spend some time changing all the occurrences of the message. You'd use a clipboard, of course, but it wouldn't make your life much easier. It's obvious that you'd probably make some mistakes during the amendment process, and you, and your boss, would get a bit frustrated. Is it possible to separate such a *repeatable* part of the code, name it, and make it reusable? It would mean that a change made once in one place would be propagated to all the places where it's used. Of course, a code like this should work only when it's explicitly launched. Yes, it's possible. This is exactly what functions are for. You need to define it. The word define is significant here. This is what the simplest function definition looks like:

```
1  def function_name():
2      function_body
3
```

It always starts with the keyword `def` (for *define*). Next after `def` goes the name of the function. The rules for naming functions are exactly the same as for naming variables. After the function name, there's a place for a pair of parentheses. they contain nothing here, but that will change soon. The line has to be ended with a colon, and the line directly after `def` begins the function body — at least one necessarily nested instruction, which will be executed every time the function is invoked; note: the function ends where the nesting ends, so you have to be careful.

We're ready to define our prompting function. We'll name it message:

```
1  def message():
2      print("Enter a value: ")
3
```

The function is extremely simple, but fully usable. We've named it message, but you can label it according to your taste. Let's use it. Our code contains the function definition now:

```
1  def message():
2      print("Enter a value: ")
3
4  print("We start here.")
5  print("We end here.")
6
```

Note that we don't use the function at all — there's no invocation of it inside the code. When you run it, you see the following output:

```
We start here.
We end here.
```

This means that Python reads the function's definitions and remembers them, but won't launch any of them without your permission. We've modified the code now — we've inserted the function's invocation between the start and end messages:

```
1  def message():
2      print("Enter a value: ")
3
4  print("We start here.")
5  message()
6  print("We end here.")
7
```

180   Chapter 17

The output looks different now:

```
We start here.
Enter a value:
We end here.
```

Test the code, modify it, experiment with it.

4.1.5 How functions work

Look at the picture on the right. It tries to show you the whole process:

- when you invoke a function, Python remembers the place where it happened and *jumps* into the invoked function;
- the body of the function is then executed;
- reaching the end of the function forces Python to return to the place directly after the point of invocation.

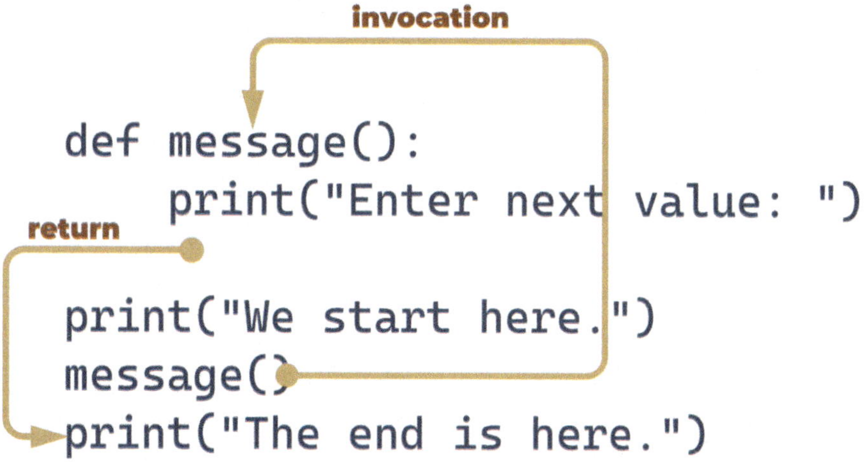

```
def message():
    print("Enter next value: ")


print("We start here.")
message()
print("The end is here.")
```

Figure 17.2

There are two, very important, catches. Here's the first of them: you mustn't invoke a function which is not known at the moment of invocation. Remember — Python reads your code from top to bottom. It's not going to look ahead in order to find a function you forgot to put in the right place. "Right" means "before invocation". We've inserted an error into the following code — can you see the difference?

```
1  print("We start here.")
2  message()
3  print("We end here.")
4
5
6  def message():
7      print("Enter a value: ")
8
```

Functions   181

We've moved the function to the end of the code. Is Python able to find it when the execution reaches the invocation? No, it isn't. The error message will read:

```
NameError: name 'message' is not defined
```

Don't try to force Python to look for functions you didn't deliver at the right time. The second catch sounds a little simpler: you mustn't have a function and a variable of the same name. The following snippet is erroneous:

```
1   def message():
2       print("Enter a value: ")
3
4   message = 1
5
```

Assigning a value to the name message causes Python to forget its previous role. The function named `message` becomes unavailable. Fortunately, you're free to mix your code with functions — you're not obliged to put all your functions at the top of your source file. Look at the snippet:

```
1   print("We start here.")
2
3
4   def message():
5       print("Enter a value: ")
6
7   message()
8
9   print("We end here.")
10
```

It may look strange, but it's completely correct, and works as intended. Let's return to our primary example, and employ the function for the right job, like here:

```
1   def message():
2       print("Enter a value: ")
3
4   message()
5   a = int(input())
6   message()
7   b = int(input())
8   message()
9   c = int(input())
10
```

Modifying the prompting message is now easy and clear — you can do it by changing the code in just one place — inside the function's body. Try it yourself.

Summary

1. A function is a block of code that performs a specific task when the function is called (invoked). You can use functions to make your code reusable, better organized, and more readable. Functions can have parameters and return values.

2. There are at least four basic types of functions in Python:

    - built-in functions which are an integral part of Python, such as the `print()` function. You can see a complete list of built-in Python functions at https://docs.python.org/3/library/functions.html;
    - the ones that come from pre-installed modules — you'll learn about them in *Python Essentials 2*;
    - user-defined functions which are written by users for users — you can write your own functions and use them freely in your code;
    - the `lambda` functions — you'll learn about them in *Python Essentials 2*.

3. You can define your own function using the `def` keyword and the following syntax:

```
1   def your_function(optional parameters):
2       # the body of the function
3
```

- You can define a function which doesn't take any arguments, e.g.:

```
1   def message():  # defining a function
2       print("Hello")  # body of the function
3
4   message()  # calling the function
5
```

- You can define a function which takes arguments, too, just like the following one-parameter function:

```
1   def hello(name):  # defining a function
2       print("Hello,", name)  # body of the function
3
4
5   name = input("Enter your name: ")
6
7   hello(name)  # calling the function
8
```

Quiz

QUESTION 1: The `input()` function is an example of a:

a) user-defined function

b) built-in function

QUESTION 2: What happens when you try to invoke a function before you define it? Example:

```
1  hi()
2
3  def hi():
4      print("hi!")
5
```

QUESTION 3: What will happen when you run the following code?

```
1  def hi():
2      print("hi")
3
4  hi(5)
5
```

EIGHTEEN
HOW FUNCTIONS COMMUNICATE WITH THEIR ENVIRONMENT

The function's full power reveals itself when it can be equipped with an interface that is able to accept data provided by the invoker. Such data can modify the function's behavior, making it more flexible and adaptable to changing conditions. A parameter is actually a variable, but there are two important factors that make parameters different and special: parameters exist only inside functions in which they have been defined, and the only place where the parameter can be defined is a space between a pair of parentheses in the `def` statement; and assigning a value to the parameter is done at the time of the function's invocation, by specifying the corresponding argument.

```
def function(parameter):
    ###
```

Don't forget that parameters live inside functions. This is their natural environment. Arguments, on the other hand, exist outside functions, and are carriers of values passed to corresponding parameters. There is a clear and unambiguous frontier between these two worlds.

Let's enrich the function with just one parameter — we're going to use it to show the user the number of a value the function asks for. We have to rebuild the `def` statement — this is what it looks like now:

```
def message(number):
    ###
```

The definition specifies that our function operates on just one parameter, named `number`. You can use it as an ordinary variable, but only inside the function — it isn't visible anywhere else. Let's now improve the function's body.

```
1   def message(number):
2       print("Enter a number:", number)
3
```

We've made use of the parameter. Note that we haven't assigned the parameter with any value. Is it correct? Yes, it is. A value for the parameter will arrive from the function's environment. Remember that specifying one or more parameters in a function's definition is also a requirement, and you have to fulfill it during invocation. You must provide as many arguments as there are defined parameters. Failure to do so will cause an error. Try to run the code. This is what you'll see in the console:

```
TypeError: message() missing 1 required positional argument:
'number'
```

This looks better, for sure:

```
1   def message(number):
2       print("Enter a number:", number)
3   message(1)
4
```

Moreover, it behaves better. The code will produce the following output:

```
Enter a number: 1
```

Can you see how it works? The value of the argument used during invocation (1) has been passed into the function, setting the initial value of the parameter named number. But we have to make you sensitive to one important circumstance. It's legal, and possible, to have a variable named the same as a function's parameter. The snippet illustrates the phenomenon:

```
1   def message(number):
2       print("Enter a number:", number)
3
4   number = 1234
5   message(1)
6   print(number)
7
```

A situation like this activates a mechanism called shadowing. Parameter x shadows any variable of the same name, but only inside the function defining the parameter. The parameter named number is a completely different entity from the variable named number. This means that the previous snippet will produce the following output:

```
Enter a number: 1
1234
```

A function can have as many parameters as you want, but the more parameters you have, the harder it is to memorize their roles and purposes. Let's modify the function — it has two parameters now:

```
def message(what, number):
    print("Enter", what, "number", number)
```

This also means that invoking the function will require two arguments. The first new parameter is intended to carry the name of the desired value. Here it is:

```
1  def message(what, number):
2      print("Enter", what, "number", number)
3
4  message("telephone", 11)
5  message("price", 5)
6  message("number", "number")
7
```

This is the output you're about to see:

```
Enter telephone number 11
Enter price number 5
Enter number number number
```

Run the code, modify it, add more parameters, and see how this affects the output.

Positional parameter passing

A technique which assigns the ith (first, second, and so on) argument to the ith (second, third, and so on) function parameter is called positional parameter passing, while arguments passed in this way are named positional arguments. You've used it already, but Python can offer a lot more. We're going to tell you about it now.

```
1  def my_function(a, b, c):
2      print(a, b, c)
3
4  my_function(1, 2, 3)
5
```

NOTE Positional parameter passing is intuitively used by people in many social occasions. For example, it may be generally accepted that when we introduce ourselves we mention our first name(s) before our last name, e.g. "My name's John Doe."

Incidentally, Hungarians do it in reverse order. Let's implement that social custom in Python. The following function will be responsible for introducing somebody:

```
1   def introduction(first_name, last_name):
2       print("Hello, my name is", first_name, last_name)
3
4   introduction("Luke", "Skywalker")
5   introduction("Jesse", "Quick")
6   introduction("Clark", "Kent")
7
```

Can you guess the output? Run the code and find out if you're right. Now imagine that the same function is being used in Hungary. In this case, the code would look like this:

```
1   def introduction(first_name, last_name):
2       print("Hello, my name is", first_name, last_name)
3
4   introduction("Skywalker", "Luke")
5   introduction("Quick", "Jesse")
6   introduction("Kent", "Clark")
7
```

The output will look different. Can you guess it? Run the code to see if you're right here, too. Are you surprised? Can you make the function more culture-independent?

Keyword argument passing

Python offers another convention for passing arguments, where the meaning of the argument is dictated by its name, not by its position — it's called keyword argument passing. Take a look at the snippet:

```
1   def introduction(first_name, last_name):
2       print("Hello, my name is", first_name, last_name)
3
4   introduction(first_name = "James", last_name = "Bond")
5   introduction(last_name = "Skywalker", first_name = "Luke")
6
```

The concept is clear — the values passed to the parameters are preceded by the target parameters' names, followed by the = sign. The position doesn't matter here — each argument's value knows its destination on the basis of the name used. You should be able to predict the output. Run the code to check if you're right. Of course, you mustn't use a non-existent parameter name. The following snippet will cause a runtime error:

```
1   def introduction(first_name, last_name):
2       print("Hello, my name is", first_name, last_name)
3
4   introduction(surname="Skywalker", first_name="Luke")
5
```

This is what Python will tell you:

```
TypeError: introduction() got an unexpected keyword argument
'surname'
```

Mixing positional and keyword arguments

You can mix both styles if you want — there is only one unbreakable rule: you have to put positional arguments before keyword arguments. If you think for a moment, you'll certainly guess why. To show you how it works, we'll use the following simple three-parameter function:

```
1  def adding(a, b, c):
2      print(a, "+", b, "+", c, "=", a + b + c)
3
```

Its purpose is to evaluate and present the sum of all its arguments. The function, when invoked in the following way:

```
1  adding(1, 2, 3)
2
```

will output:

```
1 + 2 + 3 = 6
```

It was — as you may suspect — a pure example of positional argument passing. Of course, you can replace such an invocation with a purely keyword variant, like this:

```
1  adding(c = 1, a = 2, b = 3)
2
```

Our program will output a line like this:

```
2 + 3 + 1 = 6
```

Note the order of the values. Let's try to mix both styles now. Look at the following function invocation:

```
1  adding(3, c = 1, b = 2)
2
```

Let's analyze it: the argument (3) for the a parameter is passed using the positional way; and the arguments for c and b are specified as keyword ones.

This is what you'll see in the console:

```
3 + 2 + 1 = 6
```

Be careful, and beware of mistakes. If you try to pass more than one value to one argument, all you'll get is a runtime error. Look at the following invocation — it seems that we've tried to set a twice:

```
1  adding(3, a = 1, b = 2)
2
```

Python's response:

```
TypeError: adding() got multiple values for argument 'a'
```

Look at the following snippet. A code like this is fully correct, but it doesn't make much sense:

```
1  adding(4, 3, c = 2)
2
```

Everything is right, but leaving in just one keyword argument looks a bit weird — what do you think?

Parametrized functions – more details

It happens at times that a particular parameter's values are in use more often than others. Such arguments may have their default or predefined values taken into consideration when their corresponding arguments have been omitted. They say that the most popular English last name is *Smith*. Let's try to take this into account. The default parameter's value is set using clear and pictorial syntax:

```
1  def introduction(first_name, last_name="Smith"):
2      print("Hello, my name is", first_name, last_name)
3
```

You only have to extend the parameter's name with the = sign, followed by the default value. Let's invoke the function as usual:

```
1  introduction("James", "Doe")
2
```

Can you guess the output of the program? Run it and check if you're right. And? Everything looks the same, but when you invoke the function in a way that looks a bit suspicious at first sight, like this:

```
1  introduction("Henry")
2
```

It may also look like this:

```
1  introduction(first_name="William")
2
```

There will be no error, and both invocations will succeed, while the console will show the following output:

```
Hello, my name is Henry Smith
Hello, my name is William Smith
```

Test it. You can go further if it's useful. Both parameters have their default values now, look at the following code:

```
1   def introduction(first_name="John", last_name="Smith"):
2       print("Hello, my name is", first_name, last_name)
3
```

This makes the following invocation absolutely valid:

```
1   introduction()
2
```

And this is the expected output:

```
Hello, my name is John Smith
```

If you use one keyword argument, the remaining one will take the default value:

```
1   introduction(last_name="Hopkins")
2
```

The output is:

```
Hello, my name is John Hopkins
```

Summary

1. You can pass information to functions by using parameters. Your functions can have as many parameters as you need.

- An example of a one-parameter function:

```
1   def hi(name):
2       print("Hi,", name)
3
4   hi("Greg")
5
```

- An example of a two-parameter function:

```
1   def hi_all(name_1, name_2):
2       print("Hi,", name_2)
3       print("Hi,", name_1)
4
5   hi_all("Sebastian", "Konrad")
6
```

- An example of a three-parameter function:

```
1   def address(street, city, postal_code):
2       print("Your address is:", street, "St.,", city, postal_
    code)
3
4   s = input("Street: ")
5   p_c = input("Postal Code: ")
6   c = input("City: ")
7   address(s, c, p_c)
8
```

2. You can pass arguments to a function using the following techniques:

- positional argument passing in which the order of arguments passed matters (Ex. 1)
- keyword (named) argument passing in which the order of arguments passed doesn't matter (Ex. 2)
- a mix of positional and keyword argument passing (Ex. 3.)

```
1    # Ex. 1
2    def subtra(a, b):
3        print(a - b)
4
5    subtra(5, 2) # outputs: 3
6    subtra(2, 5) # outputs: -3
7
8
9    # Ex. 2
10   def subtra(a, b):
11       print(a - b)
12
13   subtra(a=5, b=2) # outputs: 3
14   subtra(b=2, a=5) # outputs: 3
15
16   # Ex. 3
17   def subtra(a, b):
18       print(a - b)
19
20   subtra(5, b=2) # outputs: 3
21   subtra(5, 2) # outputs: 3
22
```

It's important to remember that positional arguments mustn't follow keyword arguments. That's why if you try to run the following snippet, Python will not let you do it by signaling a SyntaxError:

```
1   def subtra(a, b):
2       print(a - b)
3
4   subtra(5, b=2) # outputs: 3
5   subtra(a=5, 2) # Syntax Error
6
```

Chapter 18

3. You can use the keyword argument-passing technique to pre-define a value for a given argument:

```
1  def name(first_name, last_name="Smith"):
2      print(first_name, last_name)
3
4  name("Andy") # outputs: Andy Smith
5  name("Betty", "Johnson") # outputs: Betty Johnson (the keyword argument replaced by "Johnson")
6
```

Quiz

QUESTION 1: What is the output of the following snippet?

```
1  def intro(a="James Bond", b="Bond"):
2      print("My name is", b + ".", a + ".")
3
4  intro()
5
```

QUESTION 2: What is the output of the following snippet?

```
1  def intro(a="James Bond", b="Bond"):
2      print("My name is", b + ".", a + ".")
3
4  intro(b="Sean Connery")
5
```

QUESTION 3: What is the output of the following snippet?

```
1  def intro(a, b="Bond"):
2      print("My name is", b + ".", a + ".")
3
4  intro("Susan")
5
```

QUESTION 4: What is the output of the following snippet?

```
1  def add_numbers(a, b=2, c):
2      print(a + b + c)
3
4  add_numbers(a=1, c=3)
5
```

NINETEEN
RETURNING A RESULT FROM A FUNCTION

All the previously presented functions have some kind of effect — they produce some text and send it to the console. Of course, functions — like their mathematical siblings — may have results. To get functions to return a value, among other purposes, you use the `return` instruction. This word gives you a full picture of its capabilities. Note: it's a Python keyword. The `return` instruction has two different variants — let's consider them separately.

The `return` instruction

`return` without an expression

Let's consider the following function:

```
1   def happy_new_year(wishes = True):
2       print("Three...")
3       print("Two...")
4       print("One...")
5       if not wishes:
6           return
7
8       print("Happy New Year!")
9
```

Take a look at this function:

```
happy_new_year()
```

When invoked without any arguments, the function causes a little noise — the output will look like this:

```
Three...
Two...
One...
Happy New Year!
```

Providing `False` as an argument will modify the function's behavior:

```
happy_new_year(False)
```

The return instruction will cause its termination just before the wishes. This is the updated output:

```
Three...
Two...
One...
```

`return` with an expression

The second `return` variant is extended with an expression:

```
1  def function():
2      return expression
3
```

There are two consequences of using it: first, it causes the immediate termination of the function's execution. This is nothing new compared to the first variant. Second, the function will evaluate the expression's value and will return it (hence the name once again) as the function's result. Yes, we already know — this example isn't really sophisticated:

```
1  def boring_function():
2      return 123
3
4  x = boring_function()
5
6  print("The boring_function has returned its result. It's:", x)
7
```

The snippet writes the following text to the console:

```
The boring_function has returned its result. It's:
123
```

Let's investigate it for a while. Take a look at Figure 19.1. The `return` instruction, enriched with the expression (the expression is very simple here), "transports" the expression's value to the place where the function has been invoked. The result may be freely used here, for example, to be assigned to a variable. It may also be completely ignored and lost without a trace.

```
def boring_function():
    return 13
```
invocation → *return the value*

```
x = boring_function()
```

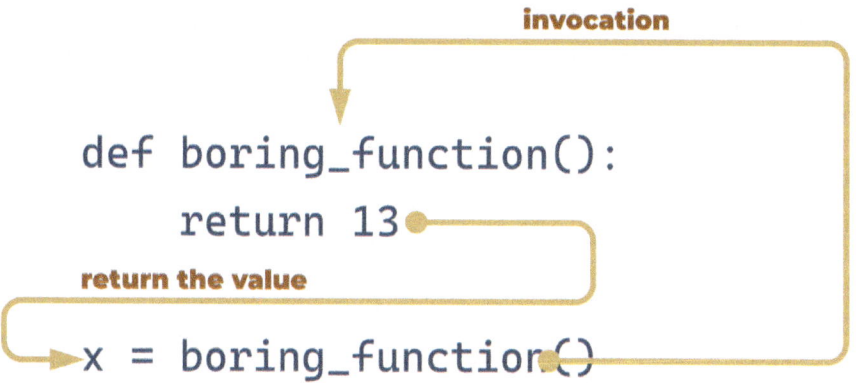

Figure 19.1

We're not being too polite here — the function returns a value, and we ignore it, that is, we don't use it in any way:

```
1  def boring_function():
2      print("'Boredom Mode' ON.")
3      return 123
4  
5  print("This lesson is interesting!")
6  boring_function()
7  print("This lesson is boring!")
8  
```

The program produces the following output:

```
This lesson is interesting!
'Boredom Mode' ON.
This lesson is boring...
```

Is it punishable? Not at all. The only disadvantage is that the result has been irretrievably lost. Don't forget that you are always allowed to ignore the function's result, and be satisfied with the function's effect, if the function has any, and if a function is intended to return a useful result, it must contain the second variant of the `return` instruction. Wait a minute — does this mean that there are useless results, too? Yes, in some sense.

A few words about None

Let us introduce you to a very curious value — to be honest, a none value — named `None`. Its data doesn't represent any reasonable value — actually, it's not a value at all; hence, it mustn't take part in any expressions. For example, a snippet like this will cause a runtime error,:

```
print(None + 2)
```

It is described by the following diagnostic message:

```
TypeError: unsupported operand type(s) for +:
'NoneType' and 'int'
```

> **NOTE** None is a keyword.

There are only two kinds of circumstances when None can be safely used: when you assign it to a variable or return it as a function's result, and when you compare it with a variable to diagnose its internal state. Just like here:

```
1  value = None
2  if value is None:
3      print("Sorry, you don't carry any value")
4
```

Don't forget this: if a function doesn't return a certain value using a return expression clause, it is assumed that it implicitly returns None. Let's test it. Take a look at the following code.

```
1  def strange_function(n):
2      if(n % 2 == 0):
3          return True
4
```

It's obvious that the `strange_function` function returns True when its argument is even. What does it return otherwise? We can use the following code to check it:

```
1  print(strange_function(2))
2  print(strange_function(1))
3
```

This is what we see in the console:

```
True
None
```

Don't be surprised next time you see None as a function result — it may be the symptom of a subtle mistake inside the function.

Effects and results: lists and functions

There are two additional questions that should be answered here. The first is: may a list be sent to a function as an argument? Of course it may! Any entity recognizable by Python can play the role of a function argument, although it has to be assured that the function is able to cope with it. So, if you pass a list to a function, the function has to handle it like a list. A function like this one here:

```
1   def list_sum(lst):
2       s = 0
3
4       for elem in lst:
5           s += elem
6
7       return s
8
```

and invoked like this:

```
1   print(list_sum([5, 4, 3]))
2
```

will return 12 as a result, but you should expect problems if you invoke it in this risky way:

```
1   print(list_sum(5))
2
```

Python's response will be unequivocal:

```
TypeError: 'int' object is not iterable
```

This is caused by the fact that a single integer value mustn't be iterated through by the for loop. The second question is: may a list be a function result? Yes, of course! Any entity recognizable by Python can be a function result. Look at the following code:

```
1   def strange_list_fun(n):
2       strange_list = []
3
4       for i in range(0, n):
5           strange_list.insert(0, i)
6
7       return strange_list
8
9   print(strange_list_fun(5))
10
```

The program's output will look like this:

```
[4, 3, 2, 1, 0]
```

Now you can write functions with and without results. Let's dive a little deeper into the issues connected with variables in functions. This is essential for creating effective and safe functions.

LAB: A leap year — writing your own functions

Your task is to write and test a function which takes one argument (a year) and returns `True` if the year is a *leap year*, or `False` otherwise. The seed of the function is already sown in the following skeleton code. We've also prepared a short testing code, which you can use to test your function. The code uses two lists — one with the test data, and the other containing the expected results. The code will tell you if any of your results are invalid.

CODE

```
 1  def is_year_leap(year):
 2      #
 3      # Write your code here.
 4      #
 5
 6  test_data = [1900, 2000, 2016, 1987]
 7  test_results = [False, True, True, False]
 8  for i in range(len(test_data)):
 9      yr = test_data[i]
10      print(yr,"->",end="")
11      result = is_year_leap(yr)
12      if result == test_results[i]:
13          print("OK")
14      else:
15          print("Failed")
16
```

LAB: How many days: writing and using your own functions

Your task is to write and test a function which takes two arguments (a year and a month) and returns the number of days for the given year-month pair. While only February is sensitive to the `year` value, your function should be universal. The initial part of the function is ready. Now, convince the function to return `None` if its arguments don't make sense. Of course, you can (and should) use the previously written and tested function (LAB: A leap year — writing your own functions). It may be very helpful. We encourage you to use a list filled with the months' lengths. You can create it inside the function — this trick will significantly shorten the code. We've prepared a testing code. Expand it to include more test cases.

CODE

```
 1  def is_year_leap(year):
 2      #
 3      # Your code from the previous LAB.
 4      #
 5
 6  def days_in_month(year, month):
 7      #
 8      # Write your new code here.
 9      #
10
```

```
11  test_years = [1900, 2000, 2016, 1987]
12  test_months = [2, 2, 1, 11]
13  test_results = [28, 29, 31, 30]
14  for i in range(len(test_years)):
15      yr = test_years[i]
16      mo = test_months[i]
17      print(yr, mo, "->", end="")
18      result = days_in_month(yr, mo)
19      if result == test_results[i]:
20          print("OK")
21      else:
22          print("Failed")
23
```

LAB: Day of the year — writing and using your own functions

Your task is to write and test a function which takes three arguments (a year, a month, and a day of the month) and returns the corresponding day of the year, or returns None if any of the arguments is invalid. Use the previously written and tested functions. Add your own test cases to the code.

CODE

```
1   def is_year_leap(year):
2       #
3       # Your code from the previous LAB.
4       #
5
6   def days_in_month(year, month):
7       #
8       # Your code from the previous lab.
9       #
10
11  def day_of_year(year, month, day):
12      #
13      # Write your new code here.
14      #
15
16  print(day_of_year(2000, 12, 31))
17
```

LAB: Prime numbers — how to find them

A natural number is prime if it is greater than 1 and has no divisors other than 1 and itself. Complicated? Not at all. For example, 8 isn't a prime number, as you can divide it by 2 and 4. We can't use divisors equal to 1 and 8, as the definition prohibits this. On the other hand, 7 is a prime number, as we can't find any legal divisors for it. Your task is to write a function checking whether a number is prime or not.

The function is called `is_prime`; it takes one argument (the value to check) and returns `True` if the argument is a prime number, and `False` otherwise.

HINT Try to divide the argument by all subsequent values (starting from 2) and check the remainder — if it's zero, your number cannot be a prime; think carefully about when you should stop the process.

If you need to know the square root of any value, you can utilize the `**` operator. Remember: the square root of `x` is the same as `x0.5`. Complete the code. Run your code and check whether your output is the same as ours.

EXPECTED OUTPUT:
```
2 3 5 7 11 13 17 19
```

CODE
```
1   def is_prime(num):
2       #
3       # Write your code here.
4       #
5
6   for i in range(1, 20):
7       if is_prime(i + 1):
8           print(i + 1, end=" ")
9   print()
10
```

LAB: Converting fuel consumption

A car's fuel consumption may be expressed in many different ways. For example, in Europe, it is shown as the amount of fuel consumed per 100 kilometers. In the USA, it is shown as the number of miles traveled by a car using one gallon of fuel.

Your task is to write a pair of functions converting l/100km into mpg, and vice versa. The functions:

- are named `liters_100km_to_miles_gallon` and `miles_gallon_to_liters_100km` respectively;
- take one argument (the value corresponding to their names)

Complete the following code and run it to check whether your output is the same as ours. Here is some information to help you:

- 1 American mile = 1609.344 meters;
- 1 American gallon = 3.785411784 liters.

EXPECTED OUTPUT:
```
60.31143162393162
31.36194444444444
23.52145833333333
3.9007393587617467
7.490910297239916
10.009131205673757
```

CODE
```
1   def liters_100km_to_miles_gallon(liters):
2       #
3       # Write your code here.
4       #
5
6   def miles_gallon_to_liters_100km(miles):
7       #
8       # Write your code here.
9       #
10
11  print(liters_100km_to_miles_gallon(3.9))
12  print(liters_100km_to_miles_gallon(7.5))
13  print(liters_100km_to_miles_gallon(10.))
14  print(miles_gallon_to_liters_100km(60.3))
15  print(miles_gallon_to_liters_100km(31.4))
16  print(miles_gallon_to_liters_100km(23.5))
17
```

Summary

1. You can use the `return` keyword to tell a function to return some value. The `return` statement exits the function, e.g.:

```
1   def multiply(a, b):
2       return a * b
3
4   print(multiply(3, 4)) # outputs: 12
5
6
7   def multiply(a, b):
8       return
9
10  print(multiply(3, 4)) # outputs: None
11
```

2. The result of a function can be easily assigned to a variable, e.g.:

```
1   def wishes():
2       return "Happy Birthday!"
3
4   w = wishes()
5
6   print(w) # outputs: Happy Birthday!
7
```

Look at the difference in output in the following two examples:

```
1   # Example 1
2   def wishes():
3       print("My Wishes")
4       return "Happy Birthday"
5
6   wishes() # outputs: My Wishes
7
8
9   # Example 2
10  def wishes():
11      print("My Wishes")
12      return "Happy Birthday"
13
14  print(wishes())
15
16  # outputs: My Wishes
17  # Happy Birthday
18
```

3. You can use a list as a function's argument, e.g.:

```
1   def hi_everybody(my_list):
2       for name in my_list:
3           print("Hi,", name)
4
5   hi_everybody(["Adam", "John", "Lucy"])
6
```

4. A list can be a function result, too, e.g.:

```
1   def create_list(n):
2       my_list = []
3       for i in range(n):
4           my_list.append(i)
5       return my_list
6
7   print(create_list(5))
8
```

Quiz

QUESTION 1: What is the output of the following snippet?

```
1   def hi():
2       return
3       print("Hi!")
4
5   hi()
6
```

QUESTION 2: What is the output of the following snippet?

```
1   def is_int(data):
2       if type(data) == int:
3           return True
4       elif type(data) == float:
5           return False
6
7   print(is_int(5))
8   print(is_int(5.0))
9   print(is_int("5"))
10
```

QUESTION 3: What is the output of the following snippet?

```
1   def even_num_lst(ran):
2       lst = []
3       for num in range(ran):
4           if num % 2 == 0:
5               lst.append(num)
6       return lst
7
8   print(even_num_lst(11))
9
```

QUESTION 4: What is the output of the following snippet?

```
1   def list_updater(lst):
2       upd_list = []
3       for elem in lst:
4           elem **= 2
5           upd_list.append(elem)
6       return upd_list
7
8   foo = [1, 2, 3, 4, 5]
9   print(list_updater(foo))
10
```

TWENTY
SCOPES IN PYTHON

Let's start with a definition: *The scope of a name (e.g. a variable name) is the part of a code where the name is properly recognizable.* For example, the scope of a function's parameter is the function itself. The parameter is inaccessible outside the function. Let's check it. Look at the following code. What will happen when you run it?

```
1    def scope_test():
2        x = 123
3
4
5    scope_test()
6    print(x)
7
```

The program will fail when run. The error message will read:

```
NameError: name 'x' is not defined
```

This is to be expected. We're going to conduct some experiments with you to show you how Python constructs scopes, and how you can use these to your benefit. Let's start by checking whether or not a variable created outside any function is visible inside the functions. In other words, does a variable's name propagate into a function's body? Look at the following code. Our guinea pig is there.

```
1  def my_function():
2      print("Do I know that variable?", var)
3
4
5  var = 1
6  my_function()
7  print(var)
8
```

The result of the test is positive — the code outputs:

```
Do I know that variable? 1
1
```

The answer is: a variable existing outside a function has scope inside the function's body. This rule has a very important exception. Let's try to find it. Let's make a small change to the code:

```
1  def my_function():
2      var = 2
3      print("Do I know that variable?", var)
4
5
6  var = 1
7  my_function()
8  print(var)
9
```

The result has changed, too — the code produces a slightly different output now:

```
Do I know that variable? 2
1
```

What's happened? The `var` variable created inside the function is not the same as when defined outside it — it seems that there two different variables of the same name. Moreover, the function's variable shadows the variable coming from the outside world. We can make the previous rule more precise and adequate: A variable existing outside a function has scope inside the function's body, excluding those which define a variable of the same name. It also means that the scope of a variable existing outside a function is supported only when getting its value (reading). Assigning a value forces the creation of the function's own variable. Make sure you understand this well and carry out your own experiments.

Functions and scopes: the `global` keyword

Hopefully, you should now have arrived at the following question: does this mean that a function is not able to modify a variable defined outside it? This would create a lot of discomfort. Fortunately, the answer is *no*. There's a special Python method which can extend a variable's scope in a way which includes the function's body, even if you want not only to read the values, but also to modify them. Such an effect is caused by a keyword named `global`:

```
1   global name
2   global name1, name2, ...
3
```

Using this keyword inside a function with the name, or names separated with commas), of a variable or variables, forces Python to refrain from creating a new variable inside the function — the one accessible from outside will be used instead. In other words, this name becomes global. It has global scope, and it doesn't matter whether it's the subject of read or assign. Look at the following code.

```
1   def my_function():
2       global var
3       var = 2
4       print("Do I know that variable?", var)
5
6
7   var = 1
8   my_function()
9   print(var)
10
```

We've added `global` to the function. The code now outputs:

```
Do I know that variable?
2
```

This should be sufficient evidence to show that the `global` keyword does what it promises.

How the function interacts with its arguments

Now let's find out how the function interacts with its arguments. The following code should teach you something. As you can see, the function changes the value of its parameter. Does the change affect the argument?

```
1   def my_function(n):
2       print("I got", n)
3       n += 1
4       print("I have", n)
5
6
```

Scopes In Python

```
7   var = 1
8   my_function(var)
9   print(var)
10
```

Run the program and check. The code's output is:

```
I got 1
I have 2
1
```

The conclusion is obvious — changing the parameter's value doesn't propagate outside the function; in any case, not when the variable is a scalar, like in the example. This also means that a function receives the argument's value, not the argument itself. This is true for scalars. Is it worth checking how it works with lists? Do you recall the peculiarities of assigning list slices versus assigning lists as a whole? The following example will shed some light on the issue:

```
1   def my_function(my_list_1):
2       print("Print #1:", my_list_1)
3       print("Print #2:", my_list_2)
4       my_list_1 = [0, 1]
5       print("Print #3:", my_list_1)
6       print("Print #4:", my_list_2)
7
8
9   my_list_2 = [2, 3]
10  my_function(my_list_2)
11  print("Print #5:", my_list_2)
12
```

The code's output is:

```
Print #1: [2, 3]
Print #2: [2, 3]
Print #3: [0, 1]
Print #4: [2, 3]
Print #5: [2, 3]
```

It seems that the former rule still works. Finally, can you see the difference in the example:

```
1   def my_function(my_list_1):
2       print("Print #1:", my_list_1)
3       print("Print #2:", my_list_2)
4       del my_list_1[0]  # Pay attention to this line.
5       print("Print #3:", my_list_1)
6       print("Print #4:", my_list_2)
7
8
```

```
9    my_list_2 = [2, 3]
10   my_function(my_list_2)
11   print("Print #5:", my_list_2)
12
```

We don't change the value of the parameter `my_list_1` because we already know it will not affect the argument, but instead modify the list identified by it. The output may be surprising. Run the code and check:

```
Print #1: [2, 3]
Print #2: [2, 3]
Print #3: [3]
Print #4: [3]
Print #5: [3]
```

Can we explain it? Let's try. If the argument is a list, then changing the value of the corresponding parameter doesn't affect the list. Remember that variables containing lists are stored in a different way than scalars. But if you change a list identified by the parameter (note: the list, not the parameter!), the list will reflect the change. It's time to write some example functions. You'll do that in the next chapter.

Summary

1. A variable that exists outside a function has scope inside the function body (Example 1) unless the function defines a variable of the same name (Example 2 and Example 3), e.g.:

Example 1:

```
1    var = 2
2
3
4    def mult_by_var(x):
5        return x * var
6
7
8    print(mult_by_var(7))  # outputs: 14
9
```

Example 2:

```
1    def mult(x):
2        var = 5
3        return x * var
4
5
6    print(mult(7))  # outputs: 35
7
```

Example 3:

```
1  def mult(x):
2      var = 7
3      return x * var
4
5
6  var = 3
7  print(mult(7)) # outputs: 49
8
```

2. A variable that exists inside a function has scope inside the function body (Example 4), e.g.:

Example 4:

```
1  def adding(x):
2      var = 7
3      return x + var
4
5
6  print(adding(4)) # outputs: 11
7  print(var) # NameError
8
```

3. You can use the `global` keyword followed by a variable name to make the variable's scope global, e.g.:

```
1   var = 2
2   print(var) # outputs: 2
3
4
5   def return_var():
6       global var
7       var = 5
8       return var
9
10
11  print(return_var()) # outputs: 5
12  print(var) # outputs: 5
13
```

Quiz

QUESTION 1: What is the output of the following snippet?

```
1   def message():
2       alt = 1
3       print("Hello, World!")
4
5
6   print(alt)
7
```

QUESTION 2: What is the output of the following snippet?

```
1    a = 1
2
3
4    def fun():
5        a = 2
6        print(a)
7
8
9    fun()
10   print(a)
11
```

QUESTION 3: What is the output of the following snippet?

```
1    a = 1
2
3
4    def fun():
5        global a
6        a = 2
7        print(a)
8
9
10   fun()
11   a = 3
12   print(a)
13
```

Scopes In Python   213

QUESTION 4: What is the output of the following snippet?

```
1   a = 1
2
3
4   def fun():
5       global a
6       a = 2
7       print(a)
8
9
10  a = 3
11  fun()
12  print(a)
13
```

TWENTY-ONE
CREATING MULTI-PARAMETER FUNCTIONS

Let's get started on a function to evaluate the Body Mass Index (BMI). As you can see from Figure 20.1, the formula gets two values: weight, originally in kilograms, and height, originally in meters. It seems that this new function will have two parameters. Its name will be bmi, but if you prefer any other name, use it instead.

$$BMI = \frac{(\text{weight in kilograms})}{\text{height in meters}^2}$$

Figure 20.1

Let's code the function:

```
1   def bmi(weight, height):
2       return weight / height ** 2
3
4
5   print(bmi(52.5, 1.65))
6
```

The result produced by the sample invocation looks as follows:

```
19.283746556473833
```

The function fulfills our expectations, but it's a bit simple — it assumes that the values of both parameters are always meaningful. It's definitely worth checking if they're trustworthy. Let's check them both and return None if any of them looks suspicious.

Evaluating BMI and converting imperial units to metric units

Look at the following code. There are two things we need to pay attention to.

```
1   def bmi(weight, height):
2       if height < 1.0 or height > 2.5 or \
3          weight < 20 or weight > 200:
4           return None
5
6       return weight / height ** 2
7
8
9   print(bmi(352.5, 1.65))
10
```

First, the test invocation ensures that the protection works properly — the output is:

```
None
```

Second, take a look at the way the backslash (\) symbol is used. If you use it in Python code and end a line with it, it will tell Python to continue the line of code in the next line of code. It can be particularly useful when you have to deal with long lines of code and you'd like to improve code readability. Okay, but there's something we omitted too easily — the imperial measurements. This function is not too useful for people accustomed to pounds, feet, and inches. What can be done for them? We can write two simple functions to convert imperial units to metric ones. Let's start with pounds. It is a well-known fact that 1lb=0.45359237kg. We'll use this in our new function. This is our helper function, named lb_to_kg:

```
1   def lb_to_kg(lb):
2       return lb * 0.45359237
3
4
5   print(lb_to_kg(1))
6
```

The result of the test invocation looks good:

```
0.45359237
```

And now it's time for feet and inches: 1ft=0.3048m, and 1in=2.54cm=0.0254m.

216 Chapter 21

The function we've written is named ft_and_inch_to_m:

```
1  def ft_and_inch_to_m(ft, inch):
2      return ft * 0.3048 + inch * 0.0254
3
4
5  print(ft_and_inch_to_m(1, 1))
6
```

The result of a quick test is:0.3302 It looks as expected. Note that we wanted to name the second parameter just in, not inch, but we couldn't. Do you know why? in is a Python keyword — it cannot be used as a name. Let's convert *six feet* into meters:

```
1  print(ft_and_inch_to_m(6, 0))
2
```

And this is the output:

1.8288000000000002

It's quite possible that sometimes you may want to use just feet without inches. Will Python help you? Of course it will. We've modified the code a bit:

```
1  def ft_and_inch_to_m(ft, inch = 0.0):
2      return ft * 0.3048 + inch * 0.0254
3
4
5  print(ft_and_inch_to_m(6))
6
```

Now the inch parameter has its default value equal to 0.0. The code produces the following output — this is what is expected:

1.8288000000000002

Finally, the code is able to answer the question: what is the BMI of a person 5'7" tall and weighing 176 lbs? This is the code we have built:

```
1   def ft_and_inch_to_m(ft, inch = 0.0):
2       return ft * 0.3048 + inch * 0.0254
3
4
5   def lb_to_kg(lb):
6       return lb * 0.4535923
7
8
9   def bmi(weight, height):
10      if height < 1.0 or height > 2.5 or weight < 20 or weight > 200:
11          return None
```

Creating Multi-Parameter Functions   217

```
12
13        return weight / height ** 2
14
15
16  print(bmi(weight = lb_to_kg(176), height = ft_and_inch_to_
    m(5, 7)))
17
```

Here is the answer. Run the code and test it.

```
27.565214082533313
```

Sample functions: Triangles

Let's play with triangles now. We'll start with a function to check whether three sides of given lengths can build a triangle, like the one in Figure 20.2. We know from school that the sum of two arbitrary sides has to be longer than the third side. It won't be a hard challenge. The function will have three parameters — one for each side. It will return `True` if the sides can build a triangle, and `False`

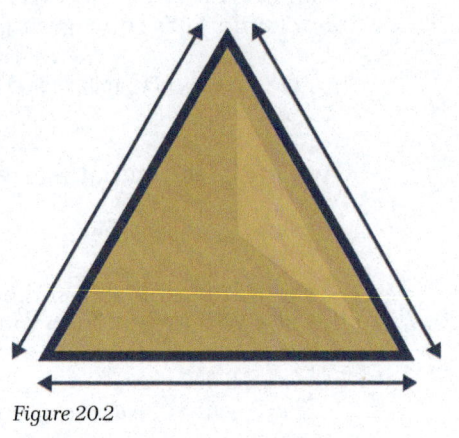

Figure 20.2

otherwise. In this case, `is_a_triangle` is a good name for such a function. Look at the following code. You can find our function there. Run the program.

```
1   def is_a_triangle(a, b, c):
2       if a + b <= c:
3           return False
4       if b + c <= a:
5           return False
6       if c + a <= b:
7           return False
8       return True
9
10
11  print(is_a_triangle(1, 1, 1))
12  print(is_a_triangle(1, 1, 3))
13
```

It seems that it works well — these are the results:

```
True
False
```

Can we make it more compact? It looks a bit wordy. This is a more compact version:

```python
1  def is_a_triangle(a, b, c):
2      if a + b <= c or b + c <= a or c + a <= b:
3          return False
4      return True
5
6
7  print(is_a_triangle(1, 1, 1))
8  print(is_a_triangle(1, 1, 3))
9
```

Can we compact it even more? Yes, we can — look:

```python
1  def is_a_triangle(a, b, c):
2      return a + b > c and b + c > a and c + a > b
3
4
5  print(is_a_triangle(1, 1, 1))
6  print(is_a_triangle(1, 1, 3))
7
```

We've negated the condition. We reversed the relational operators and replaced ors with ands, receiving a universal expression for testing triangles. Let's install the function in a larger program. It'll ask the user for three values and make use of the function.

Triangles and the Pythagorean theorem

Look at the following code. It asks the user for three values. Then it makes use of the is_a_triangle function. The code is ready to run.

```python
1   def is_a_triangle(a, b, c):
2       return a + b > c and b + c > a and c + a > b
3
4
5   a = float(input('Enter the first side\'s length: '))
6   b = float(input('Enter the second side\'s length: '))
7   c = float(input('Enter the third side\'s length: '))
8
9   if is_a_triangle(a, b, c):
10      print('Yes, it can be a triangle.')
11  else:
12      print('No, it can\'t be a triangle.')
13
```

In the second step, we'll try to ensure that a certain triangle is a right-angle triangle. We will need to make use of the Pythagorean theorem:

$c^2 = a^2 + b^2$

How do we recognize which of the three sides is the hypotenuse? The hypotenuse is the longest side. Here is the code:

```
1  def is_a_triangle(a, b, c):
2      return a + b > c and b + c > a and c + a > b
3
4
5  def is_a_right_triangle(a, b, c):
6      if not is_a_triangle(a, b, c):
7          return False
8      if c > a and c > b:
9          return c ** 2 == a ** 2 + b ** 2 if a > b and a > c:
10     if a > b and a > c:
11         return a ** 2 == b ** 2 + c ** 2
12     if b > a and b > c:
13         return b ** 2 == a ** 2 + b ** 2
14 print(is_a_right_triangle(5, 3, 4))
15 print(is_a_right_triangle(1, 3, 4))
16
```

Look at how we test the relationship between the hypotenuse and the remaining sides — we choose the longest side, and apply the Pythagorean theorem to check if everything is right. This requires three checks in total.

Evaluating a triangle's area

We can also evaluate a triangle's area. Heron's formula will be handy here:

$$s = \frac{a + b + c}{2} \qquad A = \sqrt{s(s - a)(s - b)(s - c)}$$

Figure 20.3

We're going use the exponentiation operator to find the square root — it may seem strange, but it works:

$$\sqrt{x} = x^{\frac{1}{2}}$$

Figure 20.4

This is the resulting code:

```
1  def is_a_triangle(a, b, c):
2      return a + b > c and b + c > a and c + a > b
3
4
5  def heron(a, b, c):
6      p = (a + b + c) / 2
7      return (p * (p - a) * (p - b) * (p - c)) ** 0.5
8
9
10 def area_of_triangle(a, b, c):
```

```
11      if not is_a_triangle(a, b, c):
12          return None
13      return heron(a, b, c)
14
15
16  print(area_of_triangle(1., 1., 2. ** .5))
17
```

We try it with a right-angle triangle as a half of a square with one side equal to 1. This means that its area should be equal to 0.5. It's odd — the code produces the following output:

```
0.49999999999999983
```

It's very close to 0.5, but it isn't exactly 0.5. What does it mean? Is it an error? No, it isn't. This is the specifics of floating-point calculations. We'll tell you more about it soon.

Sample functions: Factorials

Another function we're about to write is factorials. Do you remember how a factorial is defined?

```
0! = 1 (yes! it's true) 1! = 1 2! = 1 * 2 3! = 1 * 2 * 3 4! = 1 * 2 * 3 * 4 : : n! = 1 * 2 ** 3 * 4 * ... * n-1 * n
```

It's marked with an exclamation mark, and is equal to the product of all natural numbers from one up to its argument. Let's write our code. We'll create a function and call it `factorial_function`. Here is the code:

```
1   def factorial_function(n):
2       if n < 0:
3           return None
4       if n < 2:
5           return 1
6
7       product = 1
8       for i in range(2, n + 1):
9           product *= i
10      return product
11
12
13  for n in range(1, 6): # testing
14      print(n, factorial_function(n))
15
```

Notice how we mirror step-by-step the mathematical definition, and how we use the for loop to find the product. We add a simple testing code, and these are the results we get:

```
1 1
2 2
3 6
4 24
5 120
```

Fibonacci numbers

Are you familiar with Fibonacci numbers? They are a sequence of integer numbers built using a very simple rule. The first element of the sequence is equal to one (Fib_1 = 1). The second is also equal to one (Fib_2 = 1). Every subsequent number is the the_sum of the two preceding numbers: (Fib_i = Fib_{i-1} + Fib_{i-2}), Here are some of the first Fibonacci numbers:

```
fib_1 = 1
fib_2 = 1
fib_3 = 1 + 1 = 2
fib_4 = 1 + 2 = 3
fib_5 = 2 + 3 = 5
fib_6 = 3 + 5 = 8
fib_7 = 5 + 8 = 13
```

What do you think about implementing this as a function? Let's create our fib function and test it. Here it is:

```
 1  def fib(n):
 2      if n < 1:
 3          return None
 4      if n < 3:
 5          return 1
 6
 7      elem_1 = elem_2 = 1
 8      the_sum = 0
 9      for i in range(3, n + 1):
10          the_sum = elem_1 + elem_2
11          elem_1, elem_2 = elem_2, the_sum
12      return the_sum
13
14
15  for n in range(1, 10): # testing
16      print(n, "->", fib(n))
17
```

Analyze the `for` loop body carefully, and find out how we move the `elem_1` and `elem_2` variables through the subsequent Fibonacci numbers. The test part of the code produces the following output:

```
1 -> 1
2 -> 1
3 -> 2
4 -> 3
5 -> 5
6 -> 8
7 -> 13
8 -> 21
9 -> 34
```

Recursion

There's one more thing we want to show you to make everything complete — it's recursion. This term may describe many different concepts, but one of them is especially interesting — the one referring to computer programming. In this field, recursion is a technique where a function invokes itself. These two cases seem to be the best to illustrate the phenomenon – factorials and Fibonacci numbers. Especially the latter. The Fibonacci numbers definition is a clear example of recursion. We already told you that:

$Fib_i = Fib_{i-1} + Fib_{i-2}$

The definition of the ith number refers to the i-1 number, and so on, till you reach the first two. Can it be used in the code? Yes, it can. It can also make the code shorter and clearer. The second version of our fib() function makes direct use of this definition:

```
1   def fib(n):
2       if n < 1:
3           return None
4       if n < 3:
5           return 1
6       return fib(n - 1) + fib(n - 2)
7
```

The code is much clearer now. But is it really safe? Does it entail any risk? Yes, there is a little risk indeed. If you forget to consider the conditions which can stop the chain of recursive invocations, the program may enter an infinite loop. You have to be careful. The factorial has a second, recursive side too. Look:

```
n! = 1 × 2 × 3 × ... × n-1 × n
```

It's obvious that:

```
1 × 2 × 3 × ... × n-1 = (n-1)!
```

So, finally, the result is:

```
n! = (n-1)! × n
```

This is in fact a ready recipe for our new solution. Here it is. Does it work? Yes, it does. Try it for yourself.

```
1   def factorial_function(n):
2       if n < 0:
3           return None
4       if n < 2:
5           return 1
6       return n * factorial_function(n - 1)
7
```

Our short *functional* journey is almost over. The next chapter will take care of two curious Python data types: tuples and dictionaries.

```
1   def fib(n):
2       if n < 1:
3           return None
4       if n < 3:
5           return 1
6
7       elem_1 = elem_2 = 1
8       the_sum = 0
9       for i in range(3, n + 1):
10          the_sum = elem_1 + elem_2
11          elem_1, elem_2 = elem_2, the_sum
12      return the_sum
13
14
15  for n in range(1, 10):
16      print(n, "->", fib(n))
17
```

Summary

1. A function can call other functions, or even itself. When a function calls itself, this situation is known as recursion, and the function which calls itself and contains a specified termination condition (i.e. the base case — a condition which doesn't tell the function to make any further calls to that function) is called a recursive function.

2. You can use recursive functions in Python to write clean, elegant code, and divide it into smaller, organized chunks. On the other hand, you need to be very careful as it might be easy to make a mistake and create a function which never terminates. You also need to remember that recursive calls consume a lot of memory, and therefore may sometimes be inefficient. When using recursion, you need to take all its advantages and disadvantages into consideration. The factorial function is a classic example of how the concept of recursion can be put in practice:

```
1   # Recursive implementation of the factorial function.
2
3   def factorial(n):
4       if n == 1:  # The base case (termination condition.)
5           return 1
6       else:
7           return n * factorial(n - 1)
8
9
10  print(factorial(4))  # 4 * 3 * 2 * 1 = 24
11
```

Quiz

QUESTION 1: What will happen when you attempt to run the following snippet and why?

```
1   def factorial(n):
2       return n * factorial(n - 1)
3
4
5   print(factorial(4))
6
```

QUESTION 2: What is the output of the following snippet?

```
1   def fun(a):
2       if a > 30:
3           return 3
4       else:
5           return a + fun(a + 3)
6
7
8   print(fun(25))
9
```

TWENTY-TWO
TUPLES AND DICTIONARIES

Before we start talking about tuples and dictionaries, we have to introduce two important concepts: sequence types and mutability. A sequence type is a type of data in Python which is able to store more than one value. It can also store less than one, as a sequence may be empty, and these values can be browsed sequentially element by element, hence the name. As the `for` loop is a tool especially designed to iterate through sequences, we can express the definition as: a sequence is data which can be scanned by the `for` loop. You've encountered one Python sequence so far – the list. The list is a classic example of a Python sequence, although there are some other sequences worth mentioning, and we're going to present them to you now.

The second notion – mutability – is a property of any Python data that describes its readiness to be freely changed during program execution. There are two kinds of Python data: mutable and immutable. Mutable data can be freely updated at any time – we call such an operation in situ. Mutable data can be freely updated at any time – we call such an operation in situ. *In situ* is a Latin phrase that translates as literally *in position*. For example, the following instruction modifies the data in situ:

```
1    list.append(1)
2
```

Immutable data cannot be modified in this way. Imagine that a list can only be assigned and read over. You would be able neither to append an element to it, nor remove any element from it. This means that appending an element to the end of the list would require the recreation of the list from scratch. You would have to build a completely new list, consisting of the all elements of the already existing list, plus the new element. The data type we want to tell you about now is a tuple. A tuple is an immutable sequence type. It can behave like a list, but it can't be modified in situ.

Tuples

The first and the clearest distinction between lists and tuples is the syntax used to create them — tuples prefer to use parenthesis, whereas lists like to see brackets, although it's also possible to create a tuple just from a set of values separated by commas. Look at the example:

```
1   tuple_1 = (1, 2, 4, 8)
2   tuple_2 = 1., .5, .25, .125
3
```

There are two tuples, both containing four elements. Let's print them:

```
1   tuple_1 = (1, 2, 4, 8)
2   tuple_2 = 1., .5, .25, .125
3
4   print(tuple_1)
5   print(tuple_2)
6
```

This is what you should see in the console:

```
(1, 2, 4, 8)
(1.0, 0.5, 0.25, 0.125)
```

NOTE Each tuple element may be of a different type (floating-point, integer, or any other not-as-yet-introduced kind of data).

How to create a tuple

It is possible to create an empty tuple — parentheses are required then:

```
1   empty_tuple = ()
2
```

If you want to create a one-element tuple, you have to take into consideration the fact that, due to syntax reasons (a tuple has to be distinguishable from an ordinary, single value), you must end the value with a comma:

```
one_element_tuple_1 = (1, )
one_element_tuple_2 = 1.,
```

Removing the commas won't spoil the program in any syntactical sense, but you will instead get two single variables, not tuples.

How to use a tuple

If you want to get the elements of a tuple in order to read them over, you can use the same conventions to which you're accustomed while using lists. Take a look at the following code.

```
1    my_tuple = (1, 10, 100, 1000)
2
3    print(my_tuple[0])
4    print(my_tuple[-1])
5    print(my_tuple[1:])
6    print(my_tuple[:-2])
7
8    for elem in my_tuple:
9        print(elem)
10
```

The program should produce the following output – run it and check:

```
1
1000
(10, 100, 1000)
(1, 10)
1
10
100
1000
```

The similarities may be misleading – don't try to modify a tuple's contents! It's not a list! All of these instructions (except the topmost one) will cause a runtime error:

```
1    my_tuple = (1, 10, 100, 1000)
2
3    my_tuple.append(10000)
4    del my_tuple[0]
5    my_tuple[1] = -10
6
```

This is the message that Python will give you in the console window:

```
AttributeError: 'tuple' object has no attribute 'append'
```

What else can tuples do for you? The len() function accepts tuples, and returns the number of elements contained inside. The + operator can join tuples together. You've seen this already. The * operator can multiply tuples, just like lists. The in and not in operators work in the same way as in lists. The following snippet presents them all.

Tuples And Dictionaries   229

```
1   my_tuple = (1, 10, 100)
2
3   t1 = my_tuple + (1000, 10000)
4   t2 = my_tuple * 3
5
6   print(len(t2))
7   print(t1)
8   print(t2)
9   print(10 in my_tuple)
10  print(-10 not in my_tuple)
11
```

The output should look as follows:

```
9
(1, 10, 100, 1000, 10000)
(1, 10, 100, 1, 10, 100, 1, 10, 100)
True
True
```

One of the most useful tuple properties is their ability to appear on the left side of the assignment operator. You saw this phenomenon some time ago, when it was necessary to find an elegant tool to swap two variables' values. Take a look at the following snippet:

```
1   var = 123
2
3   t1 = (1, )
4   t2 = (2, )
5   t3 = (3, var)
6
7   t1, t2, t3 = t2, t3, t1
8
9   print(t1, t2, t3)
10
```

It shows three tuples interacting – in effect, the values stored in them "circulate" — t1 becomes t2, t2 becomes t3, and t3 becomes t1. Note: the example presents one more important fact: a tuple's elements can be variables, not only literals. Moreover, they can be expressions if they're on the right side of the assignment operator.

Dictionaries

The dictionary is another Python data structure. It's not a sequence type, but can be easily adapted to sequence processing, and it is mutable. To explain what the Python dictionary actually is, it is important to understand that it is literally a dictionary.

How to make a dictionary

If you want to assign some initial pairs to a dictionary, you should use the following syntax:

```
1  dictionary = {"cat": "chat", "dog": "chien", "horse": "cheval"}
2  phone_numbers = {'boss': 5551234567, 'Suzy': 22657854310}
3  empty_dictionary = {}
4
```

Tuples   **Dictionaries**

Figure 22.1

```
5  print(dictionary)
6  print(phone_numbers)
7  print(empty_dictionary)
8
```

In the first example, the dictionary uses keys and values which are both strings. In the second one, the keys are strings, but the values are integers. The reverse layout (keys ⇢ numbers, values ⇢ strings) is also possible, as well as number-number combinations. The list of pairs is surrounded by curly braces, while the pairs themselves are separated by commas, and the keys and values by colons.

The first of our dictionaries is a very simple English-French dictionary. The second — a very tiny telephone directory. The empty dictionary is constructed by an empty pair of curly braces — nothing unusual. The Python dictionary works in the same way as a bilingual dictionary. For example, you have an English word (e.g. cat) and need its French equivalent. You browse the dictionary in order to find the word. You may use different techniques to do that — it doesn't matter — and eventually you get it. Next, you check the French counterpart and it is the word "chat".

In Python's world, the word you look for is named a **key**. The word you get from the dictionary is called a **value**. This means that a dictionary is a set of key-value pairs. Note: each key must be unique — it's not possible to have more than one key of the same value; a key may be any immutable type of object, so it can be a number (integer or float), or even a string, but not a list; a dictionary is not a list because a list contains a set of numbered values, while a dictionary holds pairs of values; the `len()` function works for dictionaries, too — it returns the number of key-value elements in the dictionary; a dictionary is a one-way tool — if you have an English-French dictionary, you can look for French equivalents of English terms, but not vice versa.

Now we can show you some working examples. The dictionary as a whole can be printed with a single `print()` invocation. The snippet may produce the following output:

```
{'dog': 'chien', 'horse': 'cheval', 'cat': 'chat'}
{'Suzy': 5557654321, 'boss': 5551234567}
{}
```

Have you noticed anything surprising? The order of the printed pairs is different than in the initial assignment. What does that mean? First of all, it's a confirmation that dictionaries are not lists — they don't preserve the order of their data, as the order is completely meaningless (unlike in real, paper dictionaries). The order in which a dictionary stores its data is completely out of your control, and your expectations. That's normal.

NOTE In Python 3.6x dictionaries have become ordered collections by default. Your results may vary depending on what Python version you're using.

How to use a dictionary

Analyze the following code:

```
1  dictionary = {"cat": "chat", "dog": "chien", "horse":
   "cheval"}
2  phone_numbers = {'boss' : 5551234567, 'Suzy' : 22657854310}
3  empty_dictionary = {}
4
5  # Print the values here.
6
```

If you want to get any of the values, you have to deliver a valid key value:

```
1  print(dictionary['cat'])
2  print(phone_numbers['Suzy'])
3
```

Getting a dictionary's value resembles indexing, especially thanks to the brackets surrounding the key's value.

NOTE If the key is a string, you have to specify it as a string. Keys are case-sensitive: `'Suzy'` is something different from `'suzy'`.

The snippet outputs two lines of text:

```
chat
5557654321
```

And now the most important news: you mustn't use a non-existent key. Trying something like this will cause a runtime error. Try to do it:

```
print(phone_numbers['president'])
```

Fortunately, there's a simple way to avoid such a situation. The `in` operator, together with its companion, `not in`, can salvage this situation. The following code safely searches for some French words:

```
1  dictionary = {"cat": "chat", "dog": "chien", "horse": "cheval"}
2  words = ['cat', 'lion', 'horse']
3
4  for word in words:
5      if word in dictionary:
6          print(word, "->", dictionary[word])
7      else:
8          print(word, "is not in dictionary")
9
```

The code's output looks as follows:

```
cat -> chat
lion is not in dictionary
horse -> cheval
```

NOTE When you write a big or lengthy expression, it may be a good idea to keep it vertically aligned. This is how you can make your code more readable and more programmer-friendly, e.g.:

```
1   # Example 1:
2   dictionary = {
3                "cat": "chat",
4                "dog": "chien",
5                "horse": "cheval"
6   }
7   # Example 2:
8   phone_numbers = {'boss': 5551234567,
9                    'Suzy': 22657854310
10  }
11
```

This kind of formatting is called a hanging indent.

Dictionary methods and functions

The `keys()` method

Can dictionaries be browsed using the `for` loop, like lists or tuples? No and yes. No, because a dictionary is not a sequence type – the `for` loop is useless with it. Yes, because there are simple and very effective tools that can adapt any dictionary to the `for` loop requirements, in other words, building an intermediate link between the dictionary and a temporary sequence entity. The first of them is a method named `keys()`, possessed by each dictionary. The method returns an iterable object consisting of all the keys gathered within the dictionary. Having a group of keys enables you to access the whole dictionary in an easy and handy way. Just like here:

```
1  dictionary = {"cat": "chat", "dog": "chien", "horse": "cheval"}
2
3  for key in dictionary.keys():
4      print(key, "->", dictionary[key])
5
```

Let's now have a look at a dictionary method called `items()`. The method returns tuples where each tuple is a key-value pair. This is the first example where tuples are something more than just an example of themselves. This is how it works. Note the way in which the tuple has been used as a `for` loop variable:

```
1  dictionary = {"cat": "chat", "dog": "chien", "horse": "cheval"}
2
3  for english, french in dictionary.items():
4      print(english, "->", french)
5
```

Modifying and adding values

Assigning a new value to an existing key is simple – as dictionaries are fully mutable, there are no obstacles to modifying them. We're going to replace the value `"chat"` with `"minou"`, which is not very accurate, but it will work well with our example. Look:

```
1  dictionary = {"cat": "chat", "dog": "chien", "horse": "cheval"}
2
3  dictionary['cat'] = 'minou'
4  print(dictionary)
5
```

The code's output looks as follows:

```
horse -> cheval
dog -> chien
cat -> chat
```

The example prints:

```
cat -> chat
dog -> chien
horse -> cheval
```

The output is:

```
{'cat': 'minou', 'dog': 'chien', 'horse': 'cheval'}
```

Do you want it sorted? Just enrich the `for` loop to get such a form:

```
1  for key in sorted(dictionary.keys()):
2
```

The `sorted()` function will do its best — the output will look like this:

```
cat -> chat
dog -> chien
horse -> cheval
```

How to use a dictionary: the `items()` and `values()` methods

Another way is based on using a dictionary's method named `items()`. The method returns tuples where each tuple is a key-value pair. This is the first example where tuples are something more than just an example of themselves. This is how it works:

```
1  dictionary = {"cat": "chat", "dog": "chien", "horse": "cheval"}
2
3  for english, french in dictionary.items():
4      print(english, "->", french)
5
```

Note the way in which the tuple has been used as a `for` loop variable. The example prints:

```
cat -> chat
dog -> chien
horse -> cheval
```

There is also a method called `values()`, which works similarly to `keys()`, but returns values. Here is a simple example:

```
1  dictionary = {"cat": "chat", "dog": "chien", "horse": "cheval"}
2
3  for french in dictionary.values():
4      print(french)
5
```

Tuples And Dictionaries   235

As the dictionary is not able to automatically find a key for a given value, the role of this method is rather limited. Here is the expected output:

```
cheval
chien
chat
```

How to use a dictionary: modifying and adding values

Assigning a new value to an existing key is simple — as dictionaries are fully mutable, there are no obstacles to modifying them. We're going to replace the value `"chat"` with `"minou"`, which is not very accurate, but will work well with our example. Look:

```
1   dictionary = {"cat": "chat", "dog": "chien", "horse":
    "cheval"}
2
3   dictionary['cat'] = 'minou'
4   print(dictionary)
5
```

The output is:

```
{'cat': 'minou', 'dog': 'chien', 'horse': 'cheval'}
```

Adding a new key

Adding a new key-value pair to a dictionary is as simple as changing a value — you only have to assign a value to a new, previously non-existent key. Note that this is very different behavior compared to lists, which don't allow you to assign values to non-existing indices. Let's add a new pair of words to the dictionary – a bit weird, but still valid:

```
1   dictionary = {"cat": "chat", "dog": "chien", "horse":
    "cheval"}
2
3   dictionary['swan'] = 'cygne'
4   print(dictionary)
5
```

The example outputs:

```
{'cat': 'chat', 'dog': 'chien', 'horse': 'cheval', 'swan':
'cygne'}
```

> **NOTE** You can also insert an item to a dictionary by using the `update()` method, e.g.:

```
1    dictionary = {"cat": "chat", "dog": "chien", "horse":
     "cheval"}
2
3    dictionary.update({"duck": "canard"})
4    print(dictionary)
5
```

Removing a key

Can you guess how to remove a key from a dictionary? Note that removing a key will always cause the removal of the associated value. Values cannot exist without their keys. This is done with the `del` instruction. Here's the example:

```
1    dictionary = {"cat": "chat", "dog": "chien", "horse":
     "cheval"}
2
3    del dictionary['dog']
4    print(dictionary)
5
```

> **NOTE** Removing a non-existing key causes an error.

The example outputs:

```
{'cat': 'chat', 'horse': 'cheval'}
```

> **EXTRA** To remove the last item in a dictionary, you can use the `popitem()` method:

```
1    dictionary = {"cat": "chat", "dog": "chien", "horse":
     "cheval"}
2
3    dictionary.popitem()
4    print(dictionary) # outputs: {'cat': 'chat', 'dog':
     'chien'}
5
```

In the older versions of Python, i.e. before 3.6.7, the `popitem()` method removes a random item from a dictionary.

Tuples and dictionaries can work together

We've prepared a simple example, showing how tuples and dictionaries can work together. Let's imagine the following problem. You need a program to evaluate the students' average scores. The program should ask for the student's name, followed by her/his single score. The names may be entered in any order and entering an empty name finishes the inputting of the data. Note that entering an empty score will raise the `ValueError` exception, but don't worry about that now. You'll see how to handle such cases when we talk about exceptions in the second part of the *Python Essentials* series. Finally, a list of all names, together with the evaluated average score, should be then emitted. Look at the following code. This how to do it.

```python
school_class = {}

while True:
    name = input("Enter the student's name: ")
    if name == '':
        break

    score = int(input("Enter the student's score (0-10): "))
    if score not in range(0, 11):
        break

    if name in school_class:
        school_class[name] += (score,)
    else:
        school_class[name] = (score,)

for name in sorted(school_class.keys()):
    adding = 0
    counter = 0
    for score in school_class[name]:
        adding += score
        counter += 1
    print(name, ":", adding / counter)
```

Now, let's analyze it line by line:

- line 1: create an empty dictionary for the input data; the student's name is used as a key, while all the associated scores are stored in a tuple (the tuple may be a dictionary value – that's not a problem at all)
- line 3: enter an "infinite" loop (don't worry, it'll break at the right moment)
- line 4: read the student's name here;
- line 5-6: if the name is an empty string (), leave the loop;
- line 8: ask for one of the student's scores (an integer from the range 0-10)
- line 9-10: if the score entered is not within the range from 0 to 10, leave the loop;
- line 12-13: if the student's name is already in the dictionary, lengthen the associated tuple with the new score (note the += operator)
- line 14-15: if this is a new student (unknown to the dictionary), create a new entry – its value is a one-element tuple containing the entered score;
- line 17: iterate through the sorted students' names;

- line 18-19: initialize the data needed to evaluate the average (sum and counter)
- line 20-22: we iterate through the tuple, taking all the subsequent scores and updating the sum, together with the counter;
- line 23: evaluate and print the student's name and average score.

This is a record of the conversation we had with our program:

```
Enter the student's name: Bob
Enter the student's score (0-10): 7
Enter the student's name: Andy
Enter the student's score (0-10): 3
Enter the student's name: Bob
Enter the student's score (0-10): 2
Enter the student's name: Andy
Enter the student's score (0-10): 10
Enter the student's name: Andy
Enter the student's score (0-10): 3
Enter the student's name: Bob
Enter the student's score (0-10): 9
Enter the student's name:
Andy : 5.333333333333333
Bob : 6.0
```

Summary

Key takeaways: tuples

1. Tuples are ordered and unchangeable (immutable) collections of data. They can be thought of as immutable lists. They are written in round brackets:

```
1  my_tuple = (1, 2, True, "a string", (3, 4), [5, 6], None)
2  print(my_tuple)
3
4  my_list = [1, 2, True, "a string", (3, 4), [5, 6], None]
5  print(my_list)
6
```

- Each tuple element may be of a different type (i.e. integers, strings, booleans, etc.). What is more, tuples can contain other tuples or lists, and the other way round.

2. You can create an empty tuple like this:

```
1  empty_tuple = ()
2  print(type(empty_tuple))  # outputs: <class 'tuple'=""></class>
3
```

3. A one-element tuple may be created as follows:

```
1  one_elem_tuple_1 = ("one", ) # Brackets and a comma.
2  one_elem_tuple_2 = "one",    # No brackets, just a comma.
3
```

- If you remove the comma, you will tell Python to create a variable, not a tuple:

```
1  my_tuple_1 = 1,
2  print(type(my_tuple_1)) # outputs: <class 'tuple'=""></class>
3
4  my_tuple_2 = 1 # This is not a tuple.
5  print(type(my_tuple_2)) # outputs: <class 'int'=""></class>
6
```

4. You can access tuple elements by indexing them:

```
1  my_tuple = (1, 2.0, "string", [3, 4], (5, ), True)
2  print(my_tuple[3]) # outputs: [3, 4]
3
```

5. Tuples are immutable, which means you cannot change their elements (you cannot append tuples, or modify, or remove tuple elements). The following snippet will cause an exception:

```
1  my_tuple = (1, 2.0, "string", [3, 4], (5, ), True)
2  my_tuple[2] = "guitar" # The TypeError exception will be raised.
3
```

- However, you can delete a tuple as a whole:

```
1  my_tuple = 1, 2, 3,
2  del my_tuple
3  print(my_tuple) # NameError: name 'my_tuple' is not defined
4
```

6. You can loop through a tuple elements (Example 1), check if a specific element is (not)present in a tuple (Example 2), use the `len()` function to check how many elements there are in a tuple (Example 3), or even join/multiply tuples (Example 4):

```
1  # Example 1
2  tuple_1 = (1, 2, 3)
3  for elem in tuple_1:
4      print(elem)
5
6  # Example 2
7  tuple_2 = (1, 2, 3, 4)
8  print(5 in tuple_2)
```

```
9    print(5 not in tuple_2)
10
11   # Example 3
12   tuple_2 = (1, 2, 3, 4)
13   print(len(tuple_3))
14   print(5 not in tuple_2)
15
16   # Example 4
17   tuple_4 = tuple_1 + tuple_2
18   tuple_5 = tuple_3 * 2
19
20   print(tuple_4)
21   print(tuple_5)
22
```

EXTRA You can also create a tuple using a Python built-in function called `tuple()`. This is particularly useful when you want to convert a certain iterable (e.g. a list, range, string, etc.) to a tuple:

```
1    my_tuple = tuple((1, 2, "string"))
2    print(my_tuple)
3
4    my_list = [2, 4, 6]
5    print(my_list) # outputs: [2, 4, 6]
6    print(type(my_list)) # outputs: <class 'list'=""></class>
7    tup = tuple(my_list)
8    print(tup) # outputs: (2, 4, 6)
9    print(type(tup)) # outputs: <class 'tuple'=""></class>
10
```

By the same fashion, when you want to convert an iterable to a list, you can use a Python built-in function called `list()`:

```
1    tup = 1, 2, 3,
2    my_list = list(tup)
3    print(type(my_list)) # outputs: <class 'list'=""></class>
4
```

Key takeaways: dictionaries

1. Dictionaries are unordered*, changeable (mutable), and indexed collections of data. (*Since Python 3.6x dictionaries have become ordered by default.)

- Each dictionary is a set of *key: value* pairs. You can create it by using the following syntax:

```
1    my_dictionary = {
2        key1: value1,
3        key2: value2,
4        key3: value3,
5    }
6
```

Tuples And Dictionaries   241

2. If you want to access a dictionary item, you can do so by making a reference to its key inside a pair of square brackets (ex. 1) or by using the `get()` method (ex. 2):

```
1   pol_eng_dictionary = {
2       "kwiat": "flower",
3       "woda": "water",
4       "gleba": "soil"
5   }
6
7   item_1 = pol_eng_dictionary["gleba"] # ex. 1
8   print(item_1) # outputs: soil
9
10  item_2 = pol_eng_dictionary.get("woda") # ex. 2
11  print(item_2) # outputs: water
12
```

3. If you want to change the value associated with a specific key, you can do so by referring to the item's key name in the following way:

```
1   pol_eng_dictionary = {
2       "zamek": "castle",
3       "woda": "water",
4       "gleba": "soil"
5   }
6
7   pol_eng_dictionary["zamek"] = "lock"
8   item = pol_eng_dictionary["zamek"]
9   print(item) # outputs: lock
10
```

4. To add or remove a key (and the associated value), use the following syntax:

```
1   phonebook = {} # an empty dictionary
2
3   phonebook["Adam"] = 3456783958 # create/add a key-value pair
4   print(phonebook) # outputs: {'Adam': 3456783958}
5
6   del phonebook["Adam"]
7   print(phonebook) # outputs: {}
8
```

- You can also insert an item into a dictionary by using the `update()` method, and remove the last element by using the `popitem()` method, e.g.:

242   Chapter 22

```
1    pol_eng_dictionary = {"kwiat": "flower"}
2
3    pol_eng_dictionary.update({"gleba": "soil"})
4    print(pol_eng_dictionary) # outputs: {'kwiat': 'flower',
     'gleba': 'soil'}
5
6    pol_eng_dictionary.popitem()
7    print(pol_eng_dictionary) # outputs: {'kwiat': 'flower'}
8
```

5. You can use the `for` loop to loop through a dictionary, e.g.:

```
1    pol_eng_dictionary = {
2        "zamek": "castle",
3        "woda": "water",
4        "gleba": "soil"
5    }
6
7    for item in pol_eng_dictionary:
8        print(item)
9
10   #         woda
11   #         gleba
12
```

6. If you want to loop through a dictionary's keys and values, you can use the `items()` method, e.g.:

```
1    pol_eng_dictionary = {
2        "zamek": "castle",
3        "woda": "water",
4        "gleba": "soil"
5    }
6
7    for key, value in pol_eng_dictionary.items():
8        print("Pol/Eng ->", key, ":", value)
9
```

7. To check if a given key exists in a dictionary, you can use the `in` keyword:

```
1    pol_eng_dictionary = {
2        "zamek": "castle",
3        "woda": "water",
4        "gleba": "soil"
5    }
6
7    if "zamek" in pol_eng_dictionary:
8        print("Yes")
9    else:
10       print("No")
11
```

Tuples And Dictionaries   243

8. You can use the `del` keyword to remove a specific item, or delete a dictionary. To remove all the dictionary's items, you need to use the `clear()` method:

```
1  pol_eng_dictionary = {
2      "zamek": "castle",
3      "woda": "water",
4      "gleba": "soil"
5  }
6
7  print(len(pol_eng_dictionary)) # outputs: 3
8  del pol_eng_dictionary["zamek"] # remove an item
9  print(len(pol_eng_dictionary)) # outputs: 2
10
11 pol_eng_dictionary.clear() # removes all the items
12 print(len(pol_eng_dictionary)) # outputs: 0
13
14 del pol_eng_dictionary # removes the dictionary
15
```

9. To copy a dictionary, use the `copy()` method:

```
1  pol_eng_dictionary = {
2      "zamek": "castle",
3      "woda": "water",
4      "gleba": "soil"
5  }
6
7  copy_dictionary = pol_eng_dictionary.copy()
8
```

Quiz

QUESTION 1: What happens when you attempt to run the following snippet?

```
1   my_tup = (1, 2, 3)
2   print(my_tup[2])
3
```

QUESTION 2: What is the output of the following snippet?

```
1   tup = 1, 2, 3
2   a, b, c = tup
3
4   print(a * b * c)
5
```

QUESTION 3: Complete the code to correctly use the count() method to find the number of duplicates of 2 in the following tuple.

```
1   tup = 1, 2, 3, 2, 4, 5, 6, 2, 7, 2, 8, 9
2   duplicates = # Write your code here.
3
4   print(duplicates) # outputs: 4
5
```

QUESTION 4: Write a program that will "glue" the two dictionaries (d1 and d2) together and create a new one (d3).

```
1   d1 = {'Adam Smith': 'A', 'Judy Paxton': 'B+'}
2   d2 = {'Mary Louis': 'A', 'Patrick White': 'C'}
3   d3 = {}
4
5   for item in (d1, d2):
6       # Write your code here.
7
8   print(d3)
9
```

QUESTION 5: Write a program that will convert the my_list list to a tuple.

```
1   my_list = ["car", "Ford", "flower", "Tulip"]
2
3   t = # Write your code here.
4   print(t)
5
```

Tuples And Dictionaries   245

QUESTION 6: Write a program that will convert the colors tuple to a dictionary.

```
1   colors = (("green", "#008000"), ("blue", "#0000FF"))
2
3   # Write your code here.
4
5   print(colors_dictionary)
6
```

QUESTION 7: What will happen when you run the following code?

```
1   my_dictionary = {"A": 1, "B": 2}
2   copy_my_dictionary = my_dictionary.copy()
3   my_dictionary.clear()
4
5   print(copy_my_dictionary)
6
```

QUESTION 8: What is the output of the following program?

```
1    colors = {
2        "white": (255, 255, 255),
3        "grey": (128, 128, 128),
4        "red": (255, 0, 0),
5        "green": (0, 128, 0)
6    }
7
8    for col, rgb in colors.items():
9        print(col, ":", rgb)
10
```

TWENTY-THREE
EXCEPTIONS

It seems indisputable that all programmers, including you, want to write error-free code and do their best to achieve this goal. Unfortunately, nothing is perfect in this world and software is no exception. Pay attention to the word exception as we'll see it again very soon in a meaning that has nothing in common with the absolute. To err is human. It's impossible to make no mistakes, and it's impossible to write error-free code. Don't get us wrong — we don't want to convince you that writing messy and faulty programs is a virtue. We rather want to explain that even the most careful programmer is not able to avoid minor or major defects. It's only those who do nothing that make no mistakes.

Paradoxically, accepting this difficult truth can make you a better programmer and may improve your code quality. "How could this be possible?", you may ask. We'll try to show you.

Figure 23.1

Errors in data vs. errors in code

Dealing with programming errors has at least two sides. The one appears when you get into trouble because your — apparently correct — code is fed with bad data. For example, you expect the code will input an integer value, but your careless user enters some random letters instead. It may happen that your code will be terminated then, and the user will be left alone with a terse and ambiguous error message on the screen. The user will be unsatisfied, and you should be unsatisfied, too.

We're going to show you how to protect your code from this kind of failure and how not to provoke the user's anger.

The other side of dealing with programming errors reveals itself when undesirable code behavior is caused by mistakes you made when you were writing your program. This kind of error is commonly called a "bug", which is a manifestation of a well-established belief that if a program works badly, it must be caused by malicious bugs which live inside the computer hardware and cause short circuits or other interference. This idea is not as mad as it may look — such incidents were common in times when computers occupied large halls, consumed kilowatts of electricity, and produced enormous amounts of heat. Fortunately or not, these times are gone forever and the only bugs which can spoil your code are those you sowed in the code yourself. Therefore, we will try to show you how to find and eliminate your bugs, in other words, how to debug your code. Let's start the journey through the land of errors and bugs.

When data is not what it should be

Let's write a piece of extremely trivial code — it will read a natural number (a non-negative integer) and print its reciprocal. In this way, 2 will turn into `0.5` (½) and 4 into `0.25` (¼). Here's the program:

```
1    value = int(input('Enter a natural number: '))
2    print('The reciprocal of', value, 'is', 1/value)
3
```

Is there anything that can go wrong with it? The code is so brief and so compact that it doesn't seem like we'll find any trouble there. It seems that you already know where we are going. Yes, you're right — entering data that is not an integer — which also includes entering nothing at all- will completely ruin the program execution. This is what the code's user will see:

```
Traceback (most recent call last):
    File "code.py", line 1, in <module></module>
        value = int(input('Enter a natural number: '))
ValueError: invalid literal for int() with base 10: ''
```

All the lines Python shows you are meaningful and important, but the last line seems to be the most valuable. The first word in the line is the name of the exception which causes your code to stop. It's `ValueError` here. The rest of the line is just a brief explanation which more precisely specifies the cause of the occurred exception. How do you deal with it? How do you protect your code from termination, the user from disappointment, and yourself from the user's dissatisfaction? The very first thought that can come to your mind is to check if the data provided by the user is valid and to refuse to cooperate if the data is incorrect. In this case, the check can rely on the fact that we expect the input string to contain digits only. You should already be able to implement this check and write it yourself, shouldn't you? It is also possible to check if the `value` variable's type is an `int` Python has a special means for these kinds of checks — it's an operator named `is`. The check itself may look like this, and evaluates to `true` if the current value variable's type is `int`:

```
1    type(value) is int
2
```

Please forgive us if we don't spend any more time on it now — you will find more detailed explanations of the `is` operator in the book *Python Essentials 2*, in the part devoted to Object-Oriented Programming. You may be surprised to learn that we don't want you to do any preliminary data validation. Why? Because this is not the way Python recommends. Really.

The try-except branch

In the Python world, there is a rule that says: "It's better to beg for forgiveness than to ask for permission". Let's stop here for a moment. Don't get us wrong — we don't want you to apply the rule in your everyday life. Don't take anyone's car without permission in the hope that you can be so convincing that you will avoid conviction. The rule is about something else. Actually, the rule reads: "it's better to handle an error when it happens than to try to avoid it".

"Okay," you may say now, "but how should I beg for forgiveness when the program is terminated and there is nothing left that can be done?" This is where the exception comes on the scene. Look at the following code:

```
1    try:
2    # It's a place where
3    # you can do something
4        # without asking for permission.
5    except:
6    # It's a spot dedicated to
7        # solemnly begging for forgiveness.
8
```

You can see two branches here. The first starts with the `try` keyword — this is the place where you put the code you suspect is risky and may be terminated in case of error; note: this kind of error is called an exception, while the exception occurrence is called raising — we can say that an exception is, or was, raised. The second is the part of the code starting with the `except` keyword, which is designed to handle the exception; it's up to you what you want to do here: you can clean up the mess or you can just sweep the problem under the carpet, although we would prefer the first solution.

So, we could say that these two blocks work like this: the `try` keyword marks the place where you try to do something without permission; while the `except` keyword starts a location where you can show off your apology talents. As you can see, this approach accepts errors and treats them as a normal part of the program's life, instead of escalating efforts to avoid errors at all.

The exception proves the rule

Let's rewrite the code to adopt the Python approach to life:

```
1   try:
2       value = int(input('Enter a natural number: '))
3       print('The reciprocal of', value, 'is', 1/value)
4   except:
5       print('I do not know what to do.')
6
```

Let us summarize what we talked about: any part of the code placed between `try` and `except` is executed in a very special way – any error which occurs here won't terminate program execution. Instead, the control will immediately jump to the first line situated after the `except` keyword, and no other part of the `try` branch is executed. The code in the except branch is activated only when an exception has been encountered inside the `try` block. There is no way to get there by any other means. When either the `try` block or the `except` block is executed successfully, the control returns to the normal path of execution, and any code located beyond in the source file is executed as if nothing happened.

Now we want to ask you an innocent question: is `ValueError` the only way the control could fall into the `except` branch? Analyze the code carefully and think over your answer!

How to deal with more than one exception

The answer is obviously "no" — there is more than one possible way to raise an exception. For example, a user may enter zero as an input — can you predict what will happen next? Yes, you're right — the division placed inside the `print()` function invocation will raise the `ZeroDivisionError`. As you may expect, the code's behavior will be the same as in the previous case — the user will see the *"I do not know what to do..."* message, which seems to be quite reasonable in this context, but it's also possible that you would want to handle this kind of problem in a bit different way. Is it possible? Of course, it is. There are at least two approaches you can implement here.

The first of them is simple and complicated at the same time: you can just add two separate try blocks, one including the `input()` function invocation where the `ValueError` may be raised, and the second devoted to handling possible issues induced by the division. Both these try blocks would have their own `except` branches, and in effect you will gain full control over two different errors.

This solution is good, but it is a bit lengthy — the code becomes unnecessarily bloated. Moreover, it's not the only danger that awaits you. Note that leaving the first `try-except` block leaves a lot of uncertainty — you will have to add extra code to ensure that the value the user has entered is safe to use in division. This is how a seemingly simple solution becomes overly complicated. Fortunately, Python offers a simpler way to deal with this kind of challenge.

Two exceptions after one `try`

Look at the following code. As you can see, we've just introduced the second `except` branch. This is not the only difference — note that both branches have exception names specified. In this variant, each of the expected exceptions has its own way of handling the error, but it must be emphasized that only one of all branches can intercept the control — if one of the branches is executed, all the other branches remain idle.

```
1   try:
2       value = int(input('Enter a natural number: '))
3       print('The reciprocal of', value, 'is', 1/value)
4   except ValueError:
5       print('I do not know what to do.')
6   except ZeroDivisionError:
7       print('Division by zero is not allowed in our Universe.')
8
```

Additionally, the number of `except` branches is not limited — you can specify as many or as few of them as you need, but don't forget that none of the exceptions can be specified more than once. But this still isn't the last Python word on exceptions. Stay tuned.

The default exception and how to use it

The code has changed again — can you see the difference?

```
1   try:
2       value = int(input('Enter a natural number: '))
3       print('The reciprocal of', value, 'is', 1/value)
4   except ValueError:
5       print('I do not know what to do.')
6   except ZeroDivisionError:
7       print('Division by zero is not allowed in our Universe.')
8   except:
9       print('Something strange has happened here... Sorry!')
10
```

We've added a third `except` branch, but this time it has no exception name specified — we can say it's anonymous, or it's the default, which is closer to its actual role. You can expect that when an exception is raised and there is no `except` branch dedicated to this exception, it will be handled by the default branch.

> **NOTE** The default `except` branch must be the last `except` branch. Always!

Some useful exceptions

Let's discuss in more detail some useful, or rather, the most common, exceptions you may experience.

`ZeroDivisionError`

This appears when you try to force Python to perform any operation which provokes division in which the divider is zero, or is indistinguishable from zero. Note that there is more than one Python operator which may cause this exception to raise. Can you guess them all? Yes, they are: `/`, `//`, and `%`.

`ValueError`

Expect this exception when you're dealing with values which may be inappropriately used in some context. In general, this exception is raised when a function (like `int()` or `float()`) receives an argument of a proper type, but its value is unacceptable.

`TypeError`

This exception shows up when you try to apply a data whose type cannot be accepted in the current context. Look at the example:

```
1  short_list = [1]
2  one_value = short_list[0.5]
3
```

You're not allowed to use a float value as a list index (the same rule applies to tuples, too). `TypeError` is an adequate name to describe the problem, and an adequate exception to raise.

`AttributeError`

This exception arrives — among other occasions — when you try to activate a method which doesn't exist in an item you're dealing with. For example:

```
1  short_list = [1]
2  short_list.append(2)
3  short_list.depend(3)
4
```

The third line of our example attempts to make use of a method which isn't contained in the lists. This is the place where `AttributeError` is raised.

SyntaxError

This exception is raised when the control reaches a line of code which violates Python's grammar. It may sound strange, but some errors of this kind cannot be identified without first running the code. This kind of behavior is typical of interpreted languages — the interpreter always works in a hurry and has no time to scan the whole source code. It is content with checking the code which is currently being run. An example of such a category of issues will be presented very soon. It's a bad idea to handle this exception in your programs. You should produce code that is free of syntax errors, instead of masking the faults you've caused.

Why you can't avoid testing your code

Although we're going to wrap up our *exceptional* considerations here, don't think it's all Python can offer to help you with begging for forgiveness. Python's exception machinery is far more complex, and its capabilities allow you to build expanded error handling strategies. We'll return to these issues — we promise. Feel free to conduct your experiments and to dive into exceptions yourself.

Now we want to tell you about the second side of the never-ending struggle with errors — the inevitable destiny of a developer's life. As you are not able to avoid making bugs in your code, you must always be ready to seek out and destroy them. Don't bury your head in the sand — ignoring errors won't make them disappear. An important duty for developers is to test the newly created code, but you must not forget that testing isn't a way to prove that the code is error-free. Paradoxically, the only proof testing can provide is that your code contains errors. Don't think you can relax after a successful test.

The second important aspect of software testing is strictly psychological. It's a truth known for years that authors — even those who are reliable and self-aware — aren't able to objectively evaluate and verify their works. This is why each novelist needs an editor and each programmer needs a tester. Some say — a little spitefully but truthfully — that developers test the code to show their perfection, not to find problems that may frustrate them. Testers are free of such dilemmas, and this is why their work is more effective and profitable.

Of course, this doesn't absolve you from being attentive and careful. Test your code as best you can. Don't make the testers' work too easy. Your primary duty is to ensure that you've checked all execution paths your code can go through. Does that sound mysterious? Nothing of the kind!

Tracing the execution paths

Now look at the following code. Suppose you've just finished writing it.

```
1    temperature = float(input('Enter current temperature:'))
2
3    if temperature > 0:
4        print("Above zero")
5    elif temperature < 0:
6        print("Below zero")
7    else:
8        print("Zero")
9
```

There are three independent execution paths in the code — can you see them? They are determined by the `if-elif-else` statements. Of course, the execution paths can be built by many other statements, like loops, or even `try-except` blocks. If you're going to test your code fairly and you want to sleep soundly and to dream without nightmares (nightmares about bugs can be devastating for a developer's performance) you are obliged to prepare a test data set that will force your code to negotiate all possible paths. In our example, the set should contain at least three float values: one positive, one negative, and zero.

When Python closes its eyes

Such a test is crucial. We want to show you why you mustn't skip it. Look at the following code.

```
1    temperature = float(input('Enter current temperature:'))
2
3    if temperature > 0:
4        print("Above zero")
5    elif temperature < 0:
6        prin("Below zero")
7    else:
8        print("Zero")
9
```

We intentionally introduced an error into the code — we hope your watchful eyes noticed it immediately. Yes, we removed just one letter and in effect, the valid `print()` function invocation turns into the obviously invalid clause `prin()`. There is no such function as `prin()` in our program's scope, but is it really obvious for Python?

Run the code and enter `0`. As you can see, the code finishes its execution without any obstacles. How is that possible? Why does Python overlook such an evident developer mistake? Can you find the answers to these fundamental questions?

Tests, testing, and testers

The answer is simpler than you may expect, and a bit disappointing, too. Python — as you know for sure — is an interpreted language. This means that the source code is parsed and executed at the same time. Consequently, Python may not have time to analyze the code lines which aren't subject to execution. As an old developer's saying states: *"it's a feature, not a bug"*. Please don't use this phrase to justify your code's weird behavior.

Do you understand now why passing through all execution paths is so vital and inevitable? Let's assume that you complete your code and the tests you've made are successful. You deliver your code to the testers and — fortunately! — they found some bugs in it. We're using the word *"fortunately"* completely consciously. You need to accept that, firstly, testers are the developer's best friends — don't treat the bugs they discover as an offense or a malignancy; and, secondly, each bug the testers find is a bug that won't affect the users. Both factors are valuable and worth your attention. You already know that your code contains a bug or bugs — the latter is more likely. How do you locate them and how do you fix your code?

Bug vs. debug

The basic measure a developer can use against bugs is — unsurprisingly — a debugger, while the process during which bugs are removed from the code is called debugging. According to an old joke, debugging is a complicated mystery game in which you are simultaneously the murderer, the detective, and — the most painful part of the intrigue — the victim. Are you ready to play all these roles? Then you must arm yourself with a debugger.

A debugger is a specialized piece of software that can control how your program is executed. Using the debugger, you can execute your code line-by-line, inspect all the variables' states and change their values on demand without modifying the source code, stop program execution when certain conditions are or aren't met, and do lots of other useful tasks.

We can say that every IDE is equipped with a more or less advanced debugger. Even IDLE has one, although you may find its handling a bit complicated and troublesome. If you want to make use of IDLE's integrated debugger, you should activate it using the "Debug" entry in the main IDLE window menu bar. It's the start point for all debugger facilities.

You can see how the debugger visualizes variables and parameter values, and note the call stack which shows the chain of invocations leading from the currently executed function to the interpreter level. If you want to know more about the IDLE debugger, consult the IDLE documentation.

`print` debugging

This form of debugging, which can be applied to your code using any kind of debugger, is sometimes called interactive debugging. The meaning of the term is self-explanatory — the process needs your, that is, the developer's, interaction to be performed. Some other debugging techniques can be used to hunt bugs. It's possible that you aren't able or don't want to use a debugger. The reasons may vary. Are you helpless then? Absolutely not!

You may use one of the simplest and the oldest, but still useful, debugging tactics known as print debugging. The name speaks for itself — you just insert several additional `print()` invocations inside your code to output data which illustrates the path your code is currently negotiating. You can output the values of the variables which may affect the execution. These printouts may output meaningful text like *"I am here"*, *"I entered the `foo()` function"*, *"The result is 0"*, or they may contain sequences of characters that are legible only to you. Please don't use obscene or indecent words for the purpose, even though you may feel a strong temptation — your reputation can be ruined in a moment if these antics leak to the public.

As you can see, this kind of debugging isn't really interactive at all, or is interactive only to a small extent, when you decide to apply the `input()` function to stop or delay code execution. After the bugs are found and removed, the additional printouts may be commented out or removed — it's up to you. Don't let them be executed in the final code — they may confuse both testers and users, and bring bad karma down upon you.

Some useful tips

Here are some tips which may help you to find and eliminate the bugs. None of them is either ultimate or definitive. Use them flexibly and rely on your intuition. Don't believe yourself — check everything twice. Try to tell someone, for example, your friend or coworker, what your code is expected to do and how it actually behaves. Be concrete and don't omit details. Answer all questions your helper asks. You'll likely realize the cause of the problem while telling your story, as speaking activates these parts of your brain which remain idle during coding. If no human can help you with the problem, use a yellow rubber duck instead. We're not kidding — consult the Wikipedia article to learn more about this commonly used technique called Rubber Duck Debugging.

Try to isolate the problem. You can extract the part of your code that is suspected of being responsible for your troubles and run it separately. You can comment out parts of the code that obscure the problem. Assign concrete values to variables instead of reading them from the input. Test your functions by applying predictable argument values. Analyze the code carefully. Read it aloud.

If the bug has appeared recently and didn't show up earlier, analyze all the changes you've introduced into your code — one of them may be the reason. Take a break, drink a cup of coffee, take your dog and go for a walk, read a good book for a moment or two, make a phone call to your best friend — you'll be surprised how often it helps. Be optimistic — you'll find the bug eventually; we promise you this.

Unit testing – a higher level of coding

There is also one important and widely used programming technique that you will have to adopt sooner or later during your developer career — it's called unit testing. The name may a bit confusing, as it's not only about testing the software, but also, and most of all, about how the code is written.

To make a long story short — unit testing assumes that tests are inseparable parts of the code and preparing the test data is an inseparable part of coding. This means that when you write a function or a set of cooperating functions, you're also obliged to create a set of data for which your code's behavior is predictable and known. Moreover, you should equip your code with an interface that can be used by an automated testing environment. In this approach, any amendment made to the code (even the least significant) should be followed by the execution of all the unit tests accompanied by your source.

To standardize this approach and make it easier to apply, Python provides a dedicated module named **unittest**. We're not going to discuss it here — it's a broad and complex topic. Therefore, we've prepared a separate course and certification path for this subject. It is called "Testing Essentials with Python", and we invite you to participate in it.

Summary

1. In Python, there is a distinction between two kinds of errors:

- syntax errors (parsing errors), which occur when the parser comes across a statement that is incorrect. For example:

Try to execute the following line:

```
1   print("Hello, World!)
2
```

It will cause a **SyntaxError**, and result in the following (or similar) message being displayed in the console: Pay attention to the arrow — it indicates the place where the Python parser has run into trouble. In our case, it's the missing double quote. Did you notice it?

```
File "main.py", line 1

    print("Hello, World!)
                        ^
SyntaxError: EOL while scanning string literal
```

Exceptions, which occur even when a statement/expression is syntactically correct; these are the errors that are detected during execution when your code results in an error which is not *unconditionally fatal*. For example, try to execute the following line:

```
1    print(1/0)
2
```

It will cause a `ZeroDivisionError` exception, and result in the following, or similar, message being displayed in the console:

```
Traceback (most recent call last):
  File "main.py", line 1, in <module></module>
    print(1/0)
ZeroDivisionError: division by zero
```

Pay attention to the last line of the error message — it actually tells you what happened. There are many different types of exceptions, such as `ZeroDivisionError`, `NameError`, `TypeError`, and many more; and this part of the message informs you of what type of exception has been raised. The preceding lines show you the context in which the exception has occurred.

2. You can "catch" and handle exceptions in Python by using the `try-except` block. So, if you have a suspicion that any particular snippet may raise an exception, you can write the code that will gracefully handle it, and will not interrupt the program. Look at the example:

```
1    while True:
2        try:
3            number = int(input("Enter an integer number: "))
4            print(number/2)
5            break
6        except:
7            print("Warning: the value entered is not a valid number. Try again...")
8
```

This code asks the user for input until they enter a valid integer number. If the user enters a value that cannot be converted to an int, the program will print `Warning: the value entered is not a valid number. Try again...`, and ask the user to enter a number again. What happens in such a case? The program enters the `while` loop. The `try` block/clause is executed. The user enters a wrong value, for example: `hello!`. An exception occurs, and the rest of the `try` clause is skipped. The program jumps to the `except` block, executes it, and then continues running after the `try-except` block. If the user enters a correct value and no exception occurs, the subsequent instructions in the `try` block are executed.

3. You can handle multiple exceptions in your code block. Look at the following examples:

```
1   while True:
2       try:
3           number = int(input("Enter an int number: "))
4           print(5/number)
5           break
6       except ValueError:
7           print("Wrong value.")
8       except ZeroDivisionError:
9           print("Sorry. I cannot divide by zero.")
10      except:
11          print("I don't know what to do...")
12
```

- You can use multiple *except* blocks within one *try* statement, and specify particular exception names. If one of the except branches is executed, the other branches will be skipped. Remember: you can specify a particular built-in exception only once. Also, don't forget that the default (or generic) exception, that is the one with no name specified, should be placed at the bottom of the branch (use the more specific exceptions first, and the more general last).
- You can also specify and handle multiple built-in exceptions within a single *except* clause:

```
1   while True:
2       try:
3           number = int(input("Enter an int number: "))
4           print(5/number)
5           break
6       except (ValueError, ZeroDivisionError):
7           print("Wrong value or No division by zero rule broken.")
8       except:
9           print("Sorry, something went wrong...")
10
```

4. Some of the most useful Python built-in exceptions are: `ZeroDivisionError`, `ValueError`, `TypeError`, `AttributeError`, and `SyntaxError`. One more exception that, in our opinion, deserves your attention is the `KeyboardInterrupt` exception, which is raised when the user hits the interrupt key (*CTRL-C* or *Delete*). Run the code and hit the key combination to see what happens. To learn more about the Python built-in exceptions, consult the official Python documentation.

5. Last but not least, you should remember about testing and debugging your code. Use such debugging techniques as print debugging; if possible — ask someone to read your code and help you to find bugs in it or to improve it; try to isolate the fragment of code that is problematic and susceptible to errors: test your functions by applying

Exceptions

predictable argument values, and try to handle the situations when someone enters wrong values; comment out the parts of the code that obscure the issue. Finally, take breaks and come back to your code after some time with a fresh pair of eyes.

Quiz

QUESTION 1: What is the output of the following program if the user enters 0?

```
1   try:
2       value = int(input("Enter a value: "))
3       print(value/value)
4   except ValueError:
5       print("Bad input...")
6   except ZeroDivisionError:
7       print("Very bad input...")
8   except:
9       print("Booo!")
10
```

QUESTION 2: What is the expected behavior of the following program if the user enters 0?

```
1   value = input("Enter a value: ")
2   print(10/value)
3
```

APPENDICES

APPENDICES

Appendix A: LAB Hints

LAB 4

```
1    print("I'm\nlearning Python")
2
```

LAB 9

```
1    a = float(input("Enter first value: "))
2    b = float(input("Enter second value: "))
3
4    # output the result of addition here
5    # output the result of subtraction here
6    # output the result of multiplication here
7    # output the result of division here
8
9    print("\nThat's all, folks!")
10
```

LAB 11

```
1    hour = int(input("Starting time (hours): "))
2    mins = int(input("Starting time (minutes): "))
3    dura = int(input("Event duration (minutes): "))
4    # find the total of all minutes
5    # find the number of hours hidden in minutes and update the hour
6    # correct minutes to fall in the (0..59) range
7    # correct hours to fall in the (0..23) range
8    print(hour, ":", mins, sep='')
9
```

LAB 16

```
1    secret_number = 777
2
3    print(
4    """
5    +=================================+
6    | Welcome to my game, muggle!     |
7    | Enter an integer number         |
8    | and guess what number I've      |
9    | picked for you.                 |
10   | So, what is the secret number?  |
11   +=================================+
12   """)
13
14   # Prompt the user to enter an integer number.
15
16   # Write a while loop and the rest of your code.
17
```

Exceptions   263

LAB 17

```
1   import time
2
3   # Write a for loop that counts to five.
4       # Body of the loop - print the loop iteration number and the word "Mississippi".
5       time.sleep(1)
6
7   # Write a print function with the final message.
8
```

LAB 18

```
1   while True:
2       # Write code in the body of the loop.
3       # Put a conditional statement.
4           # Exit the loop here.
5   # Print the message.
6
```

LAB 19

```
1   user_word = input("Enter your word: ")
2   user_word = user_word.upper()
3
4   for letter in user_word:
5       # if-elif-else block, nest continue statements
6       # ...
7       # ...
8       # ...
9       else:
10          print(letter)
11
```

LAB 20

```
1   word_without_vowels = ""
2
3   user_word = input("Enter your word: ")
4   user_word = user_word.upper()
5
6   for letter in user_word:
7       if letter == "A":
8           continue
9       elif letter == "E":
10          continue
11      elif letter == "I":
12          continue
13      elif letter == "O":
14          continue
```

```
15      elif letter == "U":
16          continue
17      else:
18          # Write your code here.
19
20  # Print the word assigned to word_without_vowels.
21
```

LAB 21

```
1   blocks = int(input("Enter the number of blocks: "))
2
3   height = 0
4   in_layer = 1
5   while in_layer <= blocks:
6       # The body of the while loop.
7
8   print("The height of the pyramid:", height)
9
```

LAB 22

```
1   c0 = int(input("Enter c0: "))
2
3   if c0 > 1:
4       steps = 0
5       # The while loop goes here.
6           if c0 %2 != 0:
7               # Write your code here.
8           else:
9               cnew = c0 // 2
10          #
11          # Write your code here.
12          #
13      print("steps =",steps)
14  else:
15      print("Bad c0 value")
16
```

LAB 23

```
1   hat_list = [1, 2, 3, 4, 5]
2
3   # Step 1
4   hat_list[2] = int(input("Enter an integer number: "))
5
6   # Step 2: write a line of code that removes the last element from the list.
7
8   # Step 3: write a line of code that prints the length of the existing list.
9
10  print(hat_list)
11
```

Exceptions   265

LAB 24

```python
# step 1:
Beatles = []
#

# step 2:

Beatles.append("John Lennon")
#
#
#


# step 3:
for members in range(2):
    #
#

# step 4:
del Beatles[-1]
#
#


# step 5:
#
#
#
```

LAB 25

```python
my_list = [1, 2, 4, 4, 1, 4, 2, 6, 2, 9]
new_list = []
# Browse all numbers from the source list.
    # If the number doesn't appear within the new list...
        # ...append it here.
# Make a copy of new_list.
print("The list with unique elements only:")
print(my_list)
```

LAB 26

```python
def is_year_leap(year):
    if year % 4 != 0:
        #
    # elif statement
        #
    # elif statement
        #
    # else statement

test_data = [1900, 2000, 2016, 1987]
test_results = [False, True, True, False]
```

```
12  for i in range(len(test_data)):
13      yr = test_data[i]
14      print(yr,"-> ",end="")
15      result = is_year_leap(yr)
16      if result == test_results[i]:
17          print("OK")
18      else:
19          print("Failed")
20
```

LAB 27

```
1   def is_year_leap(year):
2       if year % 4 != 0:
3           return False
4       elif year % 100 != 0:
5           return True
6       elif year % 400 != 0:
7           return False
8       else:
9           return True
10
11  def days_in_month(year, month):
12      # if statement
13          # ...
14      days = [31, 28, 31, 30, 31, 30, 31, 31, 30, 31, 30, 31]
15      res  = days[month - 1]
16      if month == 2 and is_year_leap(year):
17          res = 29
18      return res
19
20  test_years = [1900, 2000, 2016, 1987]
21  test_months = [ 2, 2, 1, 11]
22  test_results = [28, 29, 31, 30]
23  for i in range(len(test_years)):
24      yr = test_years[i]
25      mo = test_months[i]
26      print(yr,mo,"-> ",end="")
27      result = days_in_month(yr, mo)
28      if result == test_results[i]:
29          print("OK")
30      else:
31          print("Failed")
32
```

LAB 28

```
1   def is_year_leap(year):
2       if year % 4 != 0:
3           return False
4       elif year % 100 != 0:
5           return True
6       elif year % 400 != 0:
7           return False
```

```python
        else:
            return True

def days_in_month(year,month):
    if year < 1582 or month < 1 or month > 12:
        return None
    days = [31, 28, 31, 30, 31, 30, 31, 31, 30, 31, 30, 31]
    res  = days[month - 1]
    if month == 2 and is_year_leap(year):
        res = 29
    return res

def day_of_year(year, month, day):
    days = 0
    for m in range(1, month):
        # ...
        # if statement
            # ...
        days += md
    md = days_in_month(year, month)
    if day >= 1 and day <= md:
        # ...
    else:
        # ...

print(day_of_year(2000, 12, 31))
```

LAB 29

```python
def is_prime(num):
    # the for loop
        # the if statement
            return False
    return True

for i in range(1, 20):
    if is_prime(i + 1):
        print(i + 1, end=" ")
print()
```

LAB 30

```python
# 1 American mile = 1609.344 meters
# 1 American gallon = 3.785411784 liters

def liters_100km_to_miles_gallon(liters):
    gallons = liters / 3.785411784
    miles = 100 * 1000 / 1609.344
    return miles / gallons

def miles_gallon_to_liters_100km(miles):
    # ...
```

```
11      # ...
12      # ...
13
14      print(liters_100km_to_miles_gallon(3.9))
15      print(liters_100km_to_miles_gallon(7.5))
16      print(liters_100km_to_miles_gallon(10.))
17      print(miles_gallon_to_liters_100km(60.3))
18      print(miles_gallon_to_liters_100km(31.4))
19      print(miles_gallon_to_liters_100km(23.5))
20
```

Appendix B: LAB Sample Solutions

LAB 1

```
1       # Sample Solution
2
3       print("Hello, Python!")
4       # print("Greg")
5       # print(Greg)
6       # print"Greg"
7       # print('Greg')
8       # print("Greg") print("Python")
9       # ...</sampleSolution>
10
```

LAB 2

```
1       print("Programming","Essentials","in", sep="***", end="...")
2       print("Python")
3
```

LAB 3

```
1       # Sample Solution
2
3       ###################
4       print("original version:")
5       ###################
6       print("    *")
7       print("   * *")
8       print("  *   *")
9       print(" *     *")
10      print("***     ***")
11      print("   *   *")
12      print("    *   *")
13      print("    *****")
14      ###################
15      print("with fewer 'print()' invocations:")
16      ###################
17      print("    *\n   * *\n  *   *\n *     *\n***     ***")
18      print("   *   *\n    *   *\n    *****")
19      ###################
20      print("higher:")
21      ###################
```

Exceptions   269

```
22  print("            *")
23  print("          * *")
24  print("         *    *")
25  print("        *      *")
26  print("       *        *")
27  print("      *          *")
28  print("     *            *")
29  print("    *              *")
30  print("******        ******")
31  print("        *     *")
32  print("        *     *")
33  print("        *     *")
34  print("        *     *")
35  print("        *     *")
36  print("        *     *")
37  print("         *****")
38  ###################
39  print("doubled:")
40  ###################
41  print("            *           "*2)
42  print("          * *           "*2)
43  print("         *   *          "*2)
44  print("        *     *         "*2)
45  print("       *       *        "*2)
46  print("      *         *       "*2)
47  print("     *           *      "*2)
48  print("    *             *     "*2)
49  print("******        ******"*2)
50  print("        *     *         "*2)
51  print("        *     *         "*2)
52  print("        *     *         "*2)
53  print("        *     *         "*2)
54  print("        *     *         "*2)
55  print("        *     *         "*2)
56  print("         *****          "*2)
57
```

LAB 4

```
1   print("\"I'm\"\n\"learning\"\n\"Python\"\"")
2
```

LAB 5

```
1   john = 3
2   mary = 5
3   adam = 6
4
5   print(john, mary, adam, sep=',')
6
7   total_apples = john + mary + adam
8   print(total_apples)
9
10  # peter = 12.5
```

```
11   # suzy = 2
12   # print(peter / suzy)
13   # print("Total number of apples:", total_apples)
14
```

LAB 6

```
1    kilometers = 12.25
2    miles = 7.38
3
4    miles_to_kilometers = miles * 1.61
5    kilometers_to_miles = kilometers / 1.61
6
7    print(miles, "miles is", round(miles_to_kilometers, 2), "kilometers")
8    print(kilometers, "kilometers is", round(kilometers_to_miles, 2), "miles")
9
```

LAB 7

```
1    x = 0
2    x = float(x)
3    y = 3 * x**3 - 2 * x**2 + 3 * x - 1
4    print("y =", y)
5
6    x = 1
7    x = float(x)
8    y = 3 * x**3 - 2 * x**2 + 3 * x - 1
9    print("y =", y)
10
11   x = -1
12   x = float(x)
13   y = 3 * x**3 - 2 * x**2 + 3 * x - 1
14   print("y =", y)
15
```

LAB 9

```
1    a = float(input("Enter first value: "))
2    b = float(input("Enter second value: "))
3
4    print("Addition:", a + b)
5    print("Subtraction:", a - b)
6    print("Multiplication:", a * b)
7    print("Division:", a / b)
8
9    print("\nThat's all, folks!")
10
```

LAB 10

```
1    x = float(input("Enter value for x: "))
2    y = 1./(x + 1./(x + 1./(x + 1./x)))
3    print("y =", y)
4
```

LAB 11

```
1    hour = int(input("Starting time (hours): "))
2    mins = int(input("Starting time (minutes): "))
3    dura = int(input("Event duration (minutes): "))
4    mins = mins + dura # find a total of all minutes
5    hour = hour + mins // 60 # find a number of hours hidden in minutes and update the hour
6    mins = mins % 60 # correct minutes to fall in the (0..59) range
7    hour = hour % 24 # correct hours to fall in the (0..23) range
8    print(hour, ":", mins, sep='')
9
```

LAB 12

```
1    n = int(input("Enter a number: "))
2    print(n >= 100)
3
```

LAB 13

```
1    name = input("Enter flower name: ")
2
3    if name == "Spathiphyllum":
4        print("Yes - Spathiphyllum is the best plant ever!")
5    elif name == "spathiphyllum":
6        print("No, I want a big Spathiphyllum!")
7    else:
8        print("Spathiphyllum! Not", name + "!")
9
```

LAB 14

```
1    income = float(input("Enter the annual income: "))
2
3    if income < 85528:
4        tax = income * 0.18 - 556.02
5    else:
6        tax = (income - 85528) * 0.32 + 14839.02
7
8    if tax < 0.0:
9        tax = 0.0
10
11   tax = round(tax, 0)
12   print("The tax is:", tax, "thalers")
13
```

LAB 15

```
1    year = int(input("Enter a year: "))
2
3    if year < 1582:
4        print("Not within the Gregorian calendar period")
5    else:
6        if year % 4 != 0:
```

```
7          print("Common year")
8      elif year % 100 != 0:
9          print("Leap year")
10     elif year % 400 != 0:
11         print("Common year")
12     else:
13         print("Leap year")
14
```

LAB 16

```
1    secret_number = 777
2
3    print(
4    """
5    +================================+
6    | Welcome to my game, muggle!    |
7    | Enter an integer number        |
8    | and guess what number I've     |
9    | picked for you.                |
10   | So, what is the secret number? |
11   +================================+
12   """)
13
14   user_number = int(input("Enter the number: "))
15
16   while user_number != secret_number:
17       print("Ha ha! You're stuck in my loop!")
18       user_number = int(input("Enter the number again: "))
19   print(secret_number, "Well done, muggle! You are free now.")
20
```

LAB 17

```
1    import time
2
3    for second in range(1, 6):
4        print(second, "Mississippi")
5        time.sleep(1)
6
7    print("Ready or not, here I come!")
8
```

LAB 18

```
1    while True:
2        word = input("You're stuck in an infinite loop!\nEnter the secret word to leave the loop: ")
3        if word == "chupacabra":
4            break
5    print("You've successfully left the loop!")
6
```

LAB 19

```
1   user_word = input("Enter your word: ")
2   user_word = user_word.upper()
3
4   for letter in user_word:
5       if letter == "A":
6           continue
7       elif letter == "E":
8           continue
9       elif letter == "I":
10          continue
11      elif letter == "O":
12          continue
13      elif letter == "U":
14          continue
15      else:
16          print(letter)
17
```

LAB 20

```
1   word_without_vowels = ""
2
3   user_word = input("Enter your word: ")
4   user_word = user_word.upper()
5
6   for letter in user_word:
7       if letter == "A":
8           continue
9       elif letter == "E":
10          continue
11      elif letter == "I":
12          continue
13      elif letter == "O":
14          continue
15      elif letter == "U":
16          continue
17      else:
18          word_without_vowels += letter
19
20  print(word_without_vowels)
21
```

LAB 21

```
1   blocks = int(input("Enter the number of blocks: "))
2
3   height = 0
4   in_layer = 1
5   while in_layer <= blocks:
6       height += 1
```

```
7        blocks -= in_layer
8        in_layer += 1
9    print("The height of the pyramid:", height)
10
```

LAB 22

```
1    c0 = int(input("Enter c0: "))
2
3    if c0 > 1:
4        steps = 0
5        while c0 != 1:
6            if c0 %2 != 0:
7                cnew = 3 * c0 + 1
8            else:
9                cnew = c0 // 2
10           print(c0)
11           c0 = cnew
12           steps += 1
13       print("steps =",steps)
14   else:
15       print("Bad c0 value")
16
```

LAB 23

```
1    hat_list = [1, 2, 3, 4, 5]
2
3    # Step 1
4    hat_list[2] = int(input("Enter an integer number: "))
5
6    # Step 2
7    del hat_list[-1]
8
9    # Step 3
10   print(len(hat_list))
11
```

LAB 24

```
1    # step 1:
2    Beatles = []
3    print("Step 1:", Beatles)
4
5    # step 2:
6
7    Beatles.append("John Lennon")
8    Beatles.append("Paul McCartney")
9    Beatles.append("George Harrison")
10   print("Step 2:", Beatles)
11
12   # step 3:
13   for members in range(2):
14       Beatles.append(input("New band member: "))
```

```
15  print("Step 3:", Beatles)
16
17  # step 4:
18  del Beatles[-1]
19  del Beatles[-1]
20  print("Step 4:", Beatles)
21
22  # step 5:
23  Beatles.insert(0, "RingoStarr")
24  print("Step 5:", Beatles)
25  print("The Fab:",len(Beatles))
26
```

LAB 25

```
1  my_list = [1, 2, 4, 4, 1, 4, 2, 6, 2, 9]
2  new_list = []
3  for number in my_list:   # Browse all numbers from the source list.
4      if number not in new_list:   # If the number doesn't appear within the new list...
5          new_list.append(number)   # ...append it here.
6  my_list = new_list[:]   # Make a copy of new_list.
7  print("The list with unique elements only:")
8  print(my_list)
9
```

LAB 26

```
1   def is_year_leap(year):
2       if year % 4 != 0:
3           return False
4       elif year % 100 != 0:
5           return True
6       elif year % 400 != 0:
7           return False
8       else:
9           return True
10
11  test_data = [1900, 2000, 2016, 1987]
12  test_results = [False, True, True, False]
13  for i in range(len(test_data)):
14      yr = test_data[i]
15      print(yr,"-> ",end="")
16      result = is_year_leap(yr)
17      if result == test_results[i]:
18          print("OK")
19      else:
20          print("Failed")
21
```

LAB 27

```
1   def is_year_leap(year):
2       if year % 4 != 0:
3           return False
4       elif year % 100 != 0:
5           return True
6       elif year % 400 != 0:
7           return False
8       else:
9           return True
10
11  def days_in_month(year,month):
12      if year < 1582 or month < 1 or month > 12:
13          return None
14      days = [31, 28, 31, 30, 31, 30, 31, 31, 30, 31, 30, 31]
15      res  = days[month - 1]
16      if month == 2 and is_year_leap(year):
17          res = 29
18      return res
19
20  test_years = [1900, 2000, 2016, 1987]
21  test_months = [ 2, 2, 1, 11]
22  test_results = [28, 29, 31, 30]
23  for i in range(len(test_years)):
24      yr = test_years[i]
25      mo = test_months[i]
26      print(yr,mo,"-> ",end="")
27      result = days_in_month(yr, mo)
28      if result == test_results[i]:
29          print("OK")
30      else:
31          print("Failed")
32
```

LAB 28

```
1   def is_year_leap(year):
2       if year % 4 != 0:
3           return False
4       elif year % 100 != 0:
5           return True
6       elif year % 400 != 0:
7           return False
8       else:
9           return True
10  def days_in_month(year, month):
11      if year < 1582 or month < 1 or month > 12:
12          return None
13      days = [31, 28, 31, 30, 31, 30, 31, 31, 30, 31, 30, 31]
14      res  = days[month - 1]
15      if month == 2 and is_year_leap(year):
16          res = 29
17      return res
```

```
18
19   def day_of_year(year, month, day):
20       days = 0
21       for m in range(1, month):
22           md = days_in_month(year, m)
23           if md == None:
24               return None
25           days += md
26       md = days_in_month(year, month)
27       if day >= 1 and day <= md:
28           return days + day
29       else:
30           return None
31
32   print(day_of_year(2000, 12, 31))
33
```

LAB 29

```
1    def is_prime(num):
2        for i in range(2, int(1 + num ** 0.5)):
3            if num % i == 0:
4                return False
5        return True
6
7    for i in range(1, 20):
8        if is_prime(i + 1):
9            print(i + 1, end=" ")
10   print()
11
```

LAB 30

```
1    # 1 American mile = 1609.344 meters
2    # 1 American gallon = 3.785411784 liters
3
4    def liters_100km_to_miles_gallon(liters):
5        gallons = liters / 3.785411784
6        miles = 100 * 1000 / 1609.344
7        return miles / gallons
8
9    def miles_gallon_to_liters_100km(miles):
10       km100 = miles * 1609.344 / 1000 / 100
11       liters = 3.785411784
12       return liters / km100
13
14   print(liters_100km_to_miles_gallon(3.9))
15   print(liters_100km_to_miles_gallon(7.5))
16   print(liters_100km_to_miles_gallon(10.))
17   print(miles_gallon_to_liters_100km(60.3))
18   print(miles_gallon_to_liters_100km(31.4))
19   print(miles_gallon_to_liters_100km(23.5))
20
```

Appendix C: Answers

CHAPTER 4 QUIZ
QUESTION 1
```
My
name
is
Bond. James Bond.
```

QUESTION 2
```
File "main.py", line 1
    print(sep="&", "fish", "chips")
                ^
SyntaxError: positional argument follows keyword argument
```

QUESTION 3
Line 5 will raise a `SyntaxError`, because the ' symbol in the `Greg's book.` string requires an escape character.

CHAPTER 5
SAMPLE SOLUTION 1
```
1    print('I\'m Monty Python.')
2
```

SAMPLE SOLUTION 2
```
1    print("I'm Monty Python.")
2
```

CHAPTER 6 QUESTIONS
REMAINDER (MODULO)
`3.0` — not `3` but `3.0`. The rule still works:

- `12//4.5` gives `2.0`,
- `2.0*4.5` gives `9.0`,
- `12-9.0` gives `3.0`.

OPERATORS AND THEIR BINDINGS
```
-9
-8
-9
```

LIST OF PRIORITIES
```
1
```

OPERATORS AND PARENTHESES
```
10.0
```

Chapter 5 Quiz
Question 1
They're both strings/string literals.

Question 2
The first is a string, the second is a numerical literal (a float), the third is a numerical literal (an integer), and the fourth is a boolean literal.

Question 3
It's 11, because (2**0)+(2**1)+(2**3)=11

Chapter 6 Quiz
Question 1
```
16 8.0 8
```

Question 2
```
-0.5 0.5 0 -1
```

Question 3
```
-2 2 512
```

Chapter 7 Questions
How to use a variable
```
Python version: 3.8.5
```

How to assign a new value to an already existing variable
500 — why? Well, first, the `var` variable is created and assigned a value of 100. Then, the same variable is assigned a new value: the result of adding 200 to 300, which is 500.

Solving simple mathematical problems
```
C = 5.0
```

Chapter 7 Quiz
Question 1
3

Question 2
101, m 101, del

Question 3
11

Question 4
1.0

CHAPTER 8 QUIZ
QUESTION 1
```
String #2
```

QUESTION 2
```
SyntaxError: invalid syntax
```

CHAPTER 9 QUIZ
QUESTION 1
```
    55
```

QUESTION 2
```
    <class 'str'>
```

CHAPTER 10
QUESTION 1
`True` — of course, 2 is equal to 2. Python will answer `True` (remember this pair of predefined literals, `True` and `False` — they're Python keywords, too).

QUESTION 2
This question is not as easy as the first one. Luckily, Python is able to convert the integer value into its real equivalent, and consequently, the answer is `True`.

QUESTION 3
This should be easy. The answer will be (or rather, always is) `False`.

CHAPTER 10 QUIZ
QUESTION 1
```
    False
    True
```

QUESTION 2
```
    False
    True
```

QUESTION 3
```
    True
    False
```

QUESTION 4
```
    True
    True
    else
```

QUESTION 5
```
    four
    five
```

Exceptions

Question 6
```
one
two
```

Chapter 11 Quiz
Question 1
```
for i in range(0, 11):
    if i % 2 != 0:
        print(i)
```

Question 2
```
x = 1 while x < 11:
    if x % 2 != 0:
        print(x)
    x += 1
```

Question 3
```
for ch in "john.smith@pythoninstitute.org":
    if ch == "@":
        break
    print(ch, end="")
```

Question 4
```
for digit in "0165031806510":
    if digit == "0":
        print("x", end="")
        continue
    print(digit, end="")
```

Question 5
```
4
3
2
0
```

Question 6
```
-1
0
1
2
3
```

Question 7
```
0
3
```

Chapter 12 Quiz
Question 1
```
False
```

Question 2
```
0 5 -5 1 1 16
```

CHAPTER 13 QUIZ
QUESTION 1
```
[6, 2, 3, 4, 5, 1]
```

QUESTION 2
```
[1, 3, 6, 10, 15]
```

QUESTION 3
```
NameError: name 'lst' is not defined
```

QUESTION 4
```
[2, 3]
3
```

CHAPTER 14 QUIZ
QUESTION 1
```
['A', 'D', 'F', 'Z']
```

QUESTION 2
```
[1, 2, 3]
```

QUESTION 3
```
[' ', 'C', 'B', 'A']
```

CHAPTER 15 QUIZ
QUESTION 1
```
['C']
```

QUESTION 2
```
['B', 'C']
```

QUESTION 3
```
[]
```

QUESTION 4
```
['A', 'B', 'C']
```

QUESTION 5
```python
my_list = [1, 2, "in", True, "ABC"]

print(1 in my_list) # outputs True
print("A" not in my_list) # outputs True
print(3 not in my_list) # outputs True
print(False in my_list) # outputs False

```

CHAPTER 17 QUIZ
QUESTION 1
b — it's a built-in function.

QUESTION 2
An exception is thrown (the `NameError` exception to be more precise).

QUESTION 3
An exception will be thrown (the `TypeError` exception to be more precise) — the `hi()` function doesn't take any arguments.

CHAPTER 18 QUIZ
QUESTION 1
```
My name is Bond. James Bond.
```

QUESTION 2
```
My name is Sean Connery. James Bond.
```

QUESTION 3
```
My name is Bond. Susan.
```

QUESTION 4
`SyntaxError`: non-default argument (`c`) follows default argument (b=2)

CHAPTER 19 QUIZ
QUESTION 1
The function will return an implicit `None` value.

QUESTION 2
```
True
False
None
```

QUESTION 3
```
[0, 2, 4, 6, 8, 10]
```

QUESTION 4
```
[1, 4, 9, 16, 25
```

CHAPTER 20 QUIZ
QUESTION 1
The `NameError` exception will be thrown:

```
NameError: name 'alt' is not defined
```

QUESTION 2
```
2
1
```

QUESTION 3
```
2
3
```

QUESTION 4
```
2
2
```

Chapter 21 Quiz
Question 1
The factorial function has no termination condition (no base case) so Python will raise an exception (`RecursionError: maximum recursion depth exceeded`)

Question 2
    56

Chapter 22 Quiz
Question 1
The program will print 3 to the screen.

Question 2
The program will print 6 to the screen. The `tup` tuple elements have been "unpacked" in the a, b, and c variables.

Question 3
```
tup = 1, 2, 3, 2, 4, 5, 6, 2, 7, 2, 8, 9
duplicates = tup.count(2)

print(duplicates)    # outputs: 4
```

Question 4
```
d1 = {'Adam Smith': 'A', 'Judy Paxton': 'B+'}
d2 = {'Mary Louis': 'A', 'Patrick White': 'C'}
d3 = {}

for item in (d1, d2):
    d3.update(item)

print(d3)
```

Question 5
```
my_list = ["car", "Ford", "flower", "Tulip"]

t = tuple(my_list)
print(t)
```

Question 6
```
colors = (("green", "#008000"), ("blue", "#0000FF"))

colors_dictionary = dict(colors)
print(colors_dictionary)
```

Question 7
The program will print `{'A':1,'B':2}` to the screen.

Exceptions   285

QUESTION 8
```
white : (255, 255, 255)
grey : (128, 128, 128)
red : (255, 0, 0)
green : (0, 128, 0)
```

CHAPTER 23 QUIZ
QUESTION 1
The program will output: `Very bad input....`

QUESTION 2
The program will raise the `TypeError` exception.

Appendix D: PCEP Exam Syllabus

The exam consists of four sections:

Section 1	7 items	Max Raw Score: 180 (18%)
Section 2	8 items	Max Raw Score: 290 (29%)
Section 3	7 items	Max Raw Score: 250 (25%)
Section 4	8 items	Max Raw Score: 280 (28%)

Section 1: Computer Programming and Python Fundamentals

PCEP-30-02 1.1 — Understand fundamental terms and definitions

- interpreting and the interpreter, compilation and the compiler
- lexis, syntax, and semantics

PCEP-30-02 1.2 — Understand Python's logic and structure

- keywords
- instructions
- indentation
- comments

PCEP-30-02 1.3 — Introduce literals and variables into code and use different numeral systems

- Boolean, integers, floating-point numbers
- scientific notation
- strings
- binary, octal, decimal, and hexadecimal numeral systems
- variables
- naming conventions
- implementing PEP-8 recommendations

PCEP-30-02 1.4 — Choose operators and data types adequate to the problem

- numeric operators: ** * / % // + -
- string operators: * +
- assignment and shortcut operators
- unary and binary operators
- priorities and binding
- bitwise operators: ~ & ^ | << >>
- Boolean operators: not, and, or
- Boolean expressions
- relational operators: == != > >= < <=
- the accuracy of floating-point numbers
- type casting

PCEP-30-02 1.5 — Perform Input/Output console operations

- the print() and input() functions
- the sep= and end= keyword parameters
- the int() and float() functions

Section 2: Control Flow - Conditional Blocks and Loops

PCEP-30-02 2.1 — Make decisions and branch the flow with the if instruction

- conditional statements: if, if-else, if-elif, if-elif-else
- multiple conditional statements
- nesting conditional statements

PCEP-30-02 2.2 — Perform different types of iterations

- the pass instruction
- building loops with while, for, range(), and in
- iterating through sequences
- expanding loops with while-else and for-else
- nesting loops and conditional statements
- controlling loop execution with break and continue

Section 3: Data Collections - Tuples, Dictionaries, Lists, Strings

PCEP-30-02 3.1 — Collect and process data using lists

- constructing vectors
- indexing and slicing
- the len() function
- list methods: append(), insert(), index(), etc.
- functions: len(), sorted()
- the del instruction
- iterating through lists with the for loop

- initializing loops
- the `in` and `not in` operators
- list comprehensions
- copying and cloning
- lists in lists: matrices and cubes

PCEP-30-02 3.2 — Collect and process data using tuples

- tuples: indexing, slicing, building, immutability
- tuples vs. lists: similarities and differences
- lists inside tuples and tuples inside lists

PCEP-30-02 3.3 Collect and process data using dictionaries

- dictionaries: building, indexing, adding and removing keys
- iterating through dictionaries and their keys and values
- checking the existence of keys
- methods: `keys()`, `items()`, and `values()`

PCEP-30-02 3.4 Operate with strings

- constructing strings
- indexing, slicing, immutability
- escaping using the \ character
- quotes and apostrophes inside strings
- multi-line strings
- basic string functions and methods

Section 4: Functions and Exceptions

PCEP-30-02 4.1 — Decompose the code using functions

- defining and invoking user-defined functions and generators
- the `return` keyword, returning results
- the `None` keyword
- recursion

PCEP-30-02 4.2 — Organize interaction between the function and its environment

- parameters vs. arguments
- positional, keyword, and mixed argument passing
- default parameter values
- name scopes, name hiding (shadowing), and the `global` keyword

PCEP-30-02 4.3 — Python Built-In Exceptions Hierarchy

- `BaseException`
- `Exception`

- `SystemExit`
- `KeyboardInterrupt`
- abstract exceptions
- `ArithmeticError`
- `LookupError`
- `IndexError`
- `KeyError`
- `TypeError`
- `ValueError`

PCEP-30-02 4.4 — Basics of Python Exception Handling

- `try-except` / the `try-except` Exception
- ordering the `except` branches
- propagating exceptions through function boundaries
- delegating responsibility for handling exceptions

Now that you have completed Python Essentials 1, book an exam and take the PCEP Certified Entry-Level Python Programmer Exam.

Go to https://ums.edube.org/store to purchase an exam voucher.

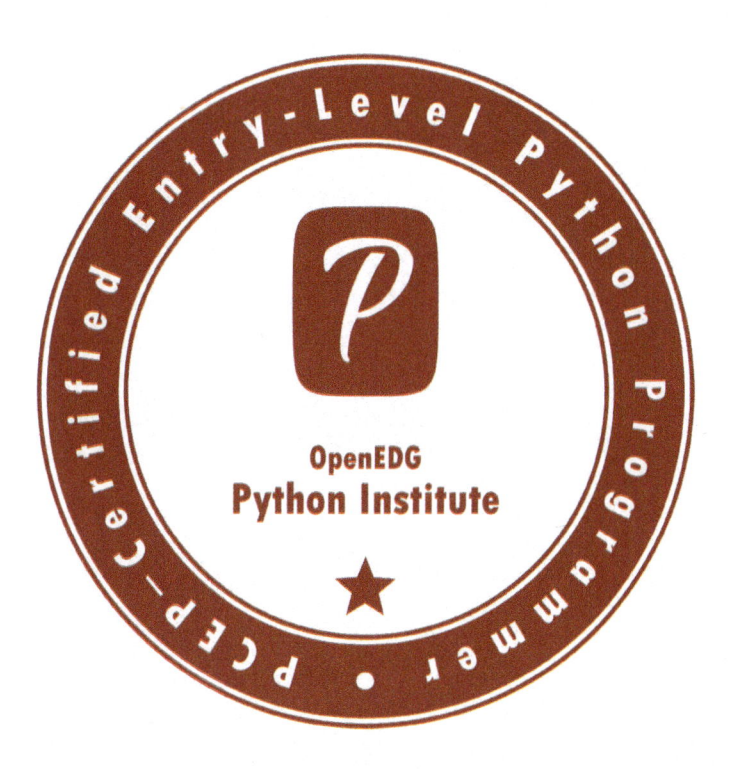

Printed in Great Britain
by Amazon